LIVING WORDS
Language, Lexicography, and the Knowledge Revolution

EXETER LANGUAGE AND LEXICOGRAPHY
General Editors: R.R.K. Hartmann and Tom McArthur

Understanding Semantics
by D. Connor Ferris, 1983

The ESP Classroom: Methodology, Materials, Expectations
edited by Gregory James, 1984

Workbook on Lexicography
by Barbara Ann Kipfer, 1984

Applied Text Linguistics
edited by Alan Turney, 1988

Lexicographers and their Works
edited by Gregory James, 1989

Lexicography in Africa
edited by R.R.K. Hartmann, 1990

Dictionary Workbooks. A Critical Evaluation
by Martin P. Stark, 1990

Sound Changes in Progress
by Anthea E. Sullivan, 1992

Chosen Words: Past and Present Problems for Dictionary Makers
by N.E. Osselton, 1995

Solving Language Problems: From General to Applied Linguistics
edited by R.R.K. Hartmann, 1996

*Communication Across Cultures: Translation Theory and Contrastive Text Linguistic*s
by Basil Hatim, 1997

LIVING WORDS
Language, Lexicography, and the Knowledge Revolution

Tom McArthur

UNIVERSITY
of
EXETER
PRESS

First published in 1998 by
University of Exeter Press
Reed Hall, Streatham Drive
Exeter, Devon EX4 4QR
UK

www.ex.ac.uk/uep/

© Tom McArthur 1998

The right of Tom McArthur to be identified as author
of this work has been asserted by him in accordance with
the Copyright Designs & Patents Act 1988.

British Library Cataloguing in Publication Data
A catalogue record of this book is available
from the British Library

Hardback ISBN 0 85989 611 0
Paperback ISBN 0 85989 620 X

Typeset in Plantin by Kestrel Data, Exeter

Printed in Great Britain by
Short Run Press Ltd, Exeter

Contents

Foreword: Reinhard Hartmann   vii

Acknowledgements   ix

Introduction   xi

LIVING WORDS

1   *Bagaba* and *carcari*: the paradox at the heart of language   3

2   Rhythm, rhyme, and reason: the power of patterned sound   10

3   The power of words: pressure, prejudice, and politics in our vocabularies and dictionaries   27

4   The word 'word'   42

5   The vocabulary-control movement in the English language, 1844–1953   50

LANGUAGE

6   Wee Jimmy and the dugs: or, where do *you* stand in the classroom?   77

7   The usage industry   89

8   Problems of purism and usage in editing *English Today*   98

9	The pedigree of Plain English	109
10	The printed word in the English-speaking world	118

LEXICOGRAPHY

11	The background and nature of ELT learners' dictionaries	133
12	Thematic lexicography	149
13	Reference materials and their formats	160
14	A mutually defining circle of words: some reflections on the making of the *Longman Lexicon of Contemporary English*	177
15	Culture-bound and trapped by technology: centuries of bias in the making of wordbooks	191
16	Guides to tomorrow's English: dictionaries for a universal language	201

THE KNOWLEDGE REVOLUTION

17	What then *is* reference science?	215
18	The scholarly guild	223
19	Knowledge, knowledge everywhere: the global library	228
20	Themes and dreams: the romance of the database	237
21	Representing knowledge for human consumption	243

Appendix: The Unabridged *Devil's Dictionary of Language Teaching*	256
References	265
Index	271

Foreword

In spite of our different backgrounds, Tom McArthur and I share many interests, and in the last fifteen years, since his return to the United Kingdom from Canada, have collaborated on a number of projects at Exeter, such as the annual InterLex Course and the M.A. Programme in Lexicography, the first of its kind in Britain.

Tom is an international authority on the English language, how it has developed, how it is studied and how it has been transmitted around the world. I am pleased that he has offered us this part of his oeuvre for publication. The mixture of personal and scholarly details in these pages is eminently readable, and the emphasis on interdisciplinary links—from linguistics to language to communication studies, and from lexicography to reference science—is commendable and exciting.

This book will initiate a new phase in the development of the series and, as we are both about to celebrate our sixtieth birthdays, I trust that there are many more successful joint ventures ahead!

Reinhard Hartmann, Exeter, April 1998

Acknowledgements

University of Exeter Press and Tom McArthur are grateful to the following publishers for permission to reprint the articles listed below in this collection.

Cambridge University Press for:
Tom McArthur, 'The usage industry', *English Today 7* (1986)
Tom McArthur, 'Problems of purism and usage in editing English today', *English Today 6* (1986)
Tom McArthur, 'The pedigree of plain English', *English Today 27* (1991)
Tom McArthur, 'The printed word in the English-speaking world', *English Today 49* (1997)
Tom McArthur, 'Guides to tomorrow's English: the shapes that dictionaries have begun to take on, in order to cope with English as a universal language', *English Today, July* (1998)

Hodder & Stoughton Educational for:
Tom McArthur, 'Rhythm, rhyme and reason: the power of patterned sound' in *Rhythm, Reading and Writing* edited by Roger Beard (1995)

Oxford University Press for:
the entry 'word' from *The Oxford Companion to the English Language* (1992)

We would also like to thank Barbara Hird warmly for her painstaking work on the index.

Introduction

Nam et ipsa scientia potestas est.
For also knowledge itself is power.
—Francis Bacon, *Meditationes Sacrae* (Sacred Meditations, 1597)

Knowledge always desires increase: it is like fire, which must first be kindled by some external agent, but which will afterwards propagate itself.
—Samuel Johnson, *Letter to William Drummon* (1766)

Bacon and Johnson lived in the forefront of the scholarship of their day. Steeped in the traditions of Western Christendom, they were yet also free to look beyond, to record what European humanity already reliably knew while considering what might yet be reliably added. Neither—or so I tell myself—would have been surprised by a collection of papers that move from a child's verbal inventions through rhythm and rhyme to the potency and nature of words themselves, then how they may best be controlled for educational purposes, then language teaching, usage, lexicography, reference science (what's *that*?), the world's scholarly élite, databases, the evolution of communication, the representation of knowledge—and a closing tribute to Ambrose Bierce, maker of the first diabolical dictionary. The encyclopedic vision of the world's Bacons and Johnsons—simultaneously specialists and generalists—may serve as a model for our own age, in which fibre-optic cables and geostationary satellites have made possible a single yet multiform worldwide information structure, in the universe of whose cells we may freely lose ourselves.

I am immensely grateful to my colleagues at the University of Exeter, in particular Reinhard Hartmann at the Dictionary Research Centre and

INTRODUCTION

Richard Willis at the University of Exeter Press, for the opportunity to bring Bacon, Johnson, Bierce, and many others together in the pages of *Living Words*. As the years and the articles accumulate, specialist writers often find that their *oeuvre*—a marvellously pretentious word, but what else is there?—has become dispersed in a spread of titles and places. If, for example, certain uniquely focused papers were published only in now hard-to-find publications, there can be one definite (and often apologetic) consequence: requests to the writer for photocopies from *bona fide* researchers. The writer may then (glad that someone cares) send back a surviving offprint or a photocopy, or even—O brave new world that has such marvels in't!—an e-mail update copied and pasted from a hard disk.

This is when a particular literary institution (genre?) comes into its own: the volume of collected papers. In such a book, for a time at least, essays can be rejuvenated even if their writers can't—and, more importantly, can be integrated in ways which were not possible before, making clearer the links among works that came into existence for different purposes, audiences, and readerships at different times and in different places, turning them at last into a coherent set of chapters. On this occasion, I have enjoyed editing myself rather than others, bringing together between one set of covers twenty-two strands in my professional life.

Apart from organizing these papers into a logical progression within and across their themes, and adding such apparatus as lead-ins, notes, and references, I have left the component parts of *Living Words* pretty much as they were, with however the following four categories of exceptions.

1. Stylistic changes

Where it has seemed to me that the *mot* was no longer quite as *juste* as I'd hoped, but that nothing substantial was going to be affected, I have for reasons of easier style or greater clarity made an occasional unsignalled change. Only in one case did I feel ambivalent—even guilty—about this, at a point in Chapter 5, which was originally published in 1978, and is the oldest text in the collection. The change I made was:

> *From*
> In 1921, Edward L. Thorndike brought out in the United States *The Teacher's Word Book*, a list of 10,000 words that an American child could expect to meet in his general reading.

INTRODUCTION

To
In 1921, Edward L. Thorndike brought out in the United States *The Teacher's Word Book*, a list of 10,000 words that American children could expect to meet in their general reading.

In cosmic terms the difference is trivial, but in sociolinguistic terms it is noteworthy. At first I thought I would leave things as they were, to be true to my original usage: an instance of generic *he*, common at the time among women writers as well as men. Then I felt that the phrasing would be out of tune in a work to be published in 1999, especially because I have for years now been using the neutral plural so as to avoid male-biased constructions. At the same time, though, I felt I *was* tampering with a little bit of reality; some sharp observer might one day compare the earlier and the later and (recalling the convulsions of political correctness in the mid-1990s) say, 'Ah hah, see what McArthur did—how sneaky can you get?' I did it anyway, but am happy to admit it in advance, and to note the evidence of change in myself. I can hardly now believe that I so unreflectingly wrote the earlier form, and this reaction itself indicates how profoundly certain practices and responses have changed in certain circles in only twenty years.

2. Information or comment added in square brackets

Where I have felt that I should leave something as it is but still make a comment, I have added that comment in square brackets after the original item. Two examples are:

Chapter 14 (original text 1997)
I can currently identify five [now six] books with a family resemblance: three non-alphabetic works and two [now three] that compromise between theme and alphabet.

Chapter 12 (original text 1986)
As a format, the alphabetic mode was practised rather haphazardly and hesitantly until the invention of the printing press in the fifteenth century, but thereafter—and particularly from around 1600—it consolidated itself [in the West and in Westernized cultures elsewhere] into the dominant tradition, in a line of development that has been well delineated by such historians as those mentioned above.

INTRODUCTION

3. Comment before, in, or after the text

Where significant additional information has been appropriate, I have usually added it before or after the text, but sometimes also as a note in the text itself. Before a text, it occurs as part of the square-bracketed introductory matter, as for example in Chapter 19 the statement that 'The text in the proceedings was an edited transcript of the tape recording of the talk, from which the following has been developed'. After a text, a comment may take such forms as a postscript, as in Chapter 3, or numbered endnotes, as in Chapter 17. In the middle of a text, a comment may be given as a square-bracketed note, as with a paragraph added to remarks on the *Longman Language Activator* in Chapter 14. A major exception to this arrangement is the updating of information at the end of Chapter 11, which deals with the history and nature of ELT learners' dictionaries. This paper first appeared in 1989, and the only way of handling the fairly extensive additional material was to integrate it fully into the text, bringing the story up to 1995.

There is inevitably an element of overlap in collections of this kind, especially where similar kinds of information have been presented with different emphases to different audiences and readerships. Thus, the work of Harold Palmer, C.K. Ogden, and Michael West is covered in both Chapters 5 and 11. Chapter 5 gives a fuller account of their work (and of the bitter conflict between West and Ogden), a significant aspect of language education in the earlier twentieth century that has been virtually forgotten as the century comes to a close; Chapter 11 ties some of the same information to a vigorous and highly profitable publishing enterprise: dictionaries for foreign learners of English.

Overlap in Chapters 19, 20, and 21 relates to my theory of the four great communicative shifts. I have left the similar elements in the three texts largely unaltered because the focus is different in each, the first addressing librarians, the second lexicographers, and the third information scientists. Such overlap can also provide an insight into the importance of a person or thing, as for example the early English lexicographer Robert Cawdrey, whose work is discussed in Chapter 7 in relation to usage books, in Chapter 9 in relation to the plain English movement, in Chapter 11 in relation to learners' dictionaries, and in Chapter 16 in relation to tomorrow's dictionaries. In such a spread, Cawdrey—long an overlooked or very minor figure in the history of the language—is accorded, it seems to me, his

INTRODUCTION

rightful place in the history of both the English language and world lexicography.

While the interplay of material across chapters has been a positive aspect of gathering these papers into their new alignment, I have also been intrigued by novel insights into older states of my own being—and been brought up short by forgotten realities. While I benefited from the opportunity to tie together some of the recurrent motifs in my professional life, I also marvelled from time to time at the nature of the past. A cardinal instance of this is a confession in Chapter 19 that I had never (1986) heard of a CD-ROM. *Never heard of a CD-ROM?* Ah, see how fast the fire of knowledge spreads.

Part 1: Living Words

1

Bagaba and *carcari*: the paradox at the heart of language

[A paper given at 'Words: An International Symposium', August 1995, organized at the University of Lund under the auspices of the Swedish Kungl. Vitterhets Historie och Antikvitets Akademien (Royal Academy of Letters, History, and Antiquities), and the opening paper of the proceedings of the same name published in Stockholm by the Academy in 1996 (with grants from the Foundation Natur och Kultur).]

The status of an item as a 'word' in any language is not dependent on how many people know it, how widely they use it, how precisely or uniformly they pronounce it, whether or not it has a single, homogeneous written and printed form, whether or not its meaning is precise, or whether it exists for an hour or a thousand years. Rather, all such matters, though important, rest on two fundamentals: that someone, regardless of age or background, employs an autonomous cluster of speech sounds (more or less within a specific phonological system) several times in ways that prompt a more or less consistent understanding in at least one other person. A nonce or *ad hoc* form is therefore as much a word as the most carefully and fully classified term in *The Oxford English Dictionary* or the most frequently occurring item in any electronic corpus. These points are primarily exemplified here in terms of two words "coined" and used by a 15-month-old child.

I will break all the rules and start with an anecdote—and a personal one at that. There is not a scrap of confirmation for anything in this anecdote in any lexicological project anywhere, and this I see not as a flaw but as an important aspect of what I want to say. In fact, I consider that the tale I want to tell you belongs at the very heart of both lexicology and the study of language acquisition and use. The story concerns my second daughter, Roshan, and a lexical adventure in which she involved us in 1969, when she was about fifteen months old. At that time, she was assembling consonants and vowels in the usual repetitive way, and experimenting with a few words she heard around her, but when speech really took off for her it centred on two items entirely of her own making.

Neither usage was English as we know it, yet they were immensely important to her and clear in their intent to my wife Feri and me. For a short time they constituted a special pair, like *bread and butter* or *yin and yang*, but one of them only lasted a few weeks while the other —suffering in no way from the loss of its partner—carried on for most of a year, a jealously guarded element in her steadily evolving and increasingly standard vocabulary.

The first of these items—the short-lived one—was *carcari*, three syllables with stress on the third, usually spoken with a rising tone of protest and often ending as a scream. *Carcari* meant something like 'I do not want my physical and mental peace disturbed, especially by being taken out of this comfortable place and bounced around in the car'. However, moving towards the car was not always the cause of disquiet, and though the word *car* was presumably the etymon of *carcari*, the cry could be evoked by other things, such as simply lifting her up (in her view suddenly) and heading for the door—any door. *Carcari* ceased to be used as soon as she concluded (as far as we could tell) that cars, journeys, and being carried off were generally at least bearable and often quite nice.

The other—longer-lasting—item began as *aba-aba*, and initially had a semantic range at least as wide and diffuse as *carcari*. It fitted any situation that pleased Roshan and referred to things that were physically still and socially or emotionally stable. By and large, if something was *carcari* it was objectionable, but if it was *aba-aba* it was fine: like being snug in her cot or on a lap or in an armchair (the last being particularly important).

Both forms are typically reduplicative, like *mama* and *dada*, but somewhat more complex, and derive from a syllabic inventory on which infants of many sociolinguistic backgrounds appear to be able to draw. Both also have broad but clear-cut situational contexts, referential meanings, and sense relations, all of which ties them in nicely with linguistic theory at large (the items are paradigmatic, syntagmatic, and contrastive), with structural semantics (they are antonyms), and of course with the arbitrary sign (she made them up herself and gave her own meanings to them, which meanings we accepted). Both were also dynamic usages to which things happened over periods of time. In addition, although she duly forgot them, *we* didn't, telling her about them years later so that as with many other families these private usages have had sporadic lives ever since. Consequently, although *carcari* and *aba-aba* belonged to no language on earth beyond Roshan's nascent idiolect and left no trace in her memory, they were successful for as long as she needed them and have left a strong trace at least in *my* memory and in my thoughts about where words come from.

After *carcari* ceased to exist, and while Roshan's vocabulary grew in the usual way, *aba-aba* went through not one but *three* changes, two phonological, one semantic. First there was the insertion of a medial stop consonant, turning *aba-aba* into a*bagaba*. Next, she simultaneously applied aphesis and stress shift to get the final—dare I call it 'canonical'?—form *bagaba*, with the accent on the final syllable. And thirdly, the range of reference narrowed until the item had only the one meaning—'chair', as in *Mummy sit Daddy bagaba* (said when Feri sat in the armchair I usually occupied). The form *bagaba* is still not English as we generally know it, but a bit of an exoticism, like *Panama* or *Woomerah*, but if Roshan's toddlerhood is compared to the rise and fall of civilizations, *carcari* constitutes a vogue expression that lasted a year or two while the usefulness of *bagaba* extends over centuries, and might perhaps include appearances in works of literature and reputable dictionaries.

In her microworld, however, the months moved on, and one day Roshan at last said 'chair', a word that her sister Meher (two years older) and everybody else had been using around her all of her life, and which she had strongly and I think deliberately resisted. So I immediately pounced, and said, 'Roshan, what happened to the bagaba?'—to which she replied firmly, but with a knowing grin: '*Bagaba gone!*' And it was. She never uttered it again, because she had put away childish things.

I have always sympathized with the nineteenth-century German zoologist Ernst Haeckel's view that ontogeny recapitulates phylogeny. This appears to happen, for example, when both the root of the tongue and the larynx of a human child are repositioned over the years from high locations comparable to those of apes to lower locations that make possible a wider range of vocal sound. In my anecdote, whatever the communicative proclivities Roshan brought with her into the world, she was demonstrating by her early second year several cultural and stylistic processes whose names and analyses are well known to lexicologists because scholars have worked on them and honed them for centuries.

Like many other toddlers, well before she was three she could invent, use, and then dispense with lexical entities entirely of her own making, suggesting that a capacity for doing such things must be very ancient indeed.

By any criteria that I can think of—including fixity of form, clear (though not necessarily precise) reference, sense relations like antonymy, intelligibility to others, and a capacity to evolve and die off—*carcari* and *bagaba* were when she used them actual *words*, just as much as *car* and *chair* and *phonology* and *lexicology* are words, although of course her words lacked validation in the wider world, particularly in the adult world, and most particularly in terms of schooling, dictionaries, and the like.

At this symposium, however, things are different, because at least for the duration of this talk *carcari* and *bagaba* are certainly behaving like words. In sociocultural terms—as opposed, importantly, to strictly communicative terms—they are more truly words than they were before, when she used them, because I am now validating them in various ways. I have, among other things, simply chosen as a lexicologist to pay public attention to them, have fitted them into sentences of standard English (which includes highlighting them in print in italic letters), have used them often enough to prevent them from being regarded as either hapax legomena or nonce words, and have (importantly) given them fixed orthographies (which might have been different, as for example *karkaree* and *buggaba*). I have also printed them out from a state-of-the-art PC by means of a laser printer, and they may well soon take up some space in the proceedings of this gathering. I have also made it possible that at some future time they could be sampled by lexicographers as low-frequency words in a corpus of linguistic texts—or even be used again for discussion purposes by other lexicologists. In other words, in a small way I have let them loose in the world.

This development is no more peculiar than George Eastman's invention of the word *Kodak* c.1888, apparently out of nowhere, or the adoption of the mathematical number *googol*, which (according to the *Random House Compact Unabridged Dictionary*, 1996) was 'allegedly' formulated in the later 1930s by the nine-year-old nephew of the American mathematician Edward Kasner, after he was asked to think of a word suggesting a really large number—in this case, 1 followed by 100 zeros. However, I suspect that *ex nihilo* coinages are more commonly made by or with small children than by photographers, mathematicians, and linguists. But my key point here is that ontogenetic creativity at the very beginning of speech—occurring in a state so raw, restricted, and fragile that it is usually available for discussion *only anecdotally*—demonstrates what lexis really is. All the rest, from the *Oxford English Dictionary* to the latest electronic corpus, is elaboration. *Bagaba* and *carcari* really are words, in the most fundamental sense of the term *word*, regardless of anything that passes or might pass in our society for lexical validation.

Let me quote at this point a comment by Dwight Bolinger on word-formation, in *Aspects of Language* (1968), where he contends that the fluid creativity of word-formation arises from casual processes generally untouched by scholarship and unvalidated by the great and the good. He discusses what he calls the 'high informality of word-making' as follows:

> Practically all words that are not imported bodily from some other language . . . are made up of old words and their parts. Sometimes those parts are pretty well standardized, like the suffix *-y* and the prefix *un-*. Other times they are only broken pieces that some inventive speaker manages to re-fit'. . . *Hamburger* yields *burger*, which is reattached in *nutburger*, *Gainesburger*, and *cheeseburger*. *Cafeteria* yields *-teria*, which is reattached in *valeteria*, *groceteria*, and *washateria*. Trade names make easy use of almost any fragment, like the *roni* of *macaroni* that is reattached in *Rice-a-Roni* and *Noodle-Roni*. The fabrication may re-use elements that have been re-used many times, or it may be a one-shot affair such as the punning reference to being a member of the *lowerarchy*, with *-archy* extracted from *hierarchy*. The principle is the same. Scientists and scholars may give themselves airs with high-bred affixes borrowed from classical languages, but they are linguistically no more sophisticated than the common speakers who are satisfied with leftovers from the vernacular. (p.54)

The expression 'leftovers from the vernacular', it seems to me, belongs very much in the worldview of the people who lend themselves airs. I appreciate why Bolinger put it that way, but would stress that the principle is indeed the same for us all, at all ages and in all avocations. We all operate with the bits and pieces of pre-existing material and —perhaps oftener than we realize—formulate *ex nihilo* products, mostly made up for the nonce and vanishing without trace. Their transience or the fact that they were coined, say, by a small child with no awareness of what she is doing need not—indeed, should not—be used in evidence against them *as words*.

A word does not need to have massive statistics, or longevity, or even a presence in print, or lexicographical validation, or precision of form and definition to be a word and to succeed. The strange creations in Lewis Carroll's poem *Jabberwocky* may be more socially valid because they are well known than if they had never been printed, published, and widely quoted, but they are not more lexicologically valid for that reason. And, published or not, they succeed as words whether or not we know precisely what they mean or whether or not Carroll knew precisely what *he* meant: in Alice's world of the looking glass, the borogoves were indeed mimsy, and the mome raths *did* outgrabe. They are words because in distinctive ways they employ the primal syllables of speech together with a semiotic that is sufficient for the intended purpose.

Pronunciation and meaning may well become more precise as more people take up and maintain a usage, but this is not necessarily so: we get by all the time with all kinds of variable pronunciations (as well as written and printed forms) and all kinds of semantic precision, imprecision, and ambiguity. The paradox at the heart of language is that its authentic lexical elements may be precise or imprecise, may be precise and imprecise at the same time (depending on need), may be more or less precise on different occasions, may be deliberately precise or deliberately imprecise or deliberately ambiguous, and may in any case be variously understood and managed (or misunderstood and mismanaged) by different people. Artifacts like standard dictionaries seek to some degree to capture this state of affairs, but they cannot easily do so, because for most of their compilers preciseness of definition is axiomatic. How many senses does a word have when it is listed in a dictionary? Many may have only one, because of the limited area in which they operate, but many more are so diffuse and difficult, or the aims of a compiler may be so particularized, that the words have different sets of numbered senses in the various dictionaries in which they appear. And there is no final arbiter.

We constantly meet up with words the length of whose pedigrees we do not know and the nature and range of whose meanings and applications are not entirely or at all clear. We understand them as best we can and often use them despite our lack of certainty. Examples abound, but I will offer only three, from different backgrounds. The first is *peristalsis*, a common enough term in physiology and medicine, but it is Greek to most speakers of English (although we all unconsciously experience what it refers to). The second is *prepone*, which is common —dare I even say 'standard'?—in Indian English, where it has a meaning opposite to *postpone*. And the third is *outwith*, a common usage among the Scots; if I say that most Anglophones live *outwith* Scotland its meaning should be clear. All three items are currently used by large numbers of speakers of English while remaining for further millions opaque, obscure, or beyond their ken. Which puts them pretty much on a par with *bagaba* and *carcari*.

2

Rhythm, rhyme, and reason: the power of patterned sound

[The opening chapter of the collection *Rhyme, Reading, and Writing*, edited by Roger Beard, Hodder & Stoughton, London, 1995, and intended primarily for mother-tongue teachers of English.]

> Mr. Fox!
> I hate this game, sir.
> This game makes
> my tongue quite lame, sir.
> Mr. Knox, sir,
> That's a shame, sir.
> We'll find something
> new to do now.
> Here is lots of
> new blue goo now.
> New goo. Blue goo.
> Gooey. Gooey.
> Blue goo. New goo.
> Gluey. Gluey.[1]

All language began as sound. Nowadays, although we can read, write, print, type, and word-process, language is still primarily vocal and auditory: anything dumbly visual can be turned 'back' into vocal sound by anyone at any time—either out loud or in the mind. In addition, 'fossilized' patterns of talk, recitation, chanting, and song survive in all written languages from the now silent ages before script was known. These patterns infect every text ever composed or likely to be composed, and the infection takes many forms, not least of which are rhythm and rhyme.

The beginnings of speech
Vocal sound appears to have originated in the service of the very young some 250 million years ago, when the first mammals evolved. At least four attributes appear to mark off the mammalia from all earlier life forms, and two of them directly relate to communication:

- *feeding:* their females feed their young from glands that produce milk
- *sound:* their young can all instinctively produce the 'mammalian isolation cry'
- *development:* their young take a long time to mature
- *hearing:* they all have a 'middle ear', a facility that enables them to hear such plaintive sounds as the mammalian isolation cry.

Because of the way they are fed, recently born mammals need to stay close to their mother. To help them do this, they produce—whether they are mice, bats, bears, humans, or anything else—specific small plaintive sounds. They can make these sounds because they have a larynx, an organ in the throat that first evolved in reptiles, not for the sake of sound at all but as a valve to close and protect the lungs from foreign matter. Mammals, however, can also use the larynx to cough and to make communicative sounds.

Apes, which evolved some seventy million years ago, make a wide range of sounds compared with most earlier mammals. As in those mammals, the ape's larynx is at the back of the mouth, a location that allows for swallowing and breathing at the same time. In addition, an ape's tongue is rooted in the mouth. These features also appear to have been true of Australopithecus, a genus with both ape-like and proto-human attributes that lived in Africa some four million years ago, but not to have been true of the first members of the genus *Homo*, or any later humans. In addition to having larger brains than apes and australopithecines, humans have larynxes that are located behind the mouth during the childhood years, as with other mammals, but move downwards as the years pass to an adult position in mid-throat. In addition, human babies have the tongue rooted in the mouth, like apes, but in older children and adults it is rooted in the pharynx, the cavity behind the mouth. Both developments allow a much greater vocal freedom than in any earlier mammal.[2]

These anatomical adaptations occurred in lockstep, as it were, with the neural developments (especially the left hemisphere of the brain) that make possible complex muscular movements in the mouth and throat and also in the dominant hand (usually the right). Such changes have not only made complex speech possible, but have also laid the foundation for the intricacies of writing—an expression of manual dexterity. It is an intriguing feature of evolution that there were physiological links between brain, mouth, and hand long before language became a dual tool, with speech and writing: indeed, before it became a triple tool, with speech, writing, and gestural signing for the deaf.

However, the various adaptations in larynx and tongue have not been entirely beneficial. Because of the altered position of the larynx, adult humans cannot swallow and breathe at the same time: they choke if they try. Because of adaptations to mouth and jaw, chewing is harder for humans than for apes, and the impacted wisdom teeth to which humans are prone can often have serious consequences. Nevertheless, the anatomy and physiology of our heads and necks, our lowered larynx, and a tongue rooted in the pharynx together make possible a range of sound beyond the ability of any other living creature. This range includes the production of:

- *syllables:* short composite sounds whose flow is generated by air pulses from the lungs
- *vowels and consonants:* contrastive 'atoms' of sound produced in the mouth and pharynx that make up the phonetic content of syllables (singly or in groups)
- *patterns* of rhythm and modulation
- *a continuum of melody* with, for most cultures, talk at one end and song at the other.

These, one can say, constitute the evolutionary building blocks from which the physical structures of language (spoken, chanted, and sung) have emerged, while the sensory, analytical, and directive apparatus of the brain provide the syntactic and semantic complex with which these physical structures mesh smoothly. The first and still primary outcome of this development has been a vast and intricate range of oral performance. Long before the means were available to store information beyond the brain (on wood, stone, clay tablets, papyrus sheets, and other surfaces), the first singers, chanters, reciters, and orators developed mnemonic and delivery techniques to help them remember and pass on their knowledge and make it as easy as possible for their listeners to understand and remember what was heard. With the exception of ancillary facial expressions and manual gestures, everything was oral and aural: the need was to find ways of achieving something as permanent as possible by means of an entirely transient medium.

The resulting 'storage speech'—which survives in full only in non-literate societies—is ancestral to many devices used in theatres and schools, such as verse patterns, stock formulas, aids to rote learning, and rhetorical tropes (such as playing with sounds and using figures of speech). Ancient singers, chanters, and reciters formalized the patterns of sound and meaning already present in ordinary language so as to develop techniques for remembering and reciting their community records, for performing social rituals (individual and choral), for narrating stories, and for singing work songs. Prominent among the tricks of this ancient oral trade were devices associated with the way in which vocal sound 'flows'.[3]

Rhythm

The English word *rhythm* derives through Latin *rhythmus* from Greek *rhuthmós*, which means 'flow', and especially 'measured flow'. The basic concept, image, or metaphor/simile of sounds that flow as if they were water is very old, and has been used and understood in slightly different ways in such fields as acoustics, music, poetics, and phonetics, bringing in such further similes, metaphors, and models as 'sound is like a wave', 'sound has a beat', 'sounds are long or short', and 'voices move':

- *in acoustics:* rhythm is wave-like, with a steady beat and elements of longer and shorter duration
- *in music:* rhythm consists of beats and lengths of notes shown as *bars* (groups of beats), the first beat of each bar being stressed
- *in poetics:* rhythm is the arrangement of syllables in more or less regular sequences of two types of verse: in languages like Latin, these are usually sequences of syllables that contain longer or shorter vowels (quantitative metre); in languages like English, they are usually sequences of stressed and unstressed syllables (accentual metre)
- *in phonetics:* rhythm is vocal movement created by the stress, quantity, and timing of syllables.

There is nothing more fundamental to a language than its rhythm: it is one of the first features to be acquired by children and one of the most difficult for adults to change, or to adopt convincingly in another language. The rhythm of language begins in the lungs, in pulses of air produced by the movement of the intercostal respiratory muscles. Phoneticians have three terms for such pulses: *chest pulses*, *breath pulses*, and *syllable pulses*. A flow of such pulses (the foundation for syllables) produces the beat heard in all normal speech. The rest of a syllable (the phonetic qualities that distinguish, say, *hi* from *ho*, *ba* from *ka*) is as it were added in the mouth, in association with pharynx and nose. However, sometimes a pulse can occur without producing any sound at all, as for example when one says '*kyou* instead of *thank you*'—a condition known as *silent stress*, in which there is still a beat even though the syllable, in this case *than*, is not pronounced. A chest pulse with greater force than usual is called a *stress pulse*, which is realised in speech as a stressed syllable. Ordinary chest pulses occur at about five per second, stress pulses less frequently.

The two kinds of pulse work differently together in different languages, producing distinctive rhythms. Phoneticians, seeking to account for differences in the timing of elements in different languages, distinguish two types: *syllable-timed* and *stress-timed languages*, depending on whether the unit of time is the syllable or the foot. Some languages fit well into these categories; others do not. Syllable-timed languages, which include French and Japanese, have a characteristic *rat-a-tat* beat, each syllable equal; stress-timed languages, which include English and Russian, have a characteristic *TUMpty-TUMpty-TUM* beat, some elements more prominent than others. Among the languages that do not fit neatly are Arabic and Hindi, and timing is in any case not uniform throughout speech in any language, for many reasons, including simply the wish on certain occasions to do things differently.

The two categories are therefore useful fictions rather than absolute facts, but the distinction has sound pedagogical value, when for example speakers of English aim for syllable-timing in their French and speakers of French aim for stress-timing in their English. Importantly, whatever kind of rhythm a language has, it will generally be more marked in recitation, chanting, and song, as part of that language's tradition of storage speech, and this is true for everything from epic recitals to nursery rhymes. And the ancient implications of storage speech will carry over into the reading of texts.

A noteworthy feature of rhythm in English is the reduction of the vowels in unstressed (weak) syllables towards a centralizing vowel, known as *schwa* and represented in phonetic script by an inverted 'e' [ə]. A gentle cough-like sound, as in the first syllable of *above* and the second syllable of *organize*, schwa is the commonest vowel sound in the language. Often the reduction of the substance in an unstressed syllable is so great that there is no vowel at all. Instead, there is a *syllabic consonant*, such as a syllabic [n] in the second spoken syllable of *happen* and a syllabic [*l*] in the second spoken syllable of *little*.

The standard orthography of English provides no clues about the rhythm of speech—especially rapid speech. There are no graphic devices for displaying inequality among spoken syllables, with the exception of certain conventions of colloquiality and verse: for example, when an apostrophe marks the loss of a sound, as in *don't* for *do not* and *cap'n* for *captain*. It is therefore important for both children and adults learning to read English to know about rhythms that are not reflected in print, and to come to terms with them—usually by oral practice and a comparison of text and sound (for example, while listening to living exemplars and/or to recordings). Native-speaking children of course have a great advantage over both non-native-speaking children and adult learners, because they have learned the rhythms long before going to school. But they too need help with relating what they know—and can do 'naturally'—to what they find on a printed page or a screen. In a serious sense, when they learn to read they have to learn to supply the rhythm that is there but cannot be seen.[4]

Rhythm and rhyme

The resemblance between the words *rhythm* and *rhyme* is not accidental. They come from the same etymological stable, as do *frail* and *fragile*, *royal* and *regal*, and other such doublets—paired words with similar histories, forms, and meanings. English is particularly rich in doublets because Latin words have often come into the language along two routes:

- *indirectly* through French (usually at an earlier time)
- *directly* from Latin (usually at a later time).

For example, while *frail* came from French, considerably adapting the Latin original *fragilis* ('breakable'), *fragile* came directly from Latin and so resembles it much more closely; similarly, *royal* came through French, but *regal* came directly from *regalis* ('kingly'). Comparably, *rhyme* came through French, earlier, and *rhythm* came directly from Latin, much later. Both are from *rhythmus*, which—as noted above—had already been taken into Latin from Greek. That is a complex enough state of affairs, but the story has been further complicated by the vagaries of medieval orthography and collisions and separations of meaning.

In medieval Latin, the term *rhythmus* (usually spelled *rythmus* or *rithmus*) was not generally used in the classical sense of 'a measured flow of sound' but in three senses relating to *consonance*, as (1) the harmony or correspondence of sounds of any kind (as opposed to *dissonance*, disharmony), (2) especially the harmony of consonants (as opposed to *assonance*, the harmony of vowels), and (3) especially the harmony of consonants at the ends of words, as in the Latin phrases:

- *beati pacifici* ('blessed [are] the peace-makers'), where the same plural ending *-i* occurs twice
- *verbatim et litteratim* ('word for word and letter for letter': that is, accurately rendered), where the same adverbial ending *-atim* occurs twice
- *dabit qui dedit* ('he will give [again] who has [already] given'), where the same third-person ending *-it* occurs twice, and there is also alliteration with *d*.

Patterns of this kind, also referred to in the classical tradition as *homeoteleuton* (Greek: '[something with] the same ending [as something else]'), were common in Latin because of its wide range of inflectional word-endings. Such patterns are closely comparable to what people recognise as *rhyme* in present-day English, but are not the same, because rhyme in English depends on syllables and parts of syllables without reference to function or meaning, *not* on elements in words that are the same because they have the same function or the same meaning. In the Middle Ages, therefore, Latin *rhythmus*, although directly ancestral to English *rhythm*, did not have its present-day meaning, but meant something closer to present-day *rhyme*, of which it was the indirect ancestor.

The medieval Latin forms *rythmus* and *rithmus* were the source of the Old French noun *rime*, first attested in the twelfth century. The meaning of *rime* was the same as Latin *rythmus/rithmus*, 'consonance, particularly in the endings of two or more words', but this was extended by the thirteenth century to include verse that contains such consonance of endings—and the type of verse that was particularly noted for 'rime' had accentual rather than quantitative metre: something far commoner in English than in Latin. In this we have the beginning of the recognition of our *rhyme* and perhaps also a greater use of techniques that we can recognise as rhyme.

In the sixteenth century, Latin *rhythmus* was adapted into French as *rhythme* and came either directly or through French into English, with a very wide range of spellings, including at least *rithme, rhithme, rythme, rhythme, rithm, rhithm, rythm, rhythm* (all generally pronounced 'rime'!). The term had at that time two meanings:

- *all the senses of medieval rithmus and rime*, relating to consonance, especially of endings; in other words, it subsumed the meanings of *rime*
- *the classical and present-day sense* of 'measured flow'.

The old spelling *rime* had continued unchallenged until this time when, in addition to a flood of new words from Latin and Greek, there was a massive re-Latinization of words borrowed from Latin in earlier times. Because they had mainly been borrowed through French, they had a distinctly un-Latin look and sound, which the Latinizers felt ought to be rectified. In French, *rime* has kept its ancient indigenous spelling and pronunciation, but in English there was pressure to conform to a classical norm on the printed page whether or not people kept the old pronunciation. After 1600, however, two compromise spellings emerged, each adding an *h* to *rime* but not a *t* or a *th*. These were *rhime* and *rhyme*. The second spelling prevailed because of the strong Greek associations of the *y*: compare *hypnosis, psychic, syzygy*. The older form *rime* has, however, continued as a minority practice, favoured by some because it is the older form or is easier to spell, or both. It is also universally accepted in certain contexts, such as the full title of Samuel Taylor Coleridge's poem *The Rime of the Ancient Mariner*.

The words *rhyme* and *rhythm*, then, collided in the sixteenth century, that age of great oral and orthographic flux, and for a time the written form *rhythm* had the fundamental meanings of both words as used today. By the seventeenth century, however, *rhythm* was restricted to the flow of poetry, by the nineteenth its range expanded to include the flow of prose, and by the twentieth it covered all the measured flow detectable in the universe, from language and music to wholesale physical and social movement and change. And most importantly for our purposes, by the seventeenth century the pair *rhythm* and *rhyme* had been established, with separate spellings, pronunciations, and areas of meaning.[5]

Rhyme-1 and rhyme-2

Rhythm is clearly a universal of language (and many other things), but the status of rhyme is not so clear: or at least not of *rhyme* as the term is generally understood at the present time in English. It may, however, be possible to borrow from, and in effect formalize, the medieval sense of *rime*, proposing as a result two senses of *rhyme* that we can bear in mind today, the first containing the second, as follows:

- *Rhyme-1:* a broader sense that can also be called sound play, covering all the echoes, chimes, and resonances of language. Rhyme-1 includes such phenomena as alliteration, consonance, assonance, and homeoteleuton, as well as all the other aesthetic, euphonic, stylistic, and rhetorical devices that, as it were, sit 'on top of' rhythm, giving it added value. In this containing sense, rhyme *is* a universal of language, expressed differently in different languages. Whereas rhythm starts in the lungs, rhyme-1 belongs in the vocal apparatus of mouth, pharynx, and nose. In its echoic, chiming, mnemonic way it is as fundamental as rhythm or syntax or any other aspect of speech.
- *Rhyme-2:* a narrower sense, covering only one realization of rhyme-1, and therefore on a par with alliteration, assonance, and the other subtypes just listed. Rhyme-2 has the everyday meaning of rhyme in present-day English: 'Identity in sound of some part, esp[ecially] the end, of words or lines of verse' (the first sense of the entry *rhyme* in the *Random House Compact Unabridged Dictionary*, 1996). Rhyme-2 is only one of many ways in which the language-universal rhyme-1 is realized in a particular language or cultural tradition at any time.

This division—and its close association with rhythm—helps resolve various problematical aspects of the term *rhyme*. For example, Clark and Whitehall (1974) have commented as follows on both the medieval coverage of rhyme and the lack of universality in what it primarily refers to today:

> To trace the history of r[hyme] in Western Atlantic literatures is a discursion into the unknown, particularly since early writers integrate it with assonance, consonance, alliteration, and the like under one head. In native North America, it occurs only in one Indian language, where it is probably borrowed from Eng[lish]. Most cultures' verse lacks r[hyme] either as an organizational device or as ornament. (708)

> Systematic rhyming . . . has appeared in such widely separated
> languages (e.g. Chinese, Sanskrit, Arabic, Norse, Prov[encal],
> Celtic) that its spontaneous development in more than one of them
> can be reasonably assumed. In the rest it may have been introduced
> like any other device from the outside, and any language that had
> already acquired r[hyme], no matter how, may have learned new
> applications of it from its neighbors. (706)

Use of the terms *rhyme-1* and *rhyme-2* helps clarify the difficulties to which Clark and Whitehall point. In the first quoted paragraph, the first sentence refers to rhyme-1, the second to rhyme-2, and we are free to suppose that other Native American languages have had other ways of embodying rhyme-1 (sound play, echoes, and chimes) into their speech. The third sentence continues to discuss rhyme-2, indicating that it is not a universal feature of language. In the second paragraph, the first sentence also deals with limitations on rhyme-2: only some languages, exemplified by those listed, have rhyming verse comparable to that in English. The second sentence notes that such verse can spread from language to language through culture diffusion, and leaves undiscussed the question of what kinds of rhyme-1 (alliteration, etc.) already occur in languages that do not (yet) have rhyme-2.

Alliteration in English

Two aspects of rhyme-1 are particularly important in English, because of their high frequency of occurrence and their antithetical relationship: *alliteration*, which deals with similarity at the beginnings of words, such as the *b*s in *bread and butter* (and has for this reason sometimes been called *initial rhyme*), and *rhyme-2*, which concerns similarity at the ends of words, as with the *ing*s in *ting-a-ling*. The two occur both independently of one another and in association, and each has dominated English verse at different times: alliteration in the Old English period (with a brief renaissance in Middle English), and rhyme-2 from the seventeenth to the earlier twentieth century. Alliteration has had a wider range of use than rhyme-2; the following list, adapted from the entry *alliteration* in the *Oxford Companion to the English Language* (1992), identifies eleven areas in which it freely occurs:

- *verse:* 'O Wild West Wind, thou breath of autumn's being' (Shelley)
- *story-telling prose:* 'the great grey-green, greasy Limpopo River'

(Kipling); 'Tune the pipes to the tragedy of tallow, the bane of bulk, the calamity of corpulence' (O. Henry)
- *speech-making:* 'Do not let us speak of darker days; let us rather speak of sterner days' (Churchill)
- *advertising:* 'Guinness is good for you'; 'You can be sure of Shell'
- *tongue-twisters:* 'Peter Piper picked a peck of pickled peppers'; 'She sells sea-shells on the sea shore'
- *similes (often clichéd):* 'as cool as a cucumber'; 'as dead as a doornail'
- *reduplicated words:* 'flimflam'; 'tittle-tattle'
- *collocations, idiomatic phrases, and proverbs:* 'bed and breakfast'; 'footloose and fancy-free'; 'Look before you leap'
- *nicknames and epithets:* 'Battling Bill'; 'Tiny Tim'; 'the Broadway Butcher'
- *newspaper headlines (especially tabloid):* 'Saucy Sue brings home the bacon'.

The *Companion* also notes that alliteration is often used for emphasis, to help drive a point home in a colourful and therefore memorable way, as in 'But Pooh is loved in Consett and Calgary, in Kalamazoo and Kalgoorlie, as tenderly as in Camberley and Carshalton' (Godfrey Hodgson, *Independent*, 2 June 1990).

Rhyme in English

Although it is not as extensive as alliteration, rhyme-2 is more complex and has been thoroughly institutionalized. As with alliteration, we need two or more words or phrases to achieve the desired effect; a traditional term for these words and phrases is *rhyme fellows*, and they are generally organized as follows:

- *monosyllabically* as in *bold/gold*
- *disyllabically* (1) with stress on the second syllable, as in *amass/surpass*, and (2) with stress on the first syllable, as in *banter/canter*
- *trisyllabically* with initial stress, as in *battery/flattery*
- *phrasally* (1) with stress on the first words, as in *stayed with us/played with us*, and (2) with stress on the middle word or syllable, as in *believe me/deceive me*.

NOTE that rhyme fellows of one sort may rhyme with those of another sort: as, for example *poet* and *know it* in *I'm a poet and I don't know it*.

RHYTHM, RHYME, AND REASON

Since the sixteenth century an extensive technical vocabulary has developed for discussing the mechanics of verse rhyming in English. The major terms in this vocabulary, with specimens, are:

- *end rhyme* (the commonest form): the occurrence of rhyming words at the end of lines of verse, as in the second and fourth lines of the following stanza, but not the first and third:

    'Is there anybody there?' said the Traveller,
    Knocking on the moonlit *door*;
    And his horse in the silence champ'd the grasses
    Of the forest's ferny *floor*.
    (Walter de la Mare, *The Listeners*)

NOTE that the alliteration in *f* in the fourth line blends into the rhyme.

- *internal or interior rhyme:* the occurrence of rhyming words within a line of verse, either in their own right (first example) or with an internal word that rhymes with a terminal word (second example, in which the effect is of two short lines written as one):

    Sister, my sister, O *fleet sweet* swallow,
    Thy way is long to the sun and the south
    (Algernon Swinburne, *Itylus*)

Then a sentimental *passion* of a vegetable *fashion*
(W. S. Gilbert, *Patience*)

- *masculine or single or strong rhyme:* the occurrence of rhymed stressed syllables (often monosyllables, and usually forming a noun, verb, or adjective) at the ends of lines:

    Stands the Church clock at ten to *three*?
    And is there honey still for *tea*?
    (Rupert Brooke, *The Old Vicarage, Grantchester*)

- *feminine or double or weak rhyme:* the occurrence of rhymes that include unstressed syllables following immediately after stressed syllables:

Love is enough: though the World be a-wan*ing*,
And the woods have no voice but the voice of complain*ing*
(William Morris, *Love is enough*)

- *triple rhyme*: the (rare) occurrence in verse of rhymes that include two unstressed syllables coming immediately after stressed syllables:

  I'd rather have a *tricycle*
  Than I would have a *bicycle*,
  For skidding on an *icicle*
  Is safer on a *tricycle*.
  (Anon)

- *eye or vision rhyme:* the occurrence of what appears to be rhyme but is an illusion created by a resemblance in spelling or by a desire to force a rhyme because of such a resemblance:

  A creature might forget to weep who bore
  Thy comfort long, and lose thy love *thereby*!
  But love me for love's sake, that evermore
  Thou mayst love on, through love's *eternity*.
  (Elizabeth Barrett Browning, *Sonnets from the Portuguese*)

  A certified poet from *Slough*,
  Whose methods of rhyming were *rough*,
  Retorted, 'I see
  That the letters agree
  And if that's not sufficient I'm *through*.
  (limerick, Clifford Witting)

- *imperfect or near or half or oblique rhyme, or pararhyme, or off rhyme, or slant rhyme:* terms, often with different meanings, for echoes at the ends of lines that do not fit the usual rhyme-2 patterns but belong within the circle of rhyme-1, because they are kinds of assonance, consonance, and the like. Three examples are provided without further analysis:

  It seemed that out of battle I *escaped*
  Down some profound long tunnel, long since scooped
  Through granites which titanic wars had *groined*.
  Yet also there encumbered sleepers *groaned*,
  Too fast in thought or death to be bestirred.
  (Wilfred Owen, *Strange Meeting*)

And when to the chase his court would *crowd*,
The poor flung ploughshares on his *road*,
And shrieked, 'Our cry is from King to *God*!'
(Dante Gabriel Rossetti, *The White Ship*)

One dignity delays *for all*—
One mited After*noon*—
None can avoid this *purple*—
None evade this *Crown*!
(Emily Dickinson)

Rhyme schemes and rhetorical devices

The above description of rhyme fellows and kinds of rhyme demonstrates a high level of organization and variation. There is, however, a higher level still, in which rhymes take on complex but highly stable patterns known as *rhyme schemes*. Such schemes have at least two functions: to provide the poet with a framework within which to work and to encourage in the reader or listener a degree of anticipation and even at times of prediction. The following three specimens are representative but by no means exhaustive, and their rhyme schemes are identified in the traditional way by means of letter formulas:

- *aabb*

I will make you brooches and toys for your delight	a
Of bird-song at morning and star-shine at night.	a
I will make a palace fit for you and me,	b
Of green days in forests and blue days at sea.	b

  I will make my kitchen, and you shall keep your room,
  Where white flows the river and bright blows the broom,
  And you shall wash your linen and keep your body white
  In rainfall at morning and dewfall at night.
  (Robert Louis Stevenson, *Romance*)

- *ababb*

Helen, thy beauty is to me	a
Like those Nicean bards of yore	b
That gently, o'er the perfumed sea,	a
The weary way-worn wanderer bore	b
To his own native shore.	b

> On desperate seas long wont to roam,
> Thy hyacinth hair, thy classic face,
> Thy Naiad airs have brought me home
> To the glory that was Greece,
> And the grandeur that was Rome.
> (Edgar Allen Poe, *To Helen*)

- *abcb*

> It is an ancient Mariner,   a
> And he stoppeth one of three.   b
> 'By thy long grey beard and glittering eye,   c
> Now wherefore stopp'st thou me?   b
>
> The Bridegroom's doors are open'd wide,
> And I am next of kin;
> The guests are met, the feast is set:
> May'st hear the merry din.'
> (Samuel Taylor Coleridge, *The Rime of the Ancient Mariner*)

Together with specific metrical patterns, such as iambic pentameter (which I will not discuss here), such rhyme schemes often serve to identify kinds of *stanzas* (groups of lines of verse), as for example a four-line stanza rhyming *aabb*. Some stanza-identifying schemes are highly complex and varied, as for example the patterns of the sonnet, a genre that consists of only one stanza of fourteen lines. One such rhyme scheme, used in Shakespeare's sonnet beginning 'Shall I compare thee to a summer's day?', is *abab/cdcd/efef/gg*, embodied in the words:

- day, temperate, May, date   abab
  shines, dimmed, declines, untrimmed   cdcd
  fade, ow'st, shade, grow'st   efef
  see, thee   gg

In addition to its organizational role, rhyme-2 has a rhetorical role. For example, in Shakespeare's plays, which are written almost entirely in blank (unrhymed) verse, a rhyming couplet is often—but not always—used to signal the end of a speech or a scene. Compare for example the last two lines of blank verse and then the closing couplet in the following, at the end of Act 5, Scene 1 of *Romeo and Juliet*. Here a grief-stricken Romeo tells the apothecary to go, saying:

- I sell thee poison; thou hast sold me none.
  Farewell, buy food, and get thyself in flesh.
  Come, cordial and not poison, go with *me*
  To Juliet's grave, for there must I use *thee*.

It is curious that, despite the vast amount of rhymed verse in English (whether literary in the case of sonnets or general and popular in the case of nursery rhymes and pop songs), the language is not rich in rhymable words. English words are very different from those of more inflected languages like Italian and Spanish. Because they lack complex, recurring inflections, English words have a very wide range of endings, so that some rhyme fellows, like *mountain/fountain*, rhyme with no other words at all—short of nonsense words such as **plountain*, created in the spirit of Lewis Carroll and Dr Seuss simply so as to produce a rhyme. Many words, such as *breadth*, *circle*, and *month*, have no rhyme fellows at all. Because of this, poets writing in English have freely made use of 'near rhymes' (known as *rhyming licences*) that involve assonance and other distant chimes, as in the above examples from the work of Owen, Rossetti, and Dickinson (under *imperfect rhyme*). Such ploys are acceptable (though only just, hence the 'imperfect') because there is simply so little to choose from. And for the same reason certain kinds of romantic and popular verse lean heavily on such clichéd rhyme fellows as *moon/June* and *love/dove*.

Conclusion

This discussion of rhyme has covered millions of years, from the first mammalian isolation cry to the specific problems of English, a language that uses rhyme a great deal yet is rather impoverished in what words and phrases can be made to rhyme. The vast canvas that I have painted, however sketchily, is probably more than most people would expect in a discussion of rhyme, but I hope I have shown that it is necessary. Certainly, dealing with English alone, I could have discussed nothing beyond the intricate aspects of what I have called *rhyme-2*. The more I thought about rhyme, however, and about phenomena close to it, such as alliteration, the more I felt: what can we know about rhyme if we only focus on rhyme, especially as the term itself is not precise and has such an odd history? I have therefore rung the changes of the centuries, in an exercise that, I hope, puts rhyme in an ancient and profoundly significant context.

For rhyme is never alone. It rests on the rhythm of breath and speech, partnered and often blended with such other sound play as alliteration, assonance, consonance, onomatopoeia, repetition, and parallelism. In turn, this playing with sound underpins and intermixes with playing with words and with rhetorical devices such as metaphor, simile, and metonymy. The result may be as elegant as a sonnet or as street-smart as rap, but there is always something primordial about it, something that has been so many thousands of years in the making that our children are born (as it were) 'wired' for it, and learn through it. They are far more like Mr Fox than Mr Knox, and are just as relentlessly in love with it all:

> Mr. Fox!
> I hate this game, sir.
> This game makes
> my tongue quite lame, sir.
> Mr. Knox, sir,
> That's a shame, sir.
> We'll find something
> new to do now.
> Here is lots of
> new blue goo now.
> New goo. Blue goo.
> Gooey. Gooey.
> Blue goo. New goo.
> Gluey. Gluey.[6]

Notes and references

1. From Dr Seuss (1960).
2. For the paleontology of speech, see Leakey and Lewin (1992), Lieberman (1991) and Gibson and Ingold (1993).
3. For storage speech, see the entry *Communicative shift* in McArthur (1992). [And the section 'Knowledge Revolution' in this work.]
4. For rhythm, syllable-timing and stress-timing see Abercrombie (1967), Couper-Kuhlen (1993), and the entries *rhythm, stress,* and *syllable* in McArthur (1992).
5. For etymologies of *rhyme, rhythm,* and *rime,* see the *Oxford English Dictionary,* Second Edition (1989), and/or the *New Shorter Oxford English Dictionary* (1993).
6. From Dr Seuss (1960).

3

The power of words: pressure, prejudice, and politics in our vocabularies and dictionaries

[A paper commissioned for, and presented at, the conference 'Language and Power: Cross-Cultural Dimensions of English in Media and Literature', August 1986, organized by the Institute of Culture and Communication, the East-West Center, Honolulu, Hawaii, US. It was published, as part of the conference proceedings, in a special issue of *World Englishes: Journal of English as an International and Intranational Language*, 5:2/3, edited by Braj B. Kachru and Larry E. Smith, Pergamon Press, Oxford & New York, 1986.]

Because the use, nature, impact, and general potency of words—whether in their free state or as listed in dictionaries—is too large a subject to cover in a paper of this length, I have limited myself to four areas that I take to be fundamental in the issue of words as tokens or counters in the various power games that we consciously or unconsciously engage in. These areas are, with their section headings:

Words and bias Bias and centricity (ego-, ethno-, Anglo-, and so forth) in our thinking, our sociocultural dispositions, and our linguistic behaviour.

Words as procedural fictions The inherently arbitrary and fictional aspect of words as contrasted with their capacity to influence us for good or for ill.

Packets of meaning and form The container-like quality of words, through which each word carries a relatively determinate fragment of our sociocultural worldview, with the results that, although technical terms like 'xenon' can be easily defined, many other words—such as 'word' itself—are virtually impossible to define in a compact and comprehensive manner.

Power over words The historical, cultural, and technological factors that have predisposed us to make certain (often implicit) assumptions about what words are and what they do, and the possibility that—with a humane application of the discoveries of linguistics—we can improve our perceptions of such things as sociolinguistic centricity as well as our skill in minimizing the frictions of (often unintended) ethnic, sexist, and élitist slurs.

Words and bias

A book with the title *The Story of Language* came out in England in 1964, with a revision in 1972. It was published by Pan paperbacks for the general reading public and its author was Dr Charles L. Barber, at the time of writing Reader of English at the University of Leeds. An impressive scholar, Barber studied at St Catharine's College, Cambridge, where he took a first-class honours degree in English. He is a widely travelled man with such varied interests as music, drama, and astronomy, and his book reflects a broad and concerned humanity.

When I read it I found it informative and satisfying in many ways, but was at the same time frustrated. Although the book informed me and helped me frame my own linguistic opinions, it also left me feeling somewhat alienated, in part because—as it emerged on closer analysis —there was something of a gulf between Barber and myself, although we are both what might be called members of the scholarly guild of the United Kingdom of Great Britain and Northern Ireland. I would like therefore to use Barber's book and my analytical response to it as a starting point here, not because I wish to do a hatchet job on the book, but because I think it serves rather well as an example of the kinds of problems with words that we all face, whether we are members of the guild of university scholars or simply people using their language as best they can. In particular, for a gathering in Hawaii in 1986 in an East-West Center, I want to start with this particular book because it illustrates certain ethnocentric matters that are significant for all of us here.

We can start with the title and the presence in it of the definite article. Barber's book is not presented as any story of language but—whether at the behest of publisher or author—as *the* story of language. This one short grammatical word is distinctly potent in what it can do and imply; we receive from it the message that absolute information is on offer here.

In the preface, however, there is a statement that appears to run counter to the absolutist title, as follows:

> This book is about the history of language: about the process of change which goes on continually in any language which is actually in use . . . Since every reader has an intimate, if unsystematic, knowledge of his own language, I have centred the book on English, and the second half of it is in effect a history of the English language. The first half deals with more general topics, such as the nature of language, its origins, the causes of linguistic change, and language families. (p.vii)

There is a great deal that can be said about the *wording*—a term that I am using deliberately—of this extract. We can accept it as an honestly intended statement of the author's position and of his plan for the book: after all, a book of this kind has to have some sort of shape and directionality. Secondly, however, and I would argue inevitably, it serves to 'fossilize' Barber into a specific stratum of the history of our species at large and Western European—especially English—scholarship in particular.

One can, for example, ask what is intended by the statement that 'every reader has an intimate, if unsystematic, knowledge of his own language'. In straightforward procedural terms, if people did not have an intimate *and a systematic* knowledge of their language, they could not perform in that language. It seems likely, therefore, that Barber is not referring to the performative level of language as such but to some other level —probably the level of conscious, educated awareness of the nature and history of a language within a given culture. If this is so—and I am pretty sure that it is so—then the author is writing from a position of considerable sociocultural strength, because he belongs to the very élite (marked by a first-class honours degree from an ancient and prestigious university) that decides just *what* a sufficient systematic and conscious awareness of a language can be. He is therefore operating in the didactic mode, talking with assurance downwards to the general reader from the high throne that we have inherited from the medieval Schoolmen. His task is, in other words, to instruct the lay brethren.

The use of 'Schoolmen' and 'lay brethren' here is of course highly charged; they have strong ecclesiastical connotations and are also resolutely masculine. Barber is masculine too in his uncomplicated use of the third person singular masculine pronoun: 'every reader has an intimate, if unsystematic, knowledge of *his* own language'. Such a pronoun could easily have been avoided by casting the sentence in the plural: 'Since readers have an intimate, if unsystematic, knowledge of their own language . . .' As we know, although I said 'easily avoided', politicians of language and stylists have argued vehemently about the most aesthetically pleasing as well as the fairest way of dealing with such constructions. Barber might very well, if he were here to defend himself, argue that the singular construction is tidier and that the traditional generic *he* has covered both men and women. The crucial point is that for the generation and tradition to which he belongs this is so, but nowadays a new generation of feminists and humanists is creating a new tradition, and within *that* tradition the use of generic *he* is not acceptable. It was acceptable to me once upon a time; now it obtrudes into my consciousness, and I avoid it in my own usage. My consciousness has been raised, which means that I have shifted my position in the politics of language. The amount of correspondence to my magazine *English Today* since it first appeared eighteen months ago indicates that this is a central issue for many people, and demonstrates cogently the power of the personal pronoun.

Next comes the overt Anglocentricity of the book, freely conceded in the extract above. It can be argued that Barber's aim here is transparent and innocuous: he is writing, as he points out, 'for the reader without any previous knowledge of the subject' and such a reader does not 'require any knowledge of foreign languages, though of course these are always a help'. As a consequence, the scholar involved in this act of meritorious popularization has 'centred the book on English', and why not? There may, however, be several good reasons why not, and particularly when writing for readers with limited technical knowledge and little or no knowledge of any linguistic system other than English. One reason is that (especially for those who do not read the introductions to books) the presentation of all language moving towards the English language may tend to reinforce the unreflecting Anglocentricity of many readers, who are not required to wrestle with anything other than English in order to follow *the* story of language. In such cases, Barber's could very well appear to be the proper, natural, and evolutionary account of the history of the human race and its languages.

Another reason is that it allows Barber to relax his own vigilance over what he says and implies about all language and the English language. He has explicitly stated that the book has been centred on English, but seems unaware that it is also strongly centred on one particular *kind* of English. This happens to be a prestigious variety with its own centre in south-east England, and the variety in which he was himself educated.

He allows this centricity to go undescribed, which suggests that there is more than bias in his presentation: the received standard of the middle class in south-east England between the two world wars is offered to the reader as 'real' English, and the structure of his chapters conforms to the pyramid of discrimination in Figure 1.

Figure 1

APEX Southern England's middle-class Standard English usage

English in particular

Germanic languages and peoples in particular

Indo-European languages and peoples in particular

Language families generally

Languages generally

BASE The phenomenon of language

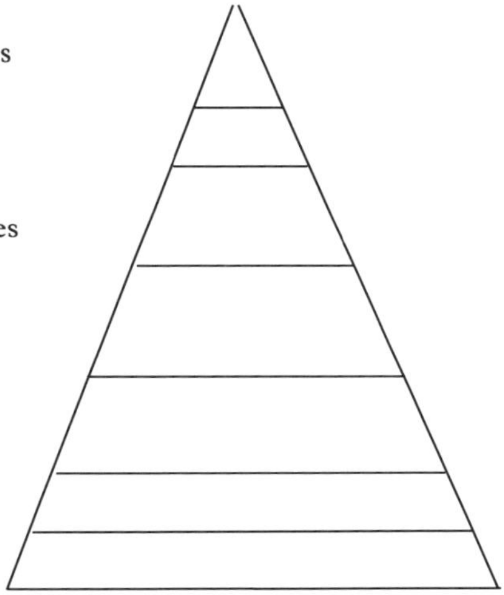

The key words of Barber's text and chapter headings contribute to this triangle of evolution, as we move from language at large up through the various narrowing levels to an apex not just of English but in effect to the norms and expectations of the community upon whom the phonetician Daniel Jones in 1917 based his *English Pronouncing Dictionary*. This work continues to be available (in fifteen successive editions and four editors) as a Britocentric guide for foreign learners of English, and has had a great influence on the phonemic models still offered to non-native users of English by the major British publishers of language materials. It is known among phoneticians and language teachers as 'Received Pronunciation' and more widely as 'BBC English', 'Oxford English', and sometimes 'The Queen's English', all terms that are centric in various important and potent ways.

At this point we can ask what effect such a pyramid might have —explicitly or implicitly—on Barber's public, or on the publics of comparable works. The answer, I imagine, is that it would reinforce the sense of security of anyone who shares Barber's centricities and expectations, but would at the same time reinforce the insecurities of others, the more so as those others feel themselves located farther and farther out and down. Crudely, it could be a discouraging book for non-white, non-Western, non-European, non-English, non-scholarly non-males.

Nobody would lose out entirely, though; the book is well-written and informative. It is, however, much less humane than the author apparently intended it to be, and this because he could not at the time move sufficiently out of the circles of his upbringing. As a result he excludes where he might have intended to include and alienates where he might have hoped to inform and edify. One reason for this is the centric potency of the words and frameworks used. It might be argued, persuasively, that what we are faced with here is culture-boundness, sociolinguistics, and social anthropology—not words as such. We are certainly dealing with all of these but, as we have seen with the use of 'the' and 'his', all such matters come to us and at us through words, and the choice of one word rather than another in one particular context rather than another. *Only* an Englishman of Barber's background would have written such a book in this way; an American, a Scot, an Arab, or a Japanese would have done it very differently (and might also have supposed that the book was *the* story of language). Barber is by no means alone: we all suffer from the flaws (if flaws they be) that I am describing. In the late 1980s, however, it may just be possible to make more of an effort *not* to suffer from them.

Not everyone of course will respond to Barber's book in quite the way that I have. I know, for example, of no revolutionary barricades set up because of it, no slogans that read 'Down with Barber's élitist pyramid!'. What happens in many cases, as far as I can tell (there has been little if any formal investigation in a field like this), is that people accept the structures and the words pretty much as they come, objecting perhaps here and there, but submitting to the whole because of the didactic mode in which it operates. Someone like Barber is an expert, and experts are experts because they have the keys of knowledge. As in other areas of education, students have tended to reflect on their own inadequacies rather than the inadequacies of teacher and system, and conclude that they belong through some rough destiny in a peripheral place. The expert's structure and words win, and in this instance the expert's inherent ethnocentricity—which is a matter of tradition, bias, and power—goes largely undiscussed.

Words as procedural fictions

Words are vexatious entities. Down the centuries, they have posed problems for grammarians, etymologists, lexicographers, philologists, and linguists alike. Indeed, one suspects that many language professionals prefer to get on with their work without inspecting words too closely. By and large, most of the participants in Western and Westernized civilization are convinced that they know what words are and do, and have no wish to be disturbed in that conviction. Certainly, many practising lexicographers feel no need to speculate about the raw materials of their trade; they simply get on with the business of presenting and defining them in time-honoured ways.

Words are also vexatious entities because they are equally the concern of literary humanists and linguistic scientists, the humanists often resenting the late intrusion of science into what was once almost exclusively their territory. Like many other master terms in the discussion of language, 'the word' is a linguistic primitive so basic and yet so elusive that it defies the best efforts of both philosophers and general linguists to trap it in a unified theory of language. It does not make a good atom of language, it cannot easily be called a language universal, it is in part an artifact of literate civilization—and yet at the same time it has a compelling reality in all the languages that identify something akin to a *lógos, verbum, mot, Wort,* or *palabra*.

Finally, words are vexatious entities because—at least in the traditions of Western Europe and its ethnocultural diasporas—the general conception of 'words' runs into the general conception of 'language': when people talk about the power of words this may be essentially the same thing as 'the power of language'. One can, however, make a useful distinction between the two, in that words are the loaded counters that can be variously slotted into the overall communicative and manipulative structures and systems of a language. We have seen this happen in a slot-and-filler way with Barber's use of *the* and *his*; he might have filled those slots in such other ways as *a* and *their*. We have also seen it happen in a particularly centric way in his approach to English as a definitive means of saying where languages are at in the world. Extending from the situation analysed in terms of Barber's book, I might choose to talk about 'the World's Englishes' rather than, say, 'World English', when looking at the role of the English language (or the English languages?) in the late twentieth century. My choice of plurality is crucial here, changing (or simply attacking) certain fundamental conceptions that most people have about English as a linguistic system. The change is a shift of sociopolitical perspective and is therefore a speech act of considerable significance. In talking about such things, we are discussing the power of language as exhibited in the power of particular words and how we choose to use them.

At the same time it is part of the received wisdom of linguistics at this time that 'words' are conventional and arbitrary things. There is no God's-Truth correlation between *pig, ghourouni, porcus, cochon, Schwein,* or *puerco* and whatever referent it serves to isolate and label. No language has a monopoly on the accurate description of 'reality', and no dictionary offers a complete list of the words and definitions that can map neatly on to the perceived bits and pieces of a puzzling universe. It is all catch-as-catch-can, a relativist's paradise.

I have no quarrel with this position, but I am interested in its implications. Nothing in the preceding paragraph means that populations—'educated' or otherwise—react to the arbitrary conventionality of words around them in the full awareness of their conventional and arbitrary nature. Most of the time, linguists (like everybody else) have their professional monitors switched off and do not use their understanding of language in any sense therapeutically or for overt consciousness-raising: they are as influenced, as insultable, as biased in broad terms, as capable of offending deliberately or by implicit failure to care, and so forth, as anybody else. Like everybody else, linguists are embedded in networks of interacting vocabulary with great power to affect them intellectually and emotionally. It could hardly be otherwise, because we have no way (as yet, or perhaps ever) of stepping outside the circle of words and seeing just what is going on.

This does not, however, mean that we cannot become more therapeutic and socially aware, and begin to transfer some of our hard-earned understanding of the arbitrariness of our word-tokens into the everyday world of better human relations. This, in effect, is what feminists ask us all to do with regard to words that are androcentrically offensive to them; it is also what people who are cosmopolitan in their outlook might care to do with regard to a whole host of ethnically loaded terms from the obvious implications of terms like *kike, wog,* and *gook* through imprecise uses of *American, English,* and *Anglo* to such apparently innocuous usages as *native speaker* (What does your communicant understand affectively by 'native' and what else does a person do besides 'speak'?) and *foreign learner* (What do we intend by 'foreign' and what status is implied by 'learn'?). We even have to be careful about the nuances of whole institutional expressions like, for example, the phrase 'English as a second language' in a world where to be bilingual can mean that one's first language loses out. The pressures, prejudices, and politics of all such words demand that we exercise caution and even seek actively to practise a greater global neutrality in the way we use words to negotiate with others.

Words, then, are procedural fictions, but because we have lived within the framework of these fictions all our lives we find it very hard indeed to substitute safer words for the words that cause harm, alienation, outrage, insecurity, and alarm. In the everyday world, *pig* is both an identifiable animal and—when one needs it to be—a label for any human being conceived as disgusting. That is an arbitrary matter too, because it depends first on our perception of the pig as an animal and then what can be isolated as disgusting among humans. In the process, the humans need not necessarily bear a close resemblance to pigs; they need only be considered socially unclean (say, among Muslims), politically nasty (among people influenced by George Orwell's *Animal Farm*), or the lackeys of entrenched power (the police as seen by many young Americans in the early 1970s). The fictive nature of the whole thing is easily demonstrated, but that makes little or no difference to the vehemence or effectiveness of the word when so used. Sticks and stones still break our bones, and names do in fact often wound us too.

Packets of meaning and form

So far I have proposed that words are works of fiction that nonetheless operate with much of the power of fact, and that a person's choice of words can be dictated by where that person stands in relation to certain socially 'centred' positions. I would now like to make a professional stab at describing how this remarkable but often unremarked state of affairs has come about.

To do this let me first of all crudely characterize *the word* as 'a minimal self-sufficient packet of linguistic form and meaning', leaving aside for the time being a whole battery of complex issues. This is a working definition and not at all a comprehensive definition (which in fact I consider impossible for a word like *word*—but see Chapter 4). By 'minimal' and 'self-sufficient' I mean that in principle words tend to be shorter rather than longer and that there are lesser elements that contribute to words and are *not* self-sufficient (like syllables on the phonic/graphic level and affixes on the morphological level). Being self-sufficient, words can operate alone or be isolated for citational purposes and still remain a coherent packet, unlike affixes and often bases and roots at a lower syntactic rank and many phrases at a higher syntactic rank. By 'packet' I am implying that a word is a kind of container just as a physical bag is a container, with a form that in some sense contains and something else that is contained—the content, usually called its 'meaning'. By this marvellously difficult word (which also in my view cannot be comprehensively defined), I intend here all the denotational and connotational value of a word, usually expressed where possible by means of pointing or depicting but more commonly simply by means of other words in the vast circularity of 'folk', 'popular', and 'academic' lexicography. This 'value' changes through time and across space, and may well have one or more distinct sense cores but is also subject to indeterminacy at its boundaries, so that, for example, one can never encapsulate in definitions the range and differences among such words as *big, large, great,* and *grand*. As a consequence, *all* definitions are operational rather than comprehensive, some definitions (as of such technical words as *titanium*) being to all intents and purposes complete and clear, others (as with *word* and *meaning*) being so wide in their applications and ancient in their signification that their definitions are more patently incomplete and less than clear.

Despite their fictive nature and their indeterminacy of meaning, however, words can be put together in strings or series which, in given contexts, can be extremely clear and effective, and it is in this two-part quality of general diffuseness but sudden contextual focus that the units we call 'words' obtain much of their power to evoke action and provoke reaction (cf. Le Page and Tabouret-Keller, 1985). Among its senses of the word *word*, the *Longman Dictionary of the English Language* (1984) has the phrase 'a meaningful unit of language', while its primary definition of *power* is 'the possession of control, authority, or influence over others'. Putting these together in order to gloss the phrase *the power of words* one gets something like 'the control, authority or influence exercised over others through meaningful units of language'. I like this gloss, because it applies equally well to a Republican politician at a rally in Texas and a 'witchdoctor' in Papua New Guinea casting a spell.

That range is important, because it reminds us of who we are and where we come from. In terms of our sociobiology, both the Republican politician and the PNG witchdoctor are highly evolved beings, but the apparent cultural gulf between them arises out of the millennia in which people have been operating with words. The witchdoctor belongs—or until recently belonged—to what Walter Ong (1982) calls 'a primary oral culture', a state of affairs which 'deeply typographic folk' like ourselves find hard to imagine. In such a culture, Ong reminds us, words have 'great power' and 'magical potency' that are tied in with people's 'sense of the word as necessarily spoken, sounded, and hence power- driven'. In addition, Ong argues that this is commonly true of oral societies, and may well have once been a universal fact of life in all such societies.

In the growth of what we call 'civilization', the next stage has been described by Elizabeth Eisenstein (1979) as 'scribal culture', societies in which a literate élite looks after relatively few written artefacts mediated to the populace at large through recitation, chanting, or simply reading aloud. In such societies, the written word was also magically potent, as is witnessed in the transformation in the European 'Dark Ages' of the Greek word *grammar* (a subject originally closely tied to alphabetic literacy) into magic as a *grimoire* (a French book of spells) and as *glamour* (a perilous attraction identified by the Scots).

In passing, one can also note the evolution of hand-copied manuscripts and codices into printed books after the evolution of the printing press in the fifteenth century. Such copied texts were largely but not entirely scripture-related, and were preponderantly in the care of monks and priests. When the presses first began to produce books, one of the most important was the Bible in both Latin and various vernacular languages, influencing the standard form of such languages for centuries afterwards. Alongside the 'scriptural' Bibles there appeared 'bibles of usage' that helped literate citizens cope with the new standard languages—and foremost among these were *dictionaries*. These 'books of dictions' (sayings, expressions, words) served to advise the more or less insecure about the 'proper' spelling, pronunciation, grammatical usage, and meanings of the words available in the standard forms of the various European languages, and benefited from the centuries-old reverence felt towards written materials. In the company of genuine Christian scripture, these dictionaries became receptacles of a new kind of lexical truth, and, even where lexicographers knew that they were not recording such a truth, users at large tended to see things differently. Lexicographers, like prescriptive grammarians, were perceived as a kind of legislator whose work was to winnow the wheat from the chaff and then provide precise definitions for the wheat.

Such attitudes towards dictionaries have persisted into our own times, despite the more objective standards of nineteenth-century academic lexicography. If this were not so then there would not have been that remarkable outburst against Webster's *Third International Dictionary* at the beginning of the 1960s. Reviewers across the United States rose up to castigate the Merriam-Webster Co. of Springfield, Massachusetts, because it had let the permissivists in and failed to live up to the standards established just after the Revolution by that arch-legislator of language,

Noah Webster. The inheritance had been betrayed (cf. Sledd and Ebbitt, 1962; McArthur, 1986: pp. 138–41; Morton, 1994).

This diachronic excursion indicates that throughout what we know of the history of our species, words have been perceived and conceived as power-laden: in primary oral cultures where they were sounded magic, in oral/scribal cultures where they could be stored on parchment and recited back into active life (again, as if by magic), and in oral-cum-scribal-cum-print cultures like our own, in which something of the potency of scripture passed into dictionaries and other wordbooks, while in the population at large words continue (despite being at root arbitrary fictions) to catch people in their web of sociocultural illusion. When *The Reader's Digest* told its customers some years ago that 'it pays to increase your wordpower', it was operating from a safe base—our built-in assumptions about words. From our earliest years we observe the manipulative capacity of words, and if Noam Chomsky is right about our coming into the world as it were 'wired' for language, then we are inclined through nature as well as nurture to value—and fall subservient to—the power of words.

Power over words

Words are versatile entities. In their conceptual sphere, they are at once containers, tools, and weapons, just as in the physical world a bag is a container, a screw-driver is a tool, and a gun is a weapon. They can serve simply for communication, but are equally likely to be used (in sharp focus) for negotiation, manipulation, domination, argument, and assault. They can do their work consciously, with the full panoply of rhetoric and suasion, or they can do their work without our conscious intent, when we use words as if we were the puppets of our social and ethnic groups. And in doing all this they benefit from a backlog of millennia in which people around the world have admired and stood in awe of the professions of the word: the shamans, genealogists, priests, gurus, and magicians; the teachers, actors, playwrights, and novelists; the philosophers, logicians, lawyers, journalists, and critics—all of whom demonstrate every day what words can be made to do and can make us do.

Curiously enough, although members of such professions as these have debated for centuries about language and words, it is only recently—a matter of a few decades—that social militants and academic investigators have begun to conclude that we ought to have more conscious control over our words than our words have control (by default) over us.

Feminists in particular, especially in North America, have led the way by arguing that it is not necessary or desirable to let certain manipulative usages continue—that these usages can be combatted and replaced. This is a novel kind of language legislation, prescriptive and proscriptive not in the name of a nation-state and its prestige language standard or of a social élite conscious of its privileges, but in the name of a broader and more inclusive 'humankind'. Additionally, in our new global village, ethnic groups have become less passive about the jokes, slurs, and accompanying assumptions that assign them to lower and more peripheral places on the pyramid of life than are commensurate with their dignity.

While militants of various kinds do such things, should language professionals simply sit on their hands and do nothing (apart perhaps from observing and taking notes)? We are now possessed of a wide range of fairly reliable information about language, and could well put this knowledge to socially valuable use. The periodicals *English Today: The International Review of the English Language* (Cambridge University Press) and *World Englishes: Journal of English as an International and Intranational Language* (Pergamon Journals [later Basil Blackwell], Oxford) are examples of a new kind of activism on the part of language professionals. Their purpose is to raise consciousness in various ways, specifically with regard to English as a global language and the other languages that English impinges upon. Such aims do not in any way compromise the academic integrity of those involved. Science has never been compromised because it has led, say, to medical breakthroughs, and is hardly likely to be compromised if it leads to new social breakthroughs with regard to language and culture, and the social pressures and prejudices inherent in many of the words we use.

In recent years there has also been some movement in this general direction among the compilers and publishers of dictionaries, particularly of the English language. Unilingual dictionaries of English are of two kinds: 'mother-tongue' dictionaries with about 400 years of tradition behind them, and 'ELT' (English Language Teaching) or EFL (English as a Foreign Language) dictionaries, whose tradition is about eighty years old. No dictionary of either kind has yet been compiled on the assumption that there is a nation-neutral 'World' Standard English; they are either UK- or US-based, accompanied by a scatter of national and regional dictionaries of Australian, Canadian, Bahamian, Jamaican, or other variety.

There has been, however, in recent years a growing-together of American and British compilations, well demonstrated in the mother-tongue *Longman Dictionary of the English Language* (cited above); it blends the expertise and databases of Merriam-Webster in the US with Longman in the UK, to produce a work that is close to nation-neutral. In addition, and demonstrating a greater generosity of spirit than has been traditional, the *Oxford Dictionary of New Zealand English* has both its cover blurb and its essay on the local English rendered in both English and Maori; such developments indicate a less imperial and ethnocentric approach to the diversity of the world's Englishes—and to the languages with which English has for so long co-existed around the world.

The EFL sector, however, has not been particularly adventurous. It is British-dominated, and still follows Daniel Jones in offering the world's students of English a model of pronunciation, syntax, and lexis that fits snugly at the top of Barber's pyramid. Some concessions have been made by Oxford and Longman to American English, but by and large, whenever a contrast is made between the two, only the American variant is labelled, the British term being left as the unmarked form: that is, it is tacitly presented as the norm. In my own *Longman Lexicon of Contemporary English* (1981), I have labelled both forms, as in *colour BrE, color AmE*, the sequence being dictated by the fact that this is a British book. This has enabled Americans to accept the book as 'mid-Atlantic', where they have turned away from the *Longman Dictionary of Contemporary English* (1978) as 'too British'. To cover the gap, Longman brought out an avowedly American version of the dictionary several years later. A more open and inclusive approach in the early stages might have obviated this.

There is still some distance to go lexicographically before dictionaries of English present a balanced global picture of the language as it is currently constituted, either to mother-tongue or other consumers. To assist towards that end, however, research in the adequate delineation of the less powerful varieties of English—in terms of both syntactic and lexical distinctness—would be a great help. This could include the creation of more works like the *Dictionary of Bahamian English* (Lexik House, US) or the *Dictionary of Newfoundland English* (University of Toronto Press, Canada), or at least of well-structured glossaries of particular varieties. All such works could help towards the development of international dictionaries that are freer of specific national patronage than is currently the case. Here are some examples, in a necessarily simplified form, of the kinds of coverage we could be seeing in the next ten years or so of English lexicography:

Anglo 1 *esp SW of USA* someone who speaks English, esp if of Northern European background [short for Spanish *anglo-americano*] 2 *Canada, esp Quebec* someone who speaks English, through background or choice [short for *Anglophone*: see].

burn *ScoE* a stream

godown *S & E Asia* a warehouse

goonda *IndE* a scoundrel or thief

loch *ScoE,* **lough** *IrE* a lake

mahalo *HawE* alternate for 'thank you'

Metis, Métis *CanE* a person ('s' not pronounced) or persons ('s' pronounced) of mixed European and indigenous Indian stock

riding 1 *England* any one of three divisions into which the county of Yorkshire was formerly divided: *the North Riding, East Riding, West Riding.* 2 *Canada* a political constituency for the election of one Member of Parliament to the House of Commons in Ottawa

utie *NZE colloq abbrev* a utility vehicle

wog *derog, esp in UK* someone of Eastern, esp. Arab, appearance and background

zilch *slang, esp in US* nothing; zero

Words are vexatious and versatile entities, and so are the people who use them. The inertia of our past has conditioned us to go on using our vocabularies for egocentric, ethnocentric, and other often manipulative purposes. This will continue, but it is equally possible that, even though we cannot break free of the web of our words, we can alter the relationships within that web, and calculate more carefully the price of our freely expressed centricities. We might even be able to change the centricities themselves in the process, towards something that is decently centred in the species as a whole and not in some caste or cartel that for its own advantage arranges words like armies.

4

The word 'word'

[The entry *word*, from the *Oxford Companion to the English Language*, Oxford University Press, 1992. In the preliminary information to the invitees of the Lund 'Words' symposium, 1995 (see the introduction to Chapter 1), the organizer, Jan Svartvik, enclosed copies of this entry and the entry *word* in the *Cambridge International Dictionary of English*, ed. Paul Procter, Cambridge University Press 1995, as recent contributions to the definition of the term. The entry has been adapted here from a two-column to a whole-page format.]

Word

[Cognate with German *Wort* word, Greek *(w)eírein* speak, Latin *verbum* word, Sanskrit *vrátam* command]. A fundamental term in both the general and the technical discussion of language. The entry on *word* in the *Oxford English Dictionary* (2nd edition, 1989) displays its senses under the three headings used in 1927 by the editor C. T. Onions:

(1) *Speech, utterance, verbal expression*, divided into eleven sense groups: speech, talk, utterance; a speech, an utterance; speech as distinct from writing; verbal expression as contrasted with thought; contention, altercation; a report, news, rumour; an order, request; a promise, undertaking; a declaration, assertion; an utterance in the form of a phrase or sentence, a saying or proverb; a divine communication, scripture, and Christ.

(2) *An element of speech*, a single twelfth sense initially defined as: 'a combination of vocal sounds, or one such sound, used in a language to express an idea (e.g. to denote a thing, attribute, or relation), and constituting an ultimate minimal element of speech having a meaning

as such'. This technical definition is followed by the seven sense groups: a name, title, idea, term; engraved or printed marks on surfaces; in contrast with the thing or idea signified; the right word for the right thing; a telegraphic message; a mathematical sequence; a string of bits in a computer.

(3) *Phrases*, a heterogeneous collection of such usages *as take a person at his word, in so many words, word of honour,* and *by word of mouth*.

Other dictionary definitions

The technical definition provided in (2) above comes twelfth in the order of *Oxford English Dictionary* senses because the dictionary was compiled on historical principles. Most twentieth-century dictionaries are, however, synchronic and tend to place their equivalent of the technical sense first. The following selection of primary definitions of *word* is drawn from recent editions of two American and two British works:

(1) *Webster's Ninth New Collegiate Dictionary* (1984): 'a speech sound or series of speech sounds that symbolizes and communicates a meaning without being divisible into smaller units capable of independent use'.

(2) *American Heritage Dictionary* (1985): 'a sound or a combination of sounds, or its representation in writing or printing, that symbolizes and communicates a meaning and may consist of a single morpheme or of a combination of morphemes'.

(3) *Collins English Dictionary* (1986): 'one of the units of speech or writing that native speakers of a language usually regard as the smallest isolable meaningful element of the language, although linguists would analyse these further into morphemes'.

(4) *Chambers English Dictionary* (1988): 'a unit of spoken language: a written sign representing such an utterance'.

Literacy and the word

The earliest known word study in the Western world took place in ancient Greece. Latin words were later analysed in terms of Greek words, the model being adapted in minor ways to fit a second but similar language, and since then the classical analysis, adapted and refined for other languages, has evolved into a model through which Western scholars analyse all languages. In Greece, word study was an inseparable part of the study of texts, which had been prompted by the invention of script.

Prior to that, *name* was a more clearly delineated concept than *word*, which was rather imprecisely associated with *speech* (apparently the meaning of *wer*, the Indo-European root underlying Latin *verbum*, Sanskrit *vrátam*, and English *word*). In oral communities, there appears generally to be no great interest in separating out 'units' of language, a lack of delimitation carried over into the early stages of alphabetic writing, in which letters followed each other in lines without spaces to separate off what are now perceived as 'words'. Spaces between groups of letters became important as the conventions of writing evolved. In alphabetic systems, spaces are now universal and as a result literate people learn to recognize 'words' as visual rather than auditory units. In a real sense, the first orthographers of a language make the decisions about how words are to be perceived in that language.

The idea that marks on a surface might also relate to speech only slowly emerged from (and coexisted with) the earlier view of words as speech itself, not elements of speech. This ancient lack of distinction between *word* and *language* continues, as in Bernard Groom's comment:

> To the imaginative writer, and especially to the poet, language is a medium for self-expression. Hard and unyielding up to a point, words can none the less be so manipulated as to bear the impress of a particular mind. (*A Short History of English Words*, 1934)

Children learn about words while learning to write, become more or less comfortable with 'the written word', and may later assume that words as they are written automatically have a place as theoretical units of both speech and script. Grammarians, philologists, and linguists, all the legatees of the Greeks, have tended to focus on words as visual entities even when analysing sound, for which phoneticians developed a special alphabet. The place of the word as an ultimate unit of language has not, however, been easy to find, with the result that many twentieth-century linguists have found it necessary to look elsewhere for key units of language: 'below' the word among phonemes and morphemes or 'above' it in sentence and discourse.

The word in different languages

The nature of words varies from language to language: *amaverunt* is one word in Latin, but cannot be translated into one word of English (in which it means either *they loved* or *they have loved*). It is a verb with a root *am*, a thematic vowel *-a-*, a marker of the perfect tense *-v-*, and a complex inflectional ending *-erunt*. The English verbs that translate it have different tenses (simple past *they loved*, present perfect *they have loved*) and bear not the slightest resemblance to the structure of their Latin equivalent. Different from both English and Latin, Swahili has a primary verb form such as *kuta* ('meet'). The forms *kutana* ('meet each other') and *kutanisha* ('cause to meet each other') may be conceived as either variations of *kuta* or as distinct words. In effect, the conception 'word' is determined afresh within the system of every language, and as a result the word-as-element-of-speech is language-specific, not language-universal. The various kinds of language have their own broadly similar words, but even so there is variation from language to language inside a category: for example, among Romance languages between French and Spanish.

Eight kinds of word

Despite such complications, however, certain features are more or less true for many if not all languages. Eight such features are fundamental to English and each has its own 'word':

(1) *The orthographic word*
The word understood in terms of alphabetic or syllabic writing systems: a visual sign with space around it. It may or may not have a canonical form: in the fourteenth century, before print encouraged standardization, *merry* was also spelled *myry, myrie, murie*, and *mery*. On occasion, the orthographic word has canonical forms for different varieties within English: BrE *colour* and AmE *color* ('the same word' in two visual forms).

(2) *The phonological word*
The word understood in terms of sound: a spoken signal that occurs more commonly as part of a longer utterance than in isolation and is subject to rhythm. Traditional spoken English is a series of stressed and unstressed syllables which behave in more or less predictable ways: where an experienced listener hears *It's no good at all* being pronounced in a relaxed, informal way, a foreigner may hear *Snow good a tall*. In the flow of speech, words do not have such distinct shapes as on paper, and syllable boundaries do not necessarily reflect grammatical boundaries: the phrases *a notion* and *an ocean* are usually homophonic and only context establishes which has in fact been said.

(3) *The morphological word*
The word in terms of form lies behind both the orthographic and the phonological word: *big* has a spelt-out realization *b-i-g* and a spoken realization /big/, but is independent of both, because it can be expressed in either medium and also in sign language. This entity is capable of realization in different 'substances'; it is distinct from such spelt-out variants as *colour* and *color* as well as from the innumerable ways in which African, American, Australian, Caribbean, English, Irish, Scottish or other people may say 'colo(u)r'. However, all such users have it in common and it is the basis of such further forms as *colourful* and *discoloured*.

(4) *The lexical word*
(also called a *full word, content word, lexeme,* and *lexical item*)
The word in terms of content relates to things, actions, and states in the world. It is usually realized by one or more morphological words, as when *do, does, doing, did, done* are taken to be five 'versions' of the one verb *DO*. Lexical words are generally fitted into the flow of language through such mechanisms as *affixation, suppletion, stress shift,* and *vowel change*, all of which have morphological and other effects. The set of such words is always open to new members, and in English embraces nouns, verbs, and adjectives, and other parts of speech when they behave like nouns, verbs, and adjectives, as in 'But me no buts'. Lexical words may be simple in structure (*cat, mouse*), or composite (*cold-bloodedness, incomprehensible, teapot, blackbird, Commonwealth, stamp collector, put up with, natural selection, Parkinson's disease*).

(5) *The grammatical word*
(also called a *form word, function word, structure word,* and in some theories a subvariety of *morpheme*)
The word in terms of syntactic function contrasts with the lexical word and is an element in the structural system of a language. It serves to link lexical words. In English, conjunctions, determiners, interjections, particles, and pronouns are grammatical words. They occur frequently and have their own semantic systems, as with such particles as *up* and *down*, which relate to position, direction, space, and time. In principle, such words are a closed set to which new items are seldom added. As lubricants, grammatical words are like affixes: the *out* in *throw out* is like the prefix *e-* in *eject*; the *before* in *before the war* means the same as *pre-* in *pre-war*. They can also function like affixes, as in *he-man* and *yes-man*.

(6) *The onomastic word*

The word in terms of naming establishes special, often unique reference: the difference between *Napoleon* and *emperor*. It may be simple like *Smith* or complex like *Smithsonian*. Names may be motivated, like *Sitting Bull* (a Sioux name derived from an omen involving a bull buffalo), or conventional, like *Smith* today (though not in the Middle Ages, when the name was occupation-based). Although such words are lexical, they are not usually listed in dictionaries and may or may not be relevant in encyclopedias. They are often regarded as apart from normal vocabulary, though they too have to be learned.

(7) *The lexicographical word*

The word in terms of dictionaries is usually presented in an alphabetic setting. Many dictionaries have an entry *did* as the past of *do*, an entry *them* as the object form of *they*, and so on, with cross-references to the representative form. There are therefore two kinds of entry: anything the compilers think anyone might look up, and the *citation forms* under which definition proceeds. The conventional citation form for nouns is the singular (unless a word is always plural) and for the verb is the bare infinitive (unless the verb only occurs as a participle, or is a modal verb).

(8) *The statistical word*

The word in terms of occurrences in texts is embodied in such instructions as 'Count all the words on the page': that is, count each letter or group of letters preceded and followed by a white space. This instruction may or may not include numbers, codes, names, and abbreviations, all of which are not necessarily part of the everyday conception of 'word'. Whatever routine is followed, the counter deals in tokens or instances and as the count is being made the emerging list turns tokens into types: for example, there could be forty-two tokens of the type *the* on a page, and four tokens of the type *dog*. Both the tokens and the types, however, are unreflectingly spoken of as words.

Other 'words'

In addition, there is a large number of more or less common expressions, some technical, some semi-technical, some general and casual, all specifying kinds of words and word-like units. They fall into overlapping groups that include: (1) Terms in which *word* appears, such as: *base word, buzz word, compound word, long word, root word*. (2) Terms based on the suffix *-ism*, such as: *Americanism, Australianism, burgessism, malapropism*. (3) Terms based on the combining form *-onym*, such as: *antonym, aptronym, characternym, eponym, hyponym, synonym*. (4) Terms that relate to form more than meaning, such as: *abbreviation, acronym, complex word, compound word, initialism, port-manteau word*. (5) Terms that relate to meaning more than form, such as: *antonym, burgessism, eponym, hard word*. (6) Terms that relate to social usage, such as: *anagram, buzz word, confusible, loanword, malapropism, nonce word, palindrome, stunt word, vogue word*. All such terms fit in various ways and at various levels into the model of the word presented above. Those with their own entries in this volume are shown in the theme list below.

Words as clusters

Because of its many dimensions, the concept 'word' is more like a cluster than an atom. On the level of theory, the cluster contains the kinds of words discussed above. On the level of practical activity, people 'know a word' not simply when they can use and understand a single item but when they know a range of variation and practices associated with it: for example, to know the word *know* entails knowing how to say, hear, read, and write its various forms and extensions, fitting them into phrases and sentences (*knows, knowing, knew, known*), relating the simple to the complex (as in *knowledge, knowledgeable, unknowing, unknowable, unknowably, unknown*), relating these to such compounds as *knowhow* and *know-all,* managing idioms (*y'know, in the know, know the ropes, know what's what, know a thing or two*), using and grasping senses, expressions, and collocations (*knowing someone or something, knowing how to do something, knowing better,* and even *knowing 'in the Biblical sense'*). This cluster, with its clear centre and hazy periphery, shares semantic space with other clusters cited as the words *understand, perceive, grasp,* and *fathom*. All operate within a system whose size and complexity defy comprehensive description, but without being beyond the reach of the everyday user of the language.

[*Postscript.* By and large I am happy with the content and organization of the *word* entry re-printed above, with one exception. I now consider that I should have included a ninth significant way in which the term *word* can be understood and assessed. This is the *translinguistic word*, as for example when people say that the forms *realitas* in Latin, *réalité* in French, *realidad* in Spanish, and *reality* in English are to all intents and purposes 'the same word'. By this they mean (and rightly, in my view) that despite significant morphological, phonological, and semantic differences, a high degree of lexical continuity survives across the linguistic divide. It is, however, impossible to cite a single omni-representative form for such a word: all the embodiments are linguistically equal.]

5

The vocabulary-control movement in the English language, 1844–1953

[A paper published in the *Indian Journal of Applied Linguistics*, 4:1, January 1978, derived from Chapter 3 of my doctoral thesis 'The English word: a critical study of some aspects of lexicography and lexicology in the English language', approved at the University of Edinburgh in 1977 on the recommendation of the internal examiner David Abercrombie and the external examiner John Sinclair.]

This paper examines the aims and achievements of various people who sought to organize part of the vocabulary of English into levels of frequency and utility. The work was pragmatic, in such areas as stenography, help for the blind, teaching reading to native speakers, and English as a foreign language. The study focuses on the work of Isaac Pitman, Edward L. Thorndike, Harold Palmer, Michael West, and C. K. Ogden, drawing on the little-known work of the Dutch researcher Herman Bongers. [NOTE This study deals in effect with the 'prehistory' of the current largescale research and development in corpus linguistics, computer corpora, and concordancing, especially in relation to lexicography and grammar. It was, however, written well before such work began, at a time when linguists of any kind had little interest in such matters.]

The special word list

The concept of vocabulary has been dominated by two features: simple arithmetic and the treatment of words not as sound but as chunks of lettering. In discussing these matters, I shall take as my starting point the October 1843 issue of the *Phonotypic Journal*, in which we find evidence that serious though informal work on frequency counts was being done by British stenographers and educationists throughout the first half of the nineteenth century (and I am grateful to Abercrombie for pointing this out to me in 1976). This information contrasts strongly with the tendency of the American investigators Charles C. Fries and A. Aileen Traver (1950) to treat the vocabulary-control movement as beginning just as the nineteenth century came to an end.

Isaac Pitman (1813–97), an English educational reformer, businessman, and the inventor of the Pitman shorthand system, in that issue of his journal presented stenographers with a list of words 'showing how often each occurs in 10,000 words, taken from 20 books, 500 from each . . . to serve as a guide in selecting grammalogues for the (shorthand) system'. His grammalogues were words which for stenographic convenience can be expressed as a single symbol (such as *and, the,* and *of*). The following list, taken from Pitman's longer alphabetic list, shows the items under S with their frequency ratings:

saw	2	so	25
say	13	spirit(ual)	13
see/sea	24	stand	6
shall	34	strength	2
short	2	sure	2

Pitman does not indicate what texts were chosen for this survey, but even the brief extract above can tell us what his approach was like. We can see that no definitions were offered for discrimination, and so *saw* can be either a tool or a past tense of *see*, or both. Similarly, the homophones *sea* and *see* are conflated, presumably because in speech they are identical and in context no stenographer could confuse them. This means that Pitman was working simultaneously with three kinds of word: (1) a graphic form or type; (2) its tokens, or the occasions on which the type is repeated; (3) a phonic parallel, the spoken version. Adopting current linguistic terminology, we can call these *graphological* (or *orthographic*) *words, statistical words,* and *phonological words* respectively. In the conflation of *spirit* and *spiritual*, however, we see something else at work: the running together of two *morphologically* distinct but related words. The Pitman exercise is revealing in its very informality, its lack of theory, and yet at the same time its practical worth. In addition, the list contains some historically interesting words like *betwixt* and *aught*, indicating to us now that such frequency lists can carry clues that relate to the period in which they were compiled and suggest certain subsequent changes in frequency and use.

The practical worth of the list was highlighted in the November edition of the same journal, where a letter from James Biden points out that a similar kind of list was made twenty years earlier by John Freeman in London. Biden observed that 'the two lists so strikingly coincide that I make free to post you a copy of all the words that occurred more than 19 times in 20,000, as a strong and gratifying confirmation of the correctness of your own laborious calculation'. He worked from a second edition of Freeman in 1820, and adds that Freeman's work was undertaken as an aid to teaching adults to read.

Credit is normally given to the work in 1898 in Germany of F.W. Kaeding in the *Haufigkeitswörterbuch der deutsches Sprache* for the development of frequency counting with a rigour and on a scale which would give it a serious objective value. Also with stenographers in mind, Kaeding organized the counting of eleven million words from a variety of texts and reduced these to their word types in alphabetic lists stating the frequency of occurrence of each. The first comparable counterpart to this in the English language was in 1923 in the United States, where George Dewey's *The Relativ Frequency of English Speech Sounds* [sic] attempted to establish for stenographers the commonest syllables of English. This undertaking was also based on written presentation and is minuscule when compared with the German work, but larger than Freeman's and Pitman's. Dewey took 100,000 statistical words from a scatter of novels, newspapers, speeches, and the like.

The idea slowly became established that the techniques of such counters had a valuable advantage over the more subjective collections of traditional lexicographers. The idea of counting tokens in a given corpus of texts, to establish undeniable patterns of frequency of occurrence, proved attractive, especially in the United States.

Educational word counts took several forms. Workers set out to organize objective lists that would help pupils in their reading, spelling, pronunciation, and general use of language, hopefully replacing the old-fashioned little spellers of those who had followed Nathaniel Bailey and Noah Webster. The Reverend J. Knowles in the United Kingdom in 1904 produced his *London Point System of Reading for the Blind*, which took 100,000 words from the Bible and other sources and abstracted the 353 commonest words. The first 72 of these were grammatical, such as pronouns and prepositions, the 73rd being the noun *man* and the 353rd being the noun *child*. Knowles claimed that his list provided three-quarters of all the words occurring in the texts assessed. In 1914 in the United States, Cook and O'Shea undertook a survey relating to the spelling needs of American children, in which the family correspondence of thirteen adults was chosen as a corpus. It was found that nine words accounted for over a quarter of the total and that 42 accounted for over one half. The observers considered that 763 words took in 90–91 per cent of the total correspondence.

Another line of interest emerges in *Six Thousand Common English Words*, by R.C. Eldridge in the US in 1911. These words were drawn from a small count of 43,000 words in American newspapers. They were garnered as a contribution towards a 'universal eclectic or polyglot vocabulary', and in this endeavour we encounter the centuries-old Esperanto-like quest for a special universal language which will surmount the difficulties of natural speech and writing.

The needs of stenography, reading, and writing, as well as the search for a universal language, led inevitably to larger questions in language teaching, both for native users and foreign learners. The initial successes made for optimism.

Thorndike and Lorge: the objective approach

In 1921, Edward L. Thorndike brought out in the United States *The Teacher's Word Book*, a list of 10,000 words that American children could expect to meet in their general reading. Thorndike, to get his words, used the basic frequency approach but added a range rating, so that the questions *How often?* and *In how many texts?* could both be answered.

Thorndike's list was derived from forty-one different sources providing four million 'running words' (that is, graphological tokens). Three million came from the Bible and the English Classics, half a million from letters, 300,000 from elementary school readers, 90,000 from newspapers, and 50,000 from general reading. The list was widely acclaimed as a breakthrough in vocabulary control and inspired numerous imitators and developers. It was chiefly used as an objective measure of the appropriateness of vocabularies in school books, and as a basis for the construction of achievement tests in vocabulary, reading, and spelling. Although not intended for such use, it was also taken as a basis for word lists for foreigners learning English.

The list embodies the basic assumptions of the objective counters. It relates entirely to written language, and behind the attractively 'objective' arithmetic is a subjective or culture-based selection of texts from which the counting can proceed. The list rests on the tacit nineteenth- and early twentieth-century Western assumption that the Bible, certain 'Classics', and a random selection from newspapers and appropriate people's letters constitute a proper sample of English at large, or at least of the best kind of English. Such a corpus either would or *should* serve as a guide to what readers may be required to know at certain ages and for certain purposes (most particularly educational examinations). In Thorndike's work, therefore, we have—behind the apparent objectivity—an implicit interventionism, a more or less undiscussed attempt to perpetuate what is taken to be the norm. The Bible's presence in the count highlights this. It is interesting to speculate whether a count made, say, in 1980 [proposed here as a future date] would place the same emphasis on the Bible.

In 1931, Thorndike published an extension of the list to 20,000 words, by incorporating material from over twenty other sources, including about five million running words from other counts. This move typifies later developments in the objectivist tradition: the enlargement of lists by the integration of smaller lists and the standardization to this end of arithmetical variations among lists. It was assumed that such incorporation would cast the net wider and mean greater accuracy. In the second list, words were rated from one to twenty according to frequency amd range. In looking at this kind of development, the British commentator Henry Widdowson notes that such expansion tends to cancel out important differences among words; something counted as the same word in the Bible, one or two Classics, and a scientific text may have nuances of meaning and use which cannot be exhibited by so blunt a method: 'This neutralizing of individual differences comes as a result of concentrating on comprehensiveness at the expense of discrimination' (1968:133f). Just how blunt the instrument might be, however, emerges in the fact that for arithmetical convenience Thorndike allowed his counters to treat traditional homographs as the same, much like Pitman with *saw*: thus, *bear* the animal and *bear* meaning 'carry, support' are lumped together. A single frequency-range rating for such composite items is meaningless.

The willingness of Thorndike and his collaborators to conflate lists is additionally disturbing because of the need to seek common criteria for different counts. Some counts for example took *is, am, are, was, were,* and *be* as six different words, while others treated them as variants of the one word *be*. Conflation demanded complicated recasting to bring lists into alignment, and implied that in fact counters should re-think the whole basis of counting. If even one major fault emerged in later reviews of earlier counts (as for example the homograph situation) then logically it demanded a recount—a return to first principles—having learned from one's mistakes. But this never happened. List-makers were content to tinker with counts already made, probably because of the sheer difficulty of making counts in the days before computers could absorb the tedium. The assumption appears to have been that any count was better than no count at all, and that conflated counts (despite the anomalies) were better still.

Thorndike did not assume that his lists were absolute, any more than lexicographers have assumed that they were working from the Mosaic Tablets. There is evidence, however (in the way the lists were used), that educators tended to treat Thorndike's List as absolute, and the likelihood that people generally tend to do this kind of thing only emphasizes the need to make sure that first principles are as clear-cut as possible. The difficulty in the objectivist tradition lies in discerning any clear first principles at all, apart from the view that words are chunks of lettering with white space on each end. Of his first attempt, Thorndike observes: 'The gist of it is that the present counts are adequate to determine the first thousand words with a small probable error, and the next 4,000 well enough for many educational purposes, and the last 5,000 to an extent that is useful, though far from accurate' (1921b:348). By 1931, however, he had doubts about the ultimate accuracy of his lists, feeling that the rarer words were still not properly placed, some words having 'lower credits than they should have' (quoted in Fries and Traver, 1950:25). This comment raises a query about the theoretical/philosophical assumptions behind the count. What does *should* imply? Does it mean that the words are not really worth much in their objectivity, because subjective intuition suggests that they do not tell us anything worthwhile? Or does the self-criticism mean that Thorndike measured himself against some Platonic Ideal List, expressing frequencies and ranges known only to God?

The many other counters added little to Thorndike. The same words re-emerge in the first 500 of each list, similar to the far less sophisticated efforts of Freeman, Pitman, Knowles, and Cook and O'Shea. More and more, the statisticians questioned their findings about the rarer or 'special' words covered and urged the accuracy of that first 500. Since the first 500 consist very largely of the grammatical words of the language this is little more than an affirmation that English has a grammatical structure which uses grammatical words. The counters Faucett and Maki (1932) moved away from a pure objectivist stance by urging that personal judgement was needed for 'wide-range words', and so the objectivist lists can be adversely criticized from both ends, the commonest and the rarest.

From 1934 onwards, Thorndike turned to the problems of the homograph and the polysemic word: that is, towards some resolution of the problem of one chunk having different senses. With Irving Lorge, he embarked on a semantic count which was related to the senses of words enumerated in the *Oxford English Dictionary* (1927). Here, for the first time, the objectivists turned to a traditional wordbook for help. If successful, such a discriminating count could give the kind of overall frequency for a chunk of lettering that stenographers and spellers might want and also for its sense frequencies, the kind of thing that educational specialists might want. No inquiry was made into the absoluteness or otherwise of the *OED* division of word meanings into senses, and we can therefore take it that Thorndike and Lorge were interested in a useful construct rather than a truly objective measure of English lexical frequencies.

If this is so, then the undertaking was the finest hour of the 'objectivist' movement. Michael West certainly makes it clear (1953:xii) that the counters in this undertaking were linguistically sophisticated—probably in much the same way as the volunteer readers for the *OED*—and the results are impressive. What we have are precise statements about printed words taken from a culture-related selection of texts charted in accordance with the senses enumerated in a vast historical dictionary. Such a count could be taken as an indicator of how words appear in printed English, as a supplement to the judicious personal decisions of (say) a textbook writer, but it could not serve as an ultimate objective authority.

In 1944 appeared the third and last extension, Thorndike and Lorge's *The Teacher's Wordbook of 30,000 Words*, which had added in new material from Lorge's magazine count and Thorndike's juvenile count. The earlier criticisms still hold good, along with one not previously raised: the massive presence of personal and place names. On one page of the 1944 list, for example, randomly selected, the following names appear:

Massachusetts	Maximilian	McCormick
Matilda	May Day	McDonald
Matt	Mayo	McKinley
Matthew	Maypole	Meade
Maud(e)	McCarthy	Mecca
Max	McClellan	

Many questions could be asked about these items, each of them provided with its frequency and range. They are hardly words of pedagogic interest outside of history and geography. In their massive presence, they point to the basic misassumption of starting to count without asking what should be counted: that is, of not having an appropriate theory of the English word. They also point to the bias of the texts chosen, and ambiguity in the listing. Is *Mayo* a place or a person or both? Can McClellan be given a frequency of any kind, especially at the expense of all the other Mcs and Macs in Scottish and Irish telephone directories or even the spellings *McLellan* and *McClelland*? Can it be seriously claimed that *Massachusetts* and *Mecca* are more worthy of frequency rating than *Majorca* and *Melbourne*, which are off-listed? The literary bias of the objective counters was inevitable, but it led, as Bright and McGregor point out, to peculiar results of some importance to the teachers they were serving:

> The tape recorder had not then been invented. One result of this [reliance on the printed word] is that some everyday household words have an oddly low frequency. *Sticky* is as rare as *strew* and *doorknob* as rare as *dulcet*. Moreover the list is now out of date. The word *transistor* does not appear at all, and the frequency of *pop* takes no account of this graphic symbol's recent semantic extension. The list was designed for use in American schools and consequently has a slight American bias but even so *trousers* is much more frequent than *pants* . . . *Damsel* and *doth* are as frequent as *error* and *encounter*. (1970:17f)

Palmer and West: the subjective approach

At the same time as the American interest in frequency counts was developing, British teachers of language were experimenting with lists which could serve as lexical bases for textbooks, simplified readers, and general courses. The foremost figure in the early stages of the British tradition was Harold E. Palmer, working first in Belgium, then London, then (for his most productive period) in Japan. In his early work as a language teacher, Palmer was impressed by the elementary word lists used in the Berlitz method for teaching modern languages. After looking at the Eldridge list of 1911, he doubted the worthwhileness of frequency counts and sought instead a view of words which would make listing systematic while still subjectively based. To this end, he developed a system of three 'lexicological' units:

(1) The *monolog*: something neither more nor less than a word

(2) The *miolog*: something less than a word

(3) The *pliolog*: something more than a word

This typology, as Widdowson points out (1968:131), after sidestepping the problem of what a word is, mixes criteria, the monolog being a kind of element or substance, the miolog being something subordinate to it (an affix perhaps), and the pliolog something more structurally complex (like an idiom or set phrase). The typology certainly glosses over many issues, but it is a step towards deciding what is worth selecting or indeed counting. In practical terms, Palmer added to this typology a dichotomy of *headword* and *subword*, which has made a more lasting impact than the three 'logs'. In any list, the headword is the main entry, and the subwords are the various more complex items associated with it (such as derivatives, compounds, and idioms). An example of this approach is the following, drawn from Herman Bongers's K List (1947), which uses Palmerian principles:

absent: adj
  absence: n
  absent-minded: adj

accept: v
  acceptance: n
  acceptable: adj
  unacceptable: adj

accident: n
  accidental: adj
  accidentally: adv

Bongers claims that Palmer worked essentially from a 'vocabulary sense' developed over years of teaching, a sense which 'enabled him to determine with little hesitation the relative utility of any word . . . a typical example of the Subjective or Empirical Method of Vocabulary Selection' (1947:74). When Palmer went to Japan in 1922 as linguistic adviser to the Japanese government, he developed his methods through the medium of the Institute of Research in English Teaching (IRET), under whose auspices he prepared two interim reports. In 1934, Bongers travelled from the Dutch East Indies [now Indonesia] to Tokyo to meet him, initiating a long period of co-operation. He later noted: 'Palmer believes (and so do we) that subjective judgment and the empirical evidence of teachers is of invaluable assistance in compiling word lists that will serve more adequately than lists based upon objective findings alone' (1947:45). Palmer's approach, as laid out in the first interim IRET report (1930), received the blessing of the English critic I.A. Richards, who wrote: 'Determination of the relative frequencies of words in selected bodies of literature gives us at best only raw material. We need to know the assumptions on which they are based' (in Bongers, 1947: 204). In the report, Palmer offered certain assumptions about words which amount to a theory for their selection. The whole set of principles is not given here, but an abstraction of ten of them highlights the distinctiveness of Palmer's approach:

(1) No absolute statements should be made about certain words being *the* important words of English, but only that they *seem* to be more important than others.

(2) Inflected forms are simply variants of a given word.

(3) Headwords should not include miologs or pliologs (less-than-words or more-than-words).

(4) Variant forms, such as abbreviations, should not count as separate forms.

(5) Words of wider range should be taken to include related words of narrower range.

(6) Stylistic words should be excluded.

(7) Homonyms are separate words and senses of a given word should only be differentiated when they are so extreme as to be 'quasi-homonyms'.

(8) Selected vocabulary should be drawn up in a general list and specific lists.

(9) Each list should be given an arbitrary numerical limit (its radius). The words within that limit should constitute a zone, say, of the first hundred units, or first thousand, and so on. The supplementary lists would relate to specialized zones.

(10) Each unit in the general list is a headword together with any subwords.

With these axioms in mind, compilers of lists can proceed to use their 'vocabulary sense'.

Objectivists criticized Palmer just as he criticized them, arguing that there was no external control on his choice. With misgivings, he compromised far enough to incorporate the first 500 words of Thorndike into his work, but in the second interim IRET report (1931) he defended reason as against mechanical selection by calling attention to what he called 'constellations' of words: 'The lesson in which the word *eat* occurs for the first time contains also the word *drink*'. In such a relationship, frequency of occurrence is the product or outcome, not the promoting factor. The constellation will include *hungry* and *thirsty* and some forty other words linked by 'thought association'. He denied that many of these associated words would appear in a frequency count at anywhere near the right rating. He did not, however, develop the idea of constellations in their own right with their internal relationships marked, preferring instead his zones, expressed in alphabetic lists.

In the course of a world tour in 1931, when he met many of the foremost figures in the vocabulary-control movement, Palmer met Michael West, who had worked on word lists in Bengal and for his *New Method Readers*, written for foreigners learning English. The vocabularies of these readers, subjectively achieved, had served as a starting point for a refining procedure, an eclectic sampling and comparison of both subjective and objective lists until West achieved a special 'defining vocabulary' of 1,490 items. This metalanguage for definition is of special lexicographic interest because it was put to use in a wordbook, West's *New Method Dictionary* (1935) and in the later derived *An International Reader's Dictionary* (1965) which defines over 24,000 items within this vocabulary. The preface of the second dictionary states that the 1,490 words are 'held to be the commonest words in English or the words first learnt by foreigners'. If the list is derived from an influential series of simplified readers, on which other simplifications are founded, then the statement is a self-fulfilling prophecy: the day will arrive when it is largely true because it has been made largely true.

It is with West that the word-listers join the mainstream of alphabetic lexicography, and IRET colleagues of Palmer in Japan, A.S. Hornby, E.V. Gatenby, and H. Wakefield, followed his example with *The Idiomatic and Syntactic English Dictionary*, published in Tokyo in 1942, and work that from 1948 onwards attained international publishing stature as *The*

Advanced Learner's Dictionary of Current English (Oxford University Press). No claim is made for the *ALDCE* with regard to a finite defining vocabulary like West's, but the words used for definition purposes could in principle be added up and listed as such. They have been intuitively and pragmatically gathered for the purpose, and according to the front matter of the *ALDCE* are intentionally 'as simple as possible' (vi).

The meeting of Palmer and West was followed in 1934 by a specially convened conference in New York, under the auspices of the Carnegie Corporation. West was instrumental in bringing it about, to allow the various objective and subjective compilers to meet and share ideas. The conference was the zenith of the movement, but should not be discussed before mention is made of a controversy in which West was deeply involved, and one which reflects sadly on the whole business of vocabulary control.

Ogden: the logical approach

C.K. Ogden developed 'Basic English' in the 1920s, and whether it is discussed in a lexicological context, within the framework of artificial languages like Esperanto, or indeed the teaching of English as a second or foreign language, his work remains as challenging today as it was in the 1920s and 1930s. There are two reasons for including Basic in this study: (1) it is linked with an important work on semantics, *The Meaning of Meaning* (1923), of which Ogden was co-author with I.A. Richards; (2) Ogden made certain claims about how Basic can be used.

Basic English can be regarded as an early exercise in applied linguistics and language planning. It is the extraction from a natural language, on a logical basis, of lexical material assumed to be useful for international communication. The term 'Basic' is an acronym with the values B for British, A for American, S for Scientific, I for International, and C for Commercial, and to the acronym we can add the three claims that Ogden made on its behalf, that: (1) it is a world auxiliary language in its own right; (2) it is also a way of leading non-English users to an understanding of normal English; (3) it is a means of improving normal English for those already using it, by reminding them of the virtues of simplicity and precision.

To achieve this three-in-one language goal, Ogden isolated from 'Standard English' a simple syntax and a logically restricted vocabulary. The syntax depended on a fixed analytic word order of the type *I will put the record on the machine now*, and allowed only six affixes: *-s* for plurals, *un-* for negating adjectives, *-ed* and *-ing* with their traditional function in making participles, *-ly* for adverbs, and *-er* as a highly productive agent suffix. In addition, permissible word compounding included: (1) what are now called phrasal verbs: verb plus adverbial particles as in *get up, put on, put up with*; (2) noun plus noun structures, like *teapot* and *farmhouse*; (3) adjective plus noun structures, like *madman* and *blackbird*.

The minimal syntax was buttressed with 850 words, divided into 400 general words, 200 picturable words, 150 quality words, 82 grammatical words, and a special set of verb operators of the type *give* and *get*, which could serve as the basis for compounding and also for such combinations as *give him a push* instead of *push him*. Ogden allowed for the possibility of metaphoric extensions of the basic meanings of the 850 words, and accepted that they could be supplemented by four further categories, as it were, outside the system: (1) numbers; (2) names of animals and plants; (3) proper names; (4) scientific-cum-international words as the need arises.

Such an audacious artifact, separated out from the living language, inevitably proved contentious, and its evangelistic aim of being all things to all men may also have made it an easy target for attack. Ogden sought to resolve a multitude of problems at a stroke, combining a spirit of progress with a kind of interventionism based on the view that many people's use of Standard English was not all that it might be. It can be borne in mind, however, that Ogden's logico-semantic approach is Palmer and West's subjective method pushed to its furthest limits, and the simplicity of the end-product is impressive.

Criticism of Basic was considerable, however, and took three forms: (1) that you cannot combine an independent world auxiliary language derived from English with a medium intended to serve as a way-in to Standard English; (2) that Basic's dependence on minimal operators and combinations leads to circumlocutions unacceptable in Standard, difficult for a native user of English to master, distorting for foreign learners, and ultimately leading to a debasement of the proper language; (3) that assumptions about a minimal vocabulary obscure the polysemic and special idiomatic significance in Standard English of its commoner words: that is, that the 850 words are not as simple as they might appear at first sight to be.

The third criticism of Basic is probably the most telling. Compounds and phrasal verbs in basic often have overall meanings which are not entirely—or not at all—deducible from their parts, as in *put up* meaning 'provide accommodate for' and *put up with* meaning 'tolerate'. Such meanings are by and large idiomatic extensions, as it were, of the Basic meanings of these words, and can be taught by means of various devices such as indicating metaphoric extensions in certain situations and contexts. It remains a problem, however, to decide where Basic meanings for a word stop and non-Basic meanings begin. Fries and Traver (1950:80f), for example, have shown that the 850 words of Basic have no fewer than 18,416 senses as listed in the *OED*. They suggest that Basic did not adequately come to terms with polysemy—the radiation of meaning in different contexts.

The simplicity of these Basic words is more apparent than real. Ogden is dealing largely with an Anglo-Saxon stratum, a kind of nativistic return to the simplicities of an age earlier than the Renaissance. His choice of such structures as phrasal verbs and nominal compounds is Germanic, and his active-verb sentences turn away from the passivization common in Latinized English. Like the seventeenth-century lexicographer Robert Cawdrey he would transform (or indeed translate) Latinate verbs like *impose* into phrasal verbs like 'lay on'. It is doubtful, however, whether a phrasal verb is really simpler in its syntactic behaviour or semantic intricacy than a Latinate verb, although at first glance on paper it looks simpler to the native user, who has been familiar with such expressions since early childhood. It has seldom been so with foreign users of the language.

Michael West seriously opposed the propagation of Basic, fearing alike its success or failure. Its success, he thought, would imperil more acceptable forms of simplified English and favour a gross pidginization of the language; its failure would cast doubt on the systems he himself advocated. West's *A Critical Examination of Basic English* (1934) and Ogden's *Counter-Offensive* (1935) show how emotive the struggle became, West seeing Ogden doing humanity 'an incalculably grave disservice', while Ogden accused West of 'gross errors' and 'ludicrous' criticism in his assessment of Basic. Ogden turned down an invitation to the West-inspired Carnegie conference in New York, and Palmer (in a comment to the *Rangoon Gazette*, quoted in *Counter-Offensive*: 174) then used this refusal as an indication that Basic was doomed to failure, its exponents unwilling to meet with reasonable men.

According to Bongers (1947:133f), Harold Palmer was invited in 1943 at the behest of Winston Churchill to consider changes in Basic which would make it more useful as an international medium. Palmer suggested the addition of 'an adequate number of verbs' to those already in use, so that *give him a push* could safely return to *push him*. He advocated the addition of more grammatical words, that compounds of a non-Standard nature be replaced by their Standard equivalents, and that the number of content words also be increased. Bongers notes: 'But with these modifications it would no longer be the Basic as planned by Ogden and Richards: it would be a Basic Standard English as envisaged by those various individuals and bodies who have for so many years specialised on the subject.' Ogden is important to lexicology because he attempted to organize a clear-cut minimum vocabulary, and to lexicography because this organized vocabulary was put to use in due course in a dictionary which rivals the work of Michael West. In 1940, there appeared the *General Basic English Dictionary* (London: Evans), 'giving more than 40,000 senses for over 20,000 words', the definitions throughout being framed in Basic. The dictionary was intended for both the foreign learner and the young native user, its defining vocabulary strengthening the implication that Basic derives from a special kind of vernacular vocabulary: the kind that children learn first.

The prefatory note to the dictionary claims that the 850 words of Basic are 'naturally the key words for Dictionary purposes', as a kind of direct reply to West's defining vocabulary. The book, however, is not restricted to students of Basic as such: anyone using the dictionary and already having some training in English 'through Basic or any other system, will be able to make headway by himself with the English of Library, Radio, and Newspaper'. The dictionary claims that the circularity of definition so common in conventional dictionaries is avoided through the medium of Basic, a point which suggests that Ogden has something in common with Cawdrey.

If the West and Ogden approaches were vehement competitors for the allegiance of language teachers, then some check on their comparative merits should be possible by examining respective entries and definitions in the West and Ogden dictionaries. To test the differences, something like the following brief sample might be adopted. I have added Cawdrey, the earliest similar lexicographer, for interest's sake, to see whether there are any points where the three compilers meet. The West material is from the *International Readers' Dictionary* (1965) and the Ogden material is from the 1955 Evans edition of the *General Basic Dictionary*:

	West 1965	*Ogden 1955*	*Cawdrey 1604*
edifice	a building	building, sp. great	building
impose	lay a load or	put (tax, punishment	lay upon or put

	unpleasant duty upon someone	etc on)	on
prompt	ready, done at once at once	acting or done quickly, readily	ready, quicke
ruminate	bite food over and over again, like a cow; think	be biting the cud; be turning question over in the mind	to chew over againe, to studie earnestlie upon

The similarities between West and Ogden far outweigh the differences, and this small sample reflects a general similarity which can easily be seen in the books themselves. Syntactically, the continuous tense in Ogden is typical of Basic and one of the flaws assailed by critics. However, both Basic and West have the word *bite*, presumably through a shared unwillingness to add *chew* to either minimal vocabulary. If, however, naturalness is the criterion for assessing all three, then Cawdrey from 300 years ago wins handily. But more impressive for general lexicological speculation are the overriding similarities among all three.

The minimal nature of the differences between Ogden and West is borne out by Fries and Traver (1950:73ff) in a very suggestive analysis. In comparing seven lists (Ogden, West, Palmer, Thorndike, Faucett-Maki, Aiken, and the Carnegie list which we shall shortly discuss), Fries and Traver found that, whereas there is only a 50 per cent overlap between Thorndike's first 1,000 words and Ogden's Basic, between Basic and West the overlap is 79.2 per cent. The overlap between Basic and the West-inspired Carnegie list is the remarkably high 93 per cent, considering that Ogden was not at the New York conference. West's vocabulary has 99 of Ogden's 100 grammatical words and operators, 84 of his 100 qualities, 154 of his 200 picturable words, and 291 of his 400 general words. In every case, the later Carnegie list moves closer to Ogden, not farther away, the most startling concession being to include 369 out of Ogden's 400 general words. Ogden may not have attended the conference, but his words certainly did.

The Carnegie Report and the General Service List

In October 1934, the Carnegie Conference was held in New York, attended by West, Palmer, Thorndike, and Faucett, among others. An initial report was prepared, and was developed at a second meeting in London the following year, when arrangements were made for a tentative general list to appear. This list and the comments with it would serve as an interim report that the collaborators hoped would be the basis for future work. The conference did not seek total reconciliation or synthesis between the objectivist and subjectivist positions, but was in fact quite successful in harmonizing them:

> We noted a close correspondence between our judgement and the results of the objective method . . . within the first 1,500 words. Beyond the first 1,500 words we found neither the purely subjective nor the purely objective list satisfactory. We observed that 3,000 words is an unsatisfactory level, since above 2,500 words stylistic variants appear in such numbers that it is difficult to draw the line.

The group rejected what they called an 'island vocabulary' serving as a self-sufficient simplified language, but as we have seen this did not prevent a closer adaptation of lists towards Ogden. The conferees accepted Palmer's argument that a general list should be supplemented by special lists for specialized purposes such as the classroom, agriculture, and technology. However, such lists were never made.

Considering themselves as initiating a period of research into words and their frequencies, the Carnegie group listed twenty-one areas worth further study, including compounds, derivatives, idioms, sense differentiation, and cognate vocabularies (such as Latinate material in both French and English). As Bright and McGregor (1970:22) point out, however, the conference was 'not at the beginning of a period of work on vocabulary but nearly at the end'. It is clear from the report that certain problems stood in the mid-1930s pretty much where they had been for decades: compounding, derivation, and idioms were as much in need of clarification as ever, and homonymy, polysemy, and synonymy were as hard as ever to elucidate.

It is also interesting that, despite efforts to present a united scientific front, the group exhibited features identifiable with past etymologists, lexicographers, and educationists. They regretted 'a tendency at the present towards a loss of stylistic values' and assumed that 'a selected vocabulary offers an opportunity of purging the language of words and other items which tend to be misused'. This point of view is markedly similar to the third point in Ogden's claim for Basic: a means of improving normal English for those already using it, by reminding them of the virtues of simplicity and precision. The members also took a special view of sex roles in language, as pointed out by Bright and McGregor (1970:21), where they note with regard to the names of tools: 'Our criterion was that the tool should be such as might be found in any home and used by women as well as men. Thus we may include Saw and Hammer, but exclude Drill'.

A general list of some 2,000 items emerged, and served until the early 1970s as 'the accepted and indeed the only objective authority on what to include in syllabuses for the teaching of L2 English' (Widdowson, 1968:123), Bright and McGregor noting (1970:22) that the list has 'stood the test of time remarkably well'. It was developed in due course by West himself into *A General Service List of English Words* (*GSL*) (1953). In his preface to that work, G.B. Jeffrey rather diplomatically wrote an epitaph to word-listing when he observed:

> As a member of the distinguished band of workers in the field of vocabulary selection who attended the New York Conference in 1934, and one who has continued to interest himself in the subject, it is fitting that he [West] should bring this phase of research to what looks like a culmination, since attention is now shifting to structural problems. (West, 1953:vi)

The *GSL* was the acme of achievement in the movement, and as such it is worth comparing an entry from it with an equivalent entry in Thorndike and Lorge's 1944 compilation, in which the entry for *game* runs:

GAME   AA   700   966   700*   639

whose rather cryptic symbols can be explained as follows: AA indicates that *game* occurs over 100 times per million running words, the 700 referring to appearances of its token in the 'pure' Thorndike of 1931, the 966 to frequency in the Lorge magazine count, the second 700* to the special Thorndike Juvenile Count (the asterisk indicating an estimate rather than a precise figure), and the 639 relating to the Lorge-Thorndike Semantic Count (without details). West's 1953 entry (which incorporates elements from the Lorge semantic count) runs:

GAME 638   (1) (amusement, children's play)
Fun and games
It's not serious; it's a game   9%

(2) (with the idea of competition, e.g. cards, football, etc)
A game of football
Indoor games; outdoor games   38%

(3) (a particular contest)
We won, six games to three
I played a poor game
Playing a losing game (10.5%)   23%

(4) (games = athletic contest)
Olympic Games   8%
?(= animals, 11%; game-/, game-birds, etc, 5%
(= fun, Make fun of, 0.5%)

For the teacher or anyone else looking for some basic guiding information, West's list is highly informative, though space-consuming. His 638 refers to frequency in a count of five million running words of the Thorndike type. In 9 per cent of these occurrences it meant the first sense, and so on through the senses following the Lorge system, the question mark indicating the compiler's doubt as to the worthwhileness of teaching the residue of material in brackets. Minor meanings tend to be omitted in West's articles, and so the percentages tend not to add up to 100. West reminds the user that in studying the frequencies and their percentages, the total frequency of any word should be taken into account, 1 per cent of *pull* being worth far more than 1 per cent of *drag*. He also reminds users that it is primarily a list for the written language, and is low on colloquial, stylistic, and emotive material.

It has one other serious problem, shared with the slowly garnered *OED* and the conceptual scheme in Peter Mark Roget's *Thesaurus*. West's list is now dated, a point which I established in a study [early 1970s, when researching what became my *Longman Lexicon of Contemporary English*] of a textbook series which openly claims to draw most of the 700 words of its elementary workbook from the *GSL*: the *New Concept English* series of L.G. Alexander (Longman, 1967). A check of twelve pages of the vocabulary index in the edition for German teachers, 1969 (for the volume *First Things First*), shows that out of 354 items (that is, just over half those used), no fewer than seventy-three are non-*GSL*. Twenty items from among the seventy-three newcomers are: *baker, beef, beer, blouse, butcher, calendar, climate, dentist, fare, honey, instalment, intelligence, job, label, lavatory, licence, magazine, measles, mince, mum.*

Alexander's sound pedagogical reasons for adding these items to the list include the need to update it for more 'modern' students, but such massive infusions weakened the on-going status of the *GSL* as a general list. Without words like these it can hardly serve. Assuming failure to undertake a new frequency count either on the old lines or with some specific word theory, any adaptation such as Alexander has made becomes only one more subjective exercise in list-making, to be challenged by the first conflicting 'vocabulary sense' of the first commentator. [This view was only strengthened when I created later in the 1970s a six-staged word list for the Collins English Library of graded readers, in which my own vocabulary played games enough with West before my in-house editor, an enthusiast for classical music, sedately added *sonata* without consulting me.]

One should acknowledge that the Carnegie Report and the *GSL* stand isolated for criticism in a way not intended by the original conference members. They worked on an interim report, planning supplements and refinements that never materialized. Circumstances have made their achievements appear monolithic and authoritarian where they probably had no intention of putting them forward as such. In all probability, the compilers would concur with later observers in assessing shortcomings, even if several of them were inclined to castigate one another's approaches at the time.

Commentators on the lists

I have taken Fries and Traver in the United States and Bongers in the Netherlands as historians of the vocabulary-control movement. This is true in the incidental sense that they made historical comments while engaged in specific tasks. Fries and Traver were asked by the Committee on Modern Languages of the American Council on Education to assess the word lists. Their report is consequently entitled *English Word Lists: A Study of Their Adaptability for Instruction* (1950), and remains a classic of its kind. *Vocabulary Control* (1947), the thorough-going but little-known work by Bongers, relates to the wish to provide Dutch schools with a 3,000-word list for their four-year English course. The 'historians', therefore, do not stand clinically apart from the movement; in important ways they are themselves part of it. But a comment by Fries and Traver is apposite in any survey of the vocabulary controllers:

> One cannot survey the building of word lists . . . without appreciating the immense amount of work that has attended the creation of these lists, as well as the wide practical experience of those who have laboured upon them. It is with diffidence, therefore, that we offer the following conclusions to which we have come from this study. (1950:87)

The following is a resumé of their conclusions:

(1) A restricted list of useful words limited to useful meanings seems not only valuable but necessary in the teaching of a foreign language. In such lists, the status of the 'word' must be clear-cut, and figurative expressions should be adequately handled. People tend to forget how fluid meaning is.

(2) Word lists should be compiled primarily to obtain the symbols for things and for qualities. In this respect, Ogden's Basic English is essentially sound, with its 600 'things', some picturable, some qualities.

(3) The separateness of 'operations' from the rest of the vocabulary as in Basic is fundamentally important for foreign learners, and verbs can be classed satisfactorily along with preposition-adverbs and conjunctions for this purpose. The limitation of the number of such operators in a first list seems also a sound approach, especially when we consider how wide a range of meanings the common verbs have. The 'learning weight' of a list with verbs as vocabulary units is considerably greater than that of a list in which the verbs are reduced to a minimum.

(4) A limited list of words with a narrow range of senses, along with a basic grammar, is useful for the foreign learner, especially for his productive work. Equally clearly, the list and grammar are valuable for text simplification.

(5) Passing from such a limited vocabulary and basic grammar to an understanding of Standard English is beset with problems, and at this point other lists need to be added, influenced by quantitative information about words and their senses. There should be two distinct sides to such lists, the productive and the receptive, but Fries and Traver did not know what degree of overlap would be likely.

(6) Despite the massive amount of work done, there were areas where more research (guided by linguistic principles) was needed: (a) colloquial English, however difficult to obtain—and counters should go to the Sears-Roebuck catalogue as willingly as to the classics; (b) lists relating to diverse age levels and social situations; (c) more than anything else, quantitative and qualitative information about patterns

of derivation and compounding, extensions of meaning, shifts of meaning according to the grammatical function of a word, and the relationship in English between form and function.

Bongers experimented in the 1940s with the 3,000-word list formulated by Palmer in the second IRET report (1931). Working in three Dutch schools, he set out to ascertain how many of these words students in fact knew (presumably in at least one sense) at the time of matriculation. He concluded that between 2,500 and 2,800 were known through current methods, and this strong correlation encouraged him in the assumption (running counter to the Carnegie Report) that a 3,000-word list was a reasonable goal, and that Palmer's was the best of its kind to date.

When visiting Japan in 1934, he had been impressed by Palmer's claim that the second IRET list would cover 95 per cent of the words in any English text of a general kind. The first 1,000 would cover 85 per cent, the second 7 per cent, and the third 3 per cent. This gargantuan diminishing return on effort reminds one of the Carnegie view that once past 2,500 we are in a lexical quagmire, but Bongers kept to his goal of 3,000, agreeing that anything beyond that would be counter-productive. He checked the Palmer claim by analysing the first 1,000 running words of thirteen English works, and got the following results:

John Galsworthy, *Swan Song* 95.4 per cent
Bernard Shaw, *The Doctor's Dilemma* 95.4 per cent
Temple Thurston, *Sally Bishop* 96.9 per cent
Upton Sinclair, *The Jungle* 95.1 per cent
Arnold Bennett, *The Card* 95.2 per cent
Theodore Dreiser, *An American Tragedy* 96.1 per cent
A. Allardyce, *Unwillingly to School* 96.6 per cent
Sinclair Lewis, *Dodsworth* 94.8 per cent
H.A. Vachell, *Quinney's Adventures* 93.8 per cent
H.G. Wells, *Mr Bletsworthy on Rampole Island* 94 per cent
Rudyard Kipling, *The Bridge Builders* 94.6 per cent
Joseph Conrad, *Typhoon* and *The Lagoon* 91.3 per cent and 95.8 per cent

The success of the Palmer list is impressive. Bongers, however, wanted to improve on it by examining other lists, arranging their contents on Palmerian principles and standardizing their frequencies. It was an immense undertaking, requiring massive and ingenious manipulation of the lists (cf. 1949:140ff), his resulting derivative lists being labelled according to letters of the alphabet. The lists which he examined were:

Palmer's second IRET; the Palmer-Hornby 1,000-word English; Faucett-Maki; the Carnegie General List; Thorndike 1931; and Helen Eaton's Comparative Frequency List for Major European Languages (1934). The work of both Bongers and Fries and Traver demonstrates the incestuousness of the lists by the 1940s, but it is significant that Bongers pays no attention to Ogden's 850 words. After much re-arrangement, shifting, comparison and collation, rejection and re-alignment, Bongers emerged well down the alphabet with a K list for the first, an L list for the second, and an M list for the third 1,000 words of English [making a KLM composite only coincidentally linked with Royal Dutch Airlines]. The details of this *tour de force* can be found in his general study.

Palmer claimed for his 3,000 words a coverage of 95 per cent, and Bongers advanced this with his KLM group, broken down into 89.5 per cent for the K words, 5.6 per cent for L, and 2.4 per cent for M. A comparison with Palmer's original suggests that Bongers may have improved most on the first 1,000, where it really matters. It seems from one viewpoint a marginal increase for so much effort, but from another it is considerable. Bongers provides comparative tables to show the capacity of the six lists, Palmer's and his, to cope with various specimen texts. None of the lists does badly, and this is the ultimate justification of the whole massive effort since the beginning of the century, but the KLM lists have the following showing, over the first 1,000 words of running words in ten texts:

> An article in *The Times* (London) 96 per cent
> Grenfell, *A Labrador Doctor* 96.4 per cent
> Pearl Buck, *The Good Earth* 96.4 per cent
> James Hilton, *Good-bye, Mr Chips* 96.9 per cent
> Emily Brontë, *Wuthering Heights* 97.4 per cent
> Warwick Deeping, *Old Pybus* 97.4 per cent
> Bernard Shaw, *The Intelligent Woman's Guide to Socialism* 97.5 per cent
> Charles Dickens, *A Tale of Two Cities* 98.6 per cent
> Anna Sewell, *Black Beauty* 98.8 per cent
> Eleanor Dooly, *The Radium Woman* 99 per cent

Bongers considered that the marginal improvement was worth the effort, and in getting it pushed the collation of lists to its limits. Assuming that his KLM group suffers from ageing in the same way as West's in 1953, it remains the *pièce de résistance* of the movement. [It is therefore to be regretted that the work of Herman Bongers is virtually forgotten today.]

We are now in a position to consider Bongers's own conclusions about vocabulary control. He had a greater commitment to it than Fries and Traver, and realized that there was nothing especially new or revolutionary in trying to get at the common words of a language in order to teach them ahead of the rare ones. He thought that word counts do identify frequency but have no significance under a million running words, and even then are only the raw material for subjectivists to adjust. Indeed, he denied the reality of objective control, arguing that the selection of the texts for counting is itself subjective. To handle words during and after a count, the principles of Palmer were in his opinion the best and those of Ogden irrelevant because Basic is not really English. If 3,000 was an acceptable upper limit for school courses, then the KLM list is the best provider, and analyses of the extent to which any book conforms to that list should, in his view, be printed in the preface, to help teachers assess the usefulness of the book to any class.

The outstanding difference between Bongers and Fries and Traver (both writing about the same time) is in their attitudes to Ogden and to quantitative studies. The Americans rate Ogden highly and urged further carefully defined quantitative work. The Dutchman dismisses Ogden and suspects quantitative work, except as raw material. Bongers is relatively satisfied with Palmer's word theory, while Fries and Traver survey Palmer but do not include his view in their conclusions. Unlike Bongers but in concurrence with with the Carnegie members, Fries and Traver want more research on many aspects of lexicology. While Bongers shows an awareness of the studies done by Fries and Traver in the 1940s, the Americans on the other hand appear unaware that in the Netherlands he was pushing the minimal-vocabulary concept to its practical limits.

Conclusion

The vocabulary-control movement arose out of an interest in how and where we use words, most notably in stenography, spelling, reading, and language learning. Inevitably, this interest expressed itself in terms of the written medium, and began (somewhat crudely, but probably unavoidably) with the counting of graphological tokens. Only in later assessments, when it was in effect too late to start all over again, did it become apparent that a theory of what to count and where to do the counting was a prime necessity. Palmer and Ogden came nearest to a theory of words, but for most members of the movement a rather incestuous juggling with lists appears to have been preferable to going back to first principles.

The failures of listing in the ways described above do not necessarily mean that listing should never under any circumstances be attempted again. Mechanical aids undreamt of by the early listers now exist to take the tedium out of the work, and to provide results more rapidly: spoken language can be got at now through recording systems in a way unimaginable even in the 1930s. Some attempts at computerized word checks have been made, but success via technology, whether now or in the future, can only follow *after* the creation of a theory of words. Technology alone cannot provide such a framework.

Certain crucial areas of lexicological study must be adequately handled before counting can begin again in earnest, areas such as: sense differentiation; the relation of derivatives to the forms from which they derive; the relations of compounds to the forms from which they are compounded; the figurative extension of meanings; and, most important of all, the relationships of words one to another in what Palmer called their 'constellations'. A solution even in part to such issues could help resuscitate a brave movement that failed for want of a clear and generally agreed methodology.

Part 2: Language

6

Wee Jimmy and the dugs: or, where do *you* stand in the classroom?

[A featured session entitled 'Where do YOU stand in the classroom?' at the 17th Annual Convention of Teachers of English to Speakers of Other Languages (TESOL), Toronto, Canada, March 1983, published as the closing paper in *On TESOL '83: The Question of Control*, TESOL, Washington DC, 1984.]

When I was a small boy growing up in Scotland, I developed the conviction that Glasgow was the centre of the universe. I had no doubts about this. Most of the people present here today also had no doubts, when you were five or six years old, that the centre of the universe lay in Mechanicsburg, Pennsylvania, or Moose Jaw, Saskatchewan, or wherever you first saw the light of day. In these matters we were, all of us, confirming Jean Piaget, Erich Fromm, and other researchers in their theories of human development.[1] I am talking here, of course, about the egocentricity of the very young, developing from a vague awareness of self alone, to self with mother, then self with family, then the point when the self could link up with the general local environment. In the process of my identification with Glasgow, of course, I unreflectingly accepted the kind of *language* that that city had to offer *me*, a child of the working class.

Dugs an coos

In order to establish how things were for children like me at that time and in that place, and also to highlight some of the things I want to discuss in this paper, I would like to share with you a few choice items from the mythology of my home town. The first of these is set in a classroom in an elementary school. There is a cast of two: a well-intentioned lady teacher and an archetypal small boy whom we can call Wee Jimmy. The teacher is equipped, among other things, with a pointer and a wall-chart with pictures of animals on it. Using the pointer the teacher indicates one particular animal on the chart, an animal with four legs and a willingness to wag its tail. The dialogue is as follows:

—And what is this animal called, Jimmy?
—Please, Miss, that's a dug, Miss.
Frown.
—No, no, Jimmy. It's not *dug*. It's a *dog*.
Pause.
—That's funny. It looks like a dug.

This apocryphal tale has a fair amount of sociolinguistic dynamite packed into it. For the moment, however, I would like to consider only one aspect of it: the role of *teacher as social engineer*. The lady here represents certain social and linguistic values and expectations. In terms of these values and expectations much of what Wee Jimmy is, does, says, and thinks is deviant, if not downright vulgar and inferior. Wee Jimmy, however, only becomes aware of this slowly and after considerable exposure to a number of teachers all more or less following the same line. At first, as in our story, he is just puzzled. Following Piaget, he tries to adapt to a *dug* that is also a *dog*. He either assimilates or accommodates the new reality[2] arriving in due course at something like: 'In school a dug has to be a dog or the teacher will be angry.'

Jimmy does of course at length become aware that there is more to it than that. The teacher's and the school's ambitions for him are extensive: Wee Jimmy must give up *dugs* for all time and take to *dogs*. By doing this, however, he will separate himself from the style of speech of his parents, relatives, and friends—forever. He is maybe fuzzy about this at first, but however fuzzy there is still a choice to be made: to go along with the teacher, or to resist. For this stage, around the age of nine onwards, I have a second apocryphal tale: same classroom, same lady teacher, same wall-chart, same pointer, same Wee Jimmy—but this time the pointer indicates a rather blank-looking animal with four legs, two horns, and an udder:

—And what's that animal called, Jimmy?
Pregnant pause.
—That's a coo, Miss.
Frown.

—No, it's not. You know better than that, James. It's a *cow*!
Wee Jimmy shakes his head firmly.
—Naw, Miss. *You*'re a cow. That's a *coo*.

There is no record of what happened to our hero after he made this acute social comment. I have actually met a lot of Wee Jimmies around the world, both as children and adults, angry people from communities where special sets of values that are not their own have been pressed upon them in school or some similar institution. No doubt you have too. I have also known even more people who did not resist as such, but developed a skilful learning strategy that helped them, singly or in groups, to cope with authority and social manipulation. They create a kind of compromise situation. In Scotland, this compromise is reflected in the distinction we make between the 'classroom language' and the 'playground language'. It is a form of what Charles Ferguson called *diglossia*[3] and what I would like to call here a kind of *tactical schizophrenia*: in one situation, under one set of rules, you behave in one way, and in another situation (sufficiently sharply distinguished from the first) you behave in quite a different way. The condition relates to what TESOL nowadays calls 'the teaching of English as a second dialect', although in our case it was quite clearly 'the teaching of English as a higher dialect'.[4]

Better butter

Where there are severe social differences (often also linked with regional, historical, and political differences), the role of teacher as social engineer shades into the role of *teacher as judge and prosecutor* and finally the role of *teacher as social persecutor*. Worse, in situations where age-old resentments boil over into confrontation and even violence, roles can be reversed: the student-victim becomes the persecutor and the teacher-persecutor becomes the victim. There are many places that we all know where this kind of thing can and does happen. One of the reasons for this happening can be illustrated by means of my third and final tale from Glasgow. In it, we will assume that Wee Jimmy has submitted to pressure and now co-operates willingly in acquiring Standard English. We have moved on to elocution, to the acquisition of a 'good' or 'proper' pronunciation. In particular, we are concerned with the glottal stop, which Glasgow people know be?er as the glo?al stop. This variant in our phonology is simply a cross we have to bear, a tribulation among life's many tribulations, and a lot of time has been spent by pedagogues in the west of Scotland trying to eliminate the glottal stop, much as follows:

—Come on, Jimmy. Say 'butter'.
—Bu?er.
—No, no. BUTTER.
—BU?ER!
—BUTTER! BUTTER!
—BU?ER! BU?ER!
—Come on, Jimmy. You can do it. T. T. BUT. BUTTER.
—BUTTER!
Huge smile. Teacher relaxes.
—Tha?'s be?er, Jimmy!

Certainly it's funny. But it is also a monument to our social and linguistic insecurities, the kind of thing that investigators like Joshua Fishman, Dell Hymes, and William Labov have in recent years described so well and discussed so fully.[5] Here, no matter how we assess the role of the student, we can see that the teacher is not just social engineer, judge, prosecutor, and persecutor, but also in turn a kind of victim too, never quite able to sustain the model that he or she is required to sell. Such situations can lead too easily to an additional role: *teacher as hypocrite.*

Marketplace and monastery

These reminiscences are intended, as it were, to set the stage. They describe, graphically I hope, the central thesis of this paper: that in the normal course of events we teachers carry with us every day into the classroom certain ideologies, complete or fragmentary, willingly or with reservations. These include sets of roles and rules, value systems and worldviews that we communicate to our students through a variety of channels. They can be communicated by the kind of instructions we give and the style of language in which we couch those instructions; they can be communicated by the observations and asides we make as we work, through our facial expressions, our body language, our stance, our movements, the way we position things in the room, the way we *use* things in the room, and *above all* by our choice and use of our teaching methods and materials.

One can discern four possibilities as regards these ideologies. Sometimes the ideology is *overt* and easy to perceive, as for example when there is a crucifix, motto, or photograph of a great leader on the wall, or regular appeal is made to sacred scriptures, a social plan, or the aims of the organization that runs the school. Sometimes the ideology is *covert* and indirect, as for example the inculcation of WASP norms in North

America, or in implicit attitudes to the roles of females and males, or the prevalence of one kind of racial or class type in textbooks. Sometimes the ideology is *erratic* and ambiguous, suggesting confusion inside the teacher/ideologue. Many teachers are by no means clear about their ideologies or the messages they send. Additionally, students can get conflicting signals, as for example when a closet pacifist teaches in a military college, or a socialist teaches a course in free enterprise. Sometimes the situation is *confrontational*, where the teacher takes one point of view and the institution or the materials or even the students take another. The pacifist comes out of the closet or the socialist may contrast his or her views with the text, or someone uses a text about tobacco, alcohol, or coffee to make a personal declaration as an abstainer. A classroom, as we all very well know, can be a welter of bits and pieces of ideology, blatant or subtle, implicit or explicit, taken for granted or openly evangelical.

Clearly, this is an enormous subject, relating not just to language teaching but to all education and in the end to the whole human condition. I want to confine myself here, however, to certain aspects of general education and language teaching, and as a starting point I want to put forward two basic distinctions which, it seems to me, lie behind much of our thought and behaviour, without our ever spending much time considering them. They are built into the kind of society that we have inherited, and I will label them archetypally, as it were. The first of these archetypes is the Marketplace, and the second is the Monastery, and I want to talk as a consequence of our language-teaching work being influenced on the one hand by a *marketplace tradition* and on the other hand by a *monastery tradition*.[6]

The *marketplace tradition* relates to the rough and tumble of life, buying and selling, surviving, trading, travelling, and somehow communicating wherever you go. Everything to do with it is dictated by simple necessity and is largely unstructured. It relates to shops, stalls, streets, bazaars, trading-posts, ports—all the places where people come together from diverse backgrounds and have somehow to deal with each other. In the great cosmopolitan cities of history—Babylon, Alexandria, Marseilles, London, New York, Singapore—the procedures of the waterfront and warehouse have demanded quick practical answers to the problem of how to deal with speakers of other languages. Anything that works is welcome: a go-between if possible, gestures or pictures, your words or their words, your grammar or their grammar, anybody's words and anybody's grammar and in any combination, in order to strike a bargain and get things moving. It is a makeshift system that has always worked well enough and in the process has given rise to trade jargons, camp languages, and pidgins and creoles. These may be socially frowned on, but they are as alive as the merchants, hucksters, sailors, soldiers, whores, and harbourmasters who use them. These *interlanguages* are vitally alive, and many a respectable and matronly modern language has something of this wild blood in its family line.[7]

By contrast, the *monastery tradition* describes a situation where education in general and language learning in particular occurred for formal social and cultural reasons, usually linked with a religion and promulgated in austere colleges where the sons of the socially elect gathered together to learn how to maintain their positions in society as priests, monks, civil servants, royal retainers, military officers, and the like. They were fitted into box-like surroundings, organized in groups, homogenized as far as possible in terms of sex, age, place, and time. The method is much the same whether it is the scribes of ancient Babylon and Egypt, the monks of medieval Europe, the brahmins of India, the teaching brotherhoods and sisterhoods of Catholic schools and missions, the one-sex staff of one-sex private schools, or the co-educational day schools that we all know now. The containerization of life is unrelieved in such institutions: students working in small box-like cells (studies) or in large box-like classrooms, their time divided up into box-like periods marked by the ringing of bells, strict discipline imposed on how they comport themselves while studying box-like books organized into box-like pages and chapters, containerized portions to be committed to memory and acted upon in appropriate ways.

The marketplace is full of passions, obsessions, and strategies, but it has never provided a serious alternative to the ideological basis of the monastery tradition, which is, I would argue, the tradition in which *we* are, willingly or unwillingly, embedded. The very architecture within which we work expresses the fundamental ideology of containerization, a highly efficient means of processing human beings for particular purposes, and one which we would find very difficult indeed to dismantle if we ever wanted to do so. Indeed, the annual TESOL convention is a masterpiece of organization built largely on the foundation of the monastery tradition: speakers are out front or up high (or both), at table or lectern, committed to time-slots and measured doses of knowledge that are offered to recipients carrying schedules all neatly laid out in rectangles that specify who does what, where, and at what time. Only in the area allocated to the publishers do we to some extent get away from this ancient order into a more fluid bazaar-like atmosphere, and there is still a certain reserve in organizations like TESOL as regards the commercial people out there, a kind of necessary evil vaguely lowering the academic tone.

Six ideological styles

I have mentioned these two traditions in order to highlight the existence of a containerizing educational process that expanded out of ancient religious and élitist origins into a worldwide network of schools and colleges. Many of us firmly believe that these schools and colleges are devoted to universal education and to the pursuit of both excellence and happiness. Wee Jimmy had to operate in just such a system with his dugs, coos, and glottal stops, and found the dice weighted against him. I would now like to look at this system in a way that, I admit, is almost imbecile in its simplicity, by saying that the whole of the monastery tradition is founded on four things that many of us might feel are hardly worth discussing: a container called a 'classroom', an authority figure once called a 'master' or a 'mistress' but now usually just a 'teacher', one or more trainees originally called 'disciples' but now known as either 'pupils' or 'students', and finally some set of 'materials' through which the teacher can ameliorate the condition of the students.

My argument at this stage is that every teacher who has ever had to work in a classroom has an ideology, however unexamined, of how things ought to *be* in that classroom, and every institution has an ideology as regards classrooms, corridors, play places, and so on. Much of the teacher's ideology derives somewhat incestuously from his or her previous experience of classrooms and schools (mainly on the other side of things, as a student), and so the teacher is often—inevitably—perpetuating a more or less undiscussed tradition, accepting things as they are.

Not always, of course. There are different ideologies of classroom behaviour and organization, and one can see these ideologies in terms of how teachers organize the essential facts of life in the classroom, inside their own heads. In simple logical terms, there are six basic sequences in which the three fundamentals can be arranged:

1 teacher—students—materials
2 teacher—materials—students
3 students—teacher—materials
4 students—materials—teacher
5 materials—teacher—students
6 materials—students—teacher

These are six systems of linear priority, and each is worth a little study. Something like them lies at the heart of many individual approaches to teaching, or animates whole methodologies, especially in language teaching. Thus, traditional monastery methodology has tended to emphasize the teacher as *authorized dispenser of knowledge* to fortunate and dutiful students with the aid of a book or books (Style 1). Or, the same teacher reveals the content of a venerated book or books to a set of students who may or may not be worthy to receive that knowledge (Style 2). A contrasting and more modern approach foregrounds the students in open-plan activities, learning together with the teacher as *the Friend-Who-Knows*, using a variety of visual and other aids (Style 3). Or, the free-and-easy students exploit various well-organized and often disposable materials while, hovering here and there, is the teacher as *resource person* (Style 4). In certain other situations, such as in the military and certain kinds of factory work or professional training, there is a job to be done with certain kinds of equipment which is of paramount interest, an instructor is there (rather than a teacher properly so called) to inculcate the skills that the learners must acquire, and if they don't then other students will (Style 5). Or, such skills may be approached as a kind of *immersion procedure* with the students learning by trial and error, and the teacher there to *limit mistakes and damage* (Style 6).

These permutations have their defenders and their opponents; they express value systems especially as regards who or what comes first in the classroom and where the priorities lie. How can we, however, translate such styles or models into the immediate world of language-teaching methodology? Without too much difficulty, I would argue, as follows:

Styles 1 and 2: teacher first. These are dominant in traditional grammar-translation as well as in traditional structuralism, where the teacher leads and the students follow, using materials from which little deviation is permitted, and where in fact the teacher hardly ever improvises, being instead the vehicle for the transmission of an approved body of information by an approved means.

Styles 3 and 4: students first. These are dominant in traditional direct-method courses as well as in situational courses, and are certainly significant in the communicative approach, where the teacher decreases his or her status as an authority figure and interweaves with students at work on a wide range of possible materials, often improvising along the way and encouraging novelty and originality (moving indeed as far as possible in the direction of the marketplace as the constraints of the monastery permit).

Styles 5 and 6: materials first. These styles predominate here and there in all methods and approaches, as for example when publishers and educational systems prepare 'teacher-proof' materials that are more important than the teachers (who may be considered insufficiently skilled in the target language or the methods used); or in such settings as the language laboratory where everyone is subordinate to the equipment and the materials to be used; or, again, in a military or similar situation where large numbers of trained personnel are needed, and assembly-line techniques are applied.

Equilibrium?

These six are not the only possible permutations. People may dislike the idea of linearity or priority, and instead try to group the three elements together in a cluster that requires no predetermined dominance. The implicit message here is: 'We all matter equally, you, me, and the book, regardless of any impression to the contrary'. Such a style has pleasing overtones of democracy; it is relaxed, humane, humanistic, and can be used by a sympathetic teacher in any of the modes of language teaching: grammar-translation, direct method, structuralism, situationalism, or the communicative approach. Its detractors, however, see it as risking an anarchic free-for-all, admitting too much of the marketplace into the security of the monastery.

Our schools and colleges today, I would propose, tend to suffer because we are not very good at reconciling monastery and marketplace: we try to soften the old authoritarianism and discover permissiveness; we recoil from permissiveness and re-discover the past ('Back to the basics!'); we worry about whether we should offer academic-style courses to all, or vocational employment-orientated courses to all, or how to vary the mix without turning some people into smug élitists and others into angry underdogs. It is no surprise that many of our schools serve as battle-grounds between the two traditions rather than as centres of education, creating very considerable ideological and social confusion. In our profession particularly, we are caught between *conservative methods* on the one hand and *radical approaches* on the other. There are on the one side teachers who favour explicit grammar, direct translation, rules, rote learning, deductive reasoning, written work, literary emphases, language history, and standard language. And there are on the other side teachers who favour implicit grammar or no organized grammar at all, immersion, free-wheeling, problem-solving, 'authentic' language, inductive reasoning, oral work, vocational and social emphases, contemporary usage, and informal usage (including dialect). They are often antagonistic, argumentative, and even arrogant towards each other, each having the conviction that they are on the side of the angels.

Piaget has asserted that children—and the adults that children become—value a feeling of equilibrium in their understanding of the world they live in, and that *dis*equilibrium disturbs them and makes them search for a fresh balance and understanding. This describes pretty well how I have felt as a language teacher over the last twenty years or so, and my own suggestion as regards our models of how classrooms work is very much an attempt to achieve equilibrium. Most of us would recognise nowadays that there are very few panaceas in our profession. Proponents of THE way to salvation in the teaching of a foreign language are greeted more and more sceptically as time passes. We are close to satiation as regards claims about new methods and approaches that ask us to abandon earlier methods and approaches that we know were flawed but were not necessarily all bad. My own inclination here is towards a rationally and emotionally satisfying approach towards both methods and materials, and towards the student-teacher relationship. The classroom with all its strengths and weaknesses won't go away, and as a consequence I would like to turn the six models of linear priority and the seventh model of teachers, students, and materials all clustered together into a circle model, a rotating device where the strengths of all these models can be used and their weaknesses minimized. Imagine then a kind of triangle with the teacher at one point, the students at another, and the materials at a third, but the possibility of rotating that triangle in any direction (as in the accompanying diagram).

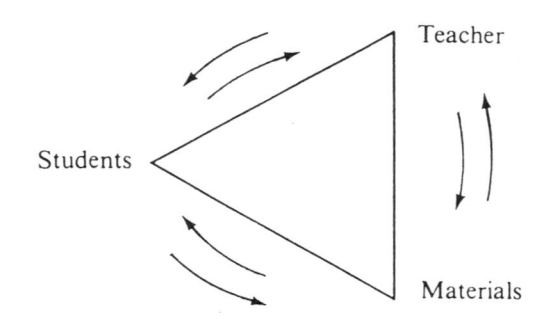

In an approach like this, which is a stylization of something I conceive as in fact much more fluid, no component is permanently dominant. Each can rotate into primary position as the need for it arises, permitting us to vary our work more consciously and also to take into account students' attention spans more coherently. For certain purposes, the teacher can perform in front of the class in such roles as *fountain-of-truth, actor, policeman, judge,* and even sometimes as *persecutor pushing the students for all they are worth*. At other times, the materials and equipment can come to the fore (films, tapes, language laboratory, television, computer, whatever), doing work that teachers cannot do, providing variety that no individual teacher can ever provide, offering an accuracy that no single human being can match. At still other times, the students are in the foreground of things, released from a single focus, on teacher, book, or machine, taking on a variety of roles in their turn, maybe even taking over the classroom and making a lot of noise, or organized in groups of various sizes for various purposes, with a variety of improvised materials, games, songs, dramas, dialogues, situations whether simulated or authentic, and from time to time spilling out of the classroom into the marketplace to try their skills.[8]

Models like these are only aids, descriptive devices for various patterns and tendencies in what we do. There is no ultimate truth in what I have been describing here; an explicit attempt, however, to talk about how we conceive our classrooms may do no harm, and may even do some good. If one is going to have ideological attitudes, they might as well be as coherent to us as possible, *and subject to overt examination*. The result might be a more truly humane approach to education in general and language education in particular. I suspect Wee Jimmy would have preferred things that way, in a world where he would be allowed both dogs *and* dugs.

Notes

1. See, among others, Piaget (1972), Fromm (1950), Donaldson (1978).
2. See Piaget (1972), Ch. 4. For a description of Piaget's triad of adaptation, assimilation, and accommodation, see Travers (1977:147–151).
3. See Ferguson (1959):325–40, reprinted in Hymes (1964), Fishman (1968).
4. I have looked more closely at the issue of 'high' and 'low' dialects in McArthur (1979) and (1983). See also Peñalosa (1981), esp. Chapters 6–10, whose focus is the situation of Chicanos (people of Mexican Spanish background in the US).
5. The field is rich. See, among others, Fishman (1968), Hymes (1964), Peñalosa (1981), and Labov (1972).

6. The concept of monastery and marketplace is discussed in more detail in McArthur (1983), Note 4:2.
7. See, in particular Hymes (1971), Valdman (1977), Bickerton (1975).
8. The triangular model proposed here appears in McArthur (1983:87). A similar but immobile triangle can be found in Dakin (1969). A more complex version of the Dakin triangle can be found in R. J(ean) Handscombe, 'The Sunrunners: ESL by TV for grade 3 in Ontario', in *TESOL Quarterly* 9:3, pp. 289–98.

7

The usage industry

[An editorial article in *English Today: The International Review of the English Language*, 7, July 1986, Cambridge University Press.]

Guides to good usage have been part of the tradition of Standard English since the seventeenth century. Such works have been a commercial success and are as abundant today as in the past. What characterizes the tradition of these 'bibles of usage'?

In 1604, the schoolmaster Robert Cawdrey brought out, in a single octavo volume, his *Table Alphabeticall of Hard, Usuall English Wordes*, and without knowing that he was doing so inaugurated the English-language usage industry, which over the centuries has created thousands of books and millions of copies of those books. The *Table* was designed for the linguistically insecure, compiled 'for the benefit and helpe of Ladies, Gentlewomen, or any other unskilfull persons'. It contained some 3,000 short entries, and was the first ever dictionary of the English language.

It appeared at a turning point in the social, literary, and linguistic history of Britain. A year before it came out, James VI, King of Scots, made the journey south to become James I, King of England—the first monarch to rule over both of the nations that used forms of the English language. At the same time, William Shakespeare, John Donne, and others were laying—also quite unwittingly—the foundations of English literature, and in 1611 there appeared, under royal sponsorship, one of the most influential books in history: the Authorized Version of the Bible, the Old Testament in Hebrew and Aramaic and the New Testament in Greek being rendered into the high English of the Tudor and Jacobean courts and clergy.

Books and standards

The invention of the printing press in the fifteenth century had already radically altered the nature of organizing and disseminating information, with an impact that can be compared to the arrival of the personal computer today. Books were no longer laboriously compiled clerical mysteries: they had rapidly become both commercially viable and highly visible in society at large. And with the coming of metal type, three parallel revolutionary developments permeated European society:

- With the example of how metal letters could be sorted efficiently by storing them alphabetically, ABC ordering caught on as a means of processing data and making it easily accessible. 'Dictionary order' became fashionable.

- With the need to organize pages of text for printing, scholars and typesetters alike became increasingly interested in consistent spelling (that is, a stable orthography) and a rational system of laying out texts (that is, a stable set of punctuation and page organization).

- Fascinated by their success with the printed word, enthusiasts began to think in terms of homogenizing the entirety of their mother tongues, to make them more like the rigorously structured Latin of scholarship throughout Western Christendom and to tame the exuberance of these vernaculars as they absorbed Latin vocabulary either by direct adoption or loan-translation. Additionally, as the new nation-states grew stronger, their centralizing governments began to contemplate the benefits of 'fixing' and 'refining' the high dialect of the court, of learning, and of the press.

In the Middle Ages, the 'king's standard' was the rallying point for his troops in the heat of battle, keeping them in good order round his high-flying banner. As the new states grew more orderly, norms for weights and measures were set up in important towns, so that people could check physically whether they were getting the correct weight and the correct measure in what they bought. By 1600 in Britain, this system of regulation too was—literally—called 'the kings Standerd', and this apt phrase was extended to other, less physical things, including in due course to 'standard-authors'. By 1759, Oliver Goldsmith could say of one such writer that he was indeed a standard-author 'because a great many very eminent authors formed their style by his'.

In such ways—crudely, in fits and starts—the idea and ideal of 'standard languages' and 'correct usage' developed and spread in Western Europe. They did not, however, develop with any great strength among either the high-born nobility or the low-born commons. Rather, middle-class professionals—merchants, teachers, printers, booksellers, lawyers, clergymen, scholars—were eager to better themselves, to know and to show all the marks of social refinement, and were in the seventeenth century much exercised by conceptions like 'good taste', 'polite society', and 'classical purity'. They were also, in their social and religious lives, constrained to adhere to custom within their particular ideological camps, whether these were Protestant, Catholic, or other. They were prone, therefore, to follow their leaders in matters of social conformity.

Among their leaders were the burgeoning new publishing houses, who saw in the middle classes a reservoir of purchasers of all kinds of improvement books, whether on social comportment and the right way to address a duchess, in elocution and etiquette, in letter-writing, in spelling, in punctuation, in grammar, in vocabulary, or in usage at large.

Bibles of usage

In the English language, one looks words up not in any dictionary but in *the* dictionary, much as one refers to something as being in such and such a book of *the* Bible: implying in effect the King James Authorized Version. Whereas, however, there was only one Bible (however translated, printed, published, and distributed), there were as time passed many dictionaries. Nonetheless, something of the medieval reverence for weighty and authoritative volumes had carried over into the age of print, and often the larger lexicons were bound in styles that were solemnly biblical. Indeed—as with Oxford and Collins today—publishers who did a good trade in bibles also brought out dictionaries and other works of reference, and were happy for them all to inspire a similar respectful awe.

In a world where men of letters were often also men of the cloth—or had been educated in school or in college by or alongside men of the cloth—it can be no surprise that wordbooks acquired (and still retain for many today) a quality of Holy Writ. Clerics and clerks, scholars and Schoolmen—there has for centuries in Europe been an interplay between the pen and the pulpit, especially when the Bible was one of the main reasons for learning to read and the main source of reading matter after one had learned. Much of the just-so sacred quality of standard literary English dates from this period, and reflects the influence of men like Samuel Johnson, who observed in the preface to his dictionary in 1755:

> As language was at its beginning merely oral, all words of necessary or common use were spoken before they were written; and while they were unfixed by any visible signs, must have been spoken with great diversity, as we now observe those who cannot read to catch sounds imperfectly, and utter them negligently. When this wild and barbarous jargon was first reduced to an alphabet, every penman endeavoured to express, as he could, the sounds which he was accustomed to pronounce or to receive, and vitiated in writing such words as were already vitiated in speech . . . From this uncertain pronunciation arise in a great part the various dialects of the same country, which will always be observed to grow fewer, and less different, as books are multiplied.

Like a true religion, the 'visible sign' triumphed over the world of 'wild and barbarous' dialects. It was itself the measure of all things, so that those who could not read—for whatever reason—deferred to those who could, and accepted both the kinder label 'unletterd' and the harsher label 'illiterate', a term as judgemental and often as abusive as 'barbarian' ever was among the Greeks.

The success of this attitude to language and to people was profound, and remains profound today. One cannot doubt the worthwhileness of the printing press, of extended literacy, of greater opportunities for education and the like, but it is important to look at the inevitable darker side of such progress, which could elevate one prestige dialect—in the case of English, the variety used among the better-off in and around London, Oxford, and Cambridge—to the position of the norm and yardstick against which all other varieties should be judged till Kingdom come. In the preface to the 1844 edition of John Walker's *A Critical Pronouncing Dictionary of the English Language* (first published in 1791), we see the nineteenth-century fruits of this situation most arrestingly laid out:

> Thus, as generations are passing away, words drop and become obsolete, and others rise into use and supply their room, while the change, although so entire, yet because it is gradual, is not attended to and the absolute alteration of the language takes place without much, at least much popular, observation . . . At first composed of a horrid mixture of all the barbarous which the various races of uncultivated conquerors, Danes, Saxons, and Normans, had

introduced, mixed up with the adulterated idioms of the native British, which they had adopted—it was a speech harsh, dissonant and uncouth. Succeeding ages smoothed down and polished it; the change has become total and complete; and there are perhaps few among the readers of the present day who admire the elegance of modern writers, who would venture to encounter the Court poet of the days of Queen Elizabeth, or could perceive much beauty or elegance in the numbers of Spencer [sic], the friend and *elevé* of the accomplished Sidney.

It is a curious argument, dismissing the monstrous past, smugly progressive, and at the same time split-minded about the days of Queen Elizabeth and King James: Edmund Spenser is dismissed, but Walker lays no sacrilegious hand on either the Authorized Version or Shakespeare. His words suggest a veritable golden age of standardization, but the dictionary itself shows that in his own terms much hard work remains to be done. He includes in it 'rules to be observed by the NATIVES of IRELAND in order to obtain a just pronunciation of English', followed by comparable rules for others. Walker had no doubts about the rightness of showing the outlandish Irish and Scots how to conform, of calling the provincial English to heel, or of exhorting errant Cockneys ('my own countrymen') not to let the side down in the heart of urbane London.

Walker's is an up-to-the-minute golden age, because 'from the wonderful and rapid improvement of modern times' it is clear that 'the *newest* Dictionary, if produced by an accomplished scholar, must always be the *best*'. No looking back to the ancients for authority and reassurance here. The best is right now, and commercial hype was as healthy in 1844 as it is today.

The coming of Henry Fowler

In the nineteenth century, howeer, the broad drift of lexicography was away from explicit hellfire-and-brimstone condemnation of usage towards the would-be objective recording of words and their usages 'on historical principles'. Something of contemporary science was added to the lexicographer's pachwork quilt. The most outstanding product of the new spirit was the dictionary of the Philological Society, that has latterly come to be known as the *Oxford English Dictionary*. Slow, sporadic, and often a source of economic heartache for the Delegates of the Press, this work has gone on from 1858 to the present day. Like all dictionaries, it has the quirks of its compilers, but it is seldom as harshly judgemental as Johnson, Webster, and Walker.

As a result, when 'standard' dictionaries began more and more to follow the philological trend and simply record usage without much overt comment, those who wanted that overt comment, direct reassurance, Calvinist condemnation of deviation, or simply guidance in a hard grammar book—that told you straight what good usage was and was not. The most famous of these appeared in 1926, also published by Oxford University Press, and like Samuel Johnson, Noah Webster, and James Murray of the *OED*, its compiler has become part of the general mythology of the Engligh language. Henry Fowler had been a schoolmaster, like so many others drawn into the web of words, and his *A Dictionary of Modern English Usage* had a most remarkable success, and remained untouched until the 1960s, not just a guide to users of the language but a model of what the twentieth-century usage book should look like: a discursive A-to-Z selection of longer and shorter essays, laced at times with wit, at times with disdain, at times with Olympian detachment. There have been many imitators and rivals.

The work of revision was given by Oxford to Sir Ernest Gowers, a civil servant who in 1948 published *Plain Words; A Guide to the Use of English*, in 1951 brought out *The ABC of Plain Words*, and in 1954 combined them as the now-classic *The Complete Plain Words*. In the preface to his 1965 edition of Fowler, he noted:

> What is the secret of its success? It is not that all Fowler's opinions are unchallengeable. It is not that he is always easy reading . . . . There are some passages that only yield [the desired sense] after what the reader may think an excessive amount of scrutiny—passages demanding hardly less concentration than one of the more obscure sections of a Finance Act . . . Nor does the secret lie in the convenience of the book as a work of reference; it hardly deserves its title of dictionary, since much of it consists of short essays on various subjects, some with fancy titles that give no clue at all to their subject.

Gowers concluded that it was the sheer idiosyncrasy of the man that made the book, something which has been true for most reference books at least since Pliny the Elder in ancient Rome. In describing something of Fowler's life, however, Gowers writes at times in a kind of in-group shorthand that cannot mean much in Nebraska or Norway, Saskatchewan or New South Wales—leave alone in the big industrial cities or rural schools of the British Isles. What he indicates in this code-like language is not just the idiosyncrasy of the man, but the idiosyncrasy of a whole social caste, dominant for so long that it takes itself and its dominance for granted:

> He was born in 1858, the son of a Cambridge Wrangler and Fellow of Christ's. From Rugby he won a scholarship to Balliol, but surprisingly failed to get a first in either Mods. or Greats. After leaving Oxford he spent seventeen years as a master at Sedbergh. His career there was ended by a difference of opinion with his headmaster, H. G. Hart (also a Rugbeian). Fowler, never a professing Christian, could not conscientiously undertake to prepare boys for confirmation.

Both Fowler and Gowers belong to, and speak on behalf of, a privileged circle within the upper echelons of British life, and have addressed themselves to others—upwardly mobile perhaps, linguistically insecure certainly—who have wanted either to confirm their places within this circle or to be as like the élite as possible. Indeed, a book by Henry Fowler and his brother Frank, preceding *Modern English Usage* by many years, and equally popular, had the straightforward title *The King's English*. Published in 1906 in optimistic Edwardian times, the book is a modern echo of Agincourt and other ancient battles where the king's standard floated high above the general din.

Standard languages manifestly do great good, but in their defence people can sometimes do great harm. Usage books like Fowler/Gowers represent this dual state of affairs when on the one hand they praise fine writing and clear speech and on the other fire their broadsides at people who are already socially weak, linguistically 'substandard', ethnically wrongfooted, and generally part of the educated white man's burden. For every person who has a soft spot for the judgemental legacy of Johnson, Walker, and Fowler/Gowers, there is another who loathes it, and there are many more whom it makes uneasy.

The present day

In recent times there has been no let-up in the production of guides to 'good' English usage. Indeed, probably more such usage books are in existence than ever before, just as there are more cook(ery) books than ever before, or books about health and diet. Since it was launched last year (1985), *English Today* has received at least a dozen new or revised usage titles for review. Some representative titles are:

- At the concise end of the spectrum, the *Chambers Pocket Guide to Good English*, 132 pages long, with no Mosaic pretensions, a broad-minded range of brief entries and useful nuggets of advice.

- At the heavyweight end of the spectrum, the quasi-biblical Reader's Digest *The Right Word at the Right Time: A Guide to the English Language and How to Use It*, which features red crosses and query marks to warn readers that certain usages are out (or very close to out) of bounds.

- In the British corner, Godfrey Howard's compact *A Guide to Good English in the 1980s* (Pelham), with cute cartoons, an amiable style, and a willingness to take on such realia as class and sex bias, ethnic slurs like *dago*, and four-letter words like *fuck*.

- In the American corner, the second edition of the hefty 641-page *Harper dictionary of Contemporary Usage*, by William and Mary Morris, who are presented as 'internationally known authorities on words and language' who in this work refer their thornier problems to a board of 'outstanding' consultants whose comments and quips enliven the enterprise.

- The paperback version of the *Oxford Guide to the English Language*, which curiously cobbles together a thematic assortment of usage issues and a pocket dictionary. The intriguing result bristles with separate lists and indexes that are hard to find and follow.

The market must be there, and yet the 1980s [were] for many reasons a time of unprecedented risk for the compilers and publishers of such lists. There are at least three reasons for this:

(1) *The scale of English.* The explosive size of the language, used every day by between three hundred million and a billion people all over the planet. Somewhere within that mass circulates and fluctuates what was once 'the King's Standard', nibbled at here, extolled there, intertwining in one place with a strong dialect, patois, or creole, in another place with a full-blown separate language like French, Spanish, Hindi, or Afrikaans. It could be argued that more than ever we *need* usage guides, to sort out the mess. It could also be argued that more than ever before it is impossible for individuals or even committees to advise the world on all the awkward issues. To do that needs the wisdom of Solomon and a

knowledge of the language's affairs which we do have all in one database for easy consultation.

(2) *The weakening of a social caste.* In the forty years since the end of the Second World War the old pillars of the temple have cracked and begun to fall. The monolithic strength and self-assurance of the caste that ran the British Empire (and had its cognates in all the English-speaking nations) has become fragmented, and the caste is itself less secure. This has to be so when in London in 1985 Michael Joseph published a counter-usage book: Dorgan Rushton's *The Queen's English: High Taw Tawk Prowpah-Leah.* Its apocryphal upper-crust consultants are cuttingly listed as Sir Vere Brayne d'Hemmidge and Lady Minah Brayne d'Hemmidge. A patented bookmark accompanies the book, with instructions on how to use it to practise clenching the teeth and stiffening the upper lip. It is, as it were, the revenge of the Cockney against the spirit of John Walker.

(3) *Blending prescription and description.* People of course are still linguistically insecure. The problem of the publishers is to cater to this insecurity while somehow blending the old conception of bibles of usage with the current need to consult language specialists who do not particularly believe in the old conception of bibles of usage. The Reader's Digest volume displays this problem strikingly; it seeks to be prescriptive, but lists as its consultants an array of descriptive linguists. The result is a neither/nor kind of book that looks back to the golden age and sideways at the cultural relativists. It clearly means well, but the result is a patchwork of old adages and warnings, new liberal-mindedness towards the colonies, moments of brilliant balance, and flashes of bad taste and inadequate research.

David Crystal brought out a book about usage not too long ago, entitled *Who Cares About English Usage?* (1984). It doesn't much resemble Fowler; it chats rather than pontificates. I'd like to close this article with the words he uses to close his book: 'I hope you will feel like finding out more about the history and variety of English—not just by collecting facts, but by trying to establish the reasons for the way things are. My approach doesn't ask you to stop being vigilant, as speaker and listener, reader and writer—but it does ask you to be considerate, while you're on watch. It asks you to care, as well as to take care. Eternal vigilance? Certainly. But in a civilized society, eternal tolerance too.'

8

Problems of purism and usage in editing *English Today*

[Some reflections on editing *English Today: The International Review of the English Language* (Cambridge University Press) that appeared in 6 (April 1986) as 'The problem of purism' and 11 (July 1987) as 'On editing *English Today*'. The original articles were prompted by letters from readers about deterioration in English and the role that *ET* could or should play in stopping the general rot.]

The problem of purism

'When books refer to Standard English, they mean English that is considered correct by most educated people for writing and speaking, in nearly all situations.' This classically straightforward description appears in Godfrey Howard's *A Guide to Good English in the 1980s*, published in 1985. Howard, however, immediately adds: 'The problem is there is no final authority on where slang and colloquial language end and Standard English begins'.

Ay, there's the usage rub. Like many other commentators on the language, Howard concludes that there are risks in laying down the law, because 'even good dictionaries take different views' on the standardness of certain words and usages. He opts for a 'standard English' without the capital S, so as to avoid suggesting 'an absolute fixed standard that everyone agrees with'. Or, from the purist point of view, that everyone should seek for and conform to when found. The only difficulty here is that people will divide even on whether the 's' should be a capital or not, advocates of the 'permissive' lower case locked in verbal combat with the defenders of the majuscule.

There appears to be no limit when it comes to defending the honour of the language, whether that language is perceived as a standard core or the whole kit and caboodle of English everywhere. The conflict dates at least from Reformation times, when purists vigorously deplored the flow of flowery Latinisms into the vernacular tongue. Latin and English, they argued, should be kept apart: further mongrelizing the already mongrel native tongue would, they asserted, spoil the purity of the breed, and was a sure sign of decadence. People were at that time already arguing about the use of 'infer' for 'imply', while innovative lexicographers were coining Anglo-Latinisms wholesale. Their method was simple: take a Latin-English dictionary, apply a few simple French-style conversion rules, and *onerosus* becomes 'onerous' and *catalogus* 'catalogue'. Words like 'alacrity' and 'ruminate' entered the language in just this way, words that nobody would blink at now; others, like 'nexible' (able to hold or knit together, cf. *nexus*) and 'bubulcitate' (to cry like a cowherd), were on offer as well, but the options weren't taken up, so some kind of filtering process appears to have been at work. The words, presumably, did have to be functional.

The editorial mail-bag of *English Today* contains its fair share of present-day protest. Much of it is aimed at 'the media', while now and again a warning shot is fired across *ET*'s bows as well. W. A. R. Hamilton, a pensioner from Bristol, states his position with admirable clarity:

> I shall not renew my subscription to *English Today*. Not being either a Phonetician nor an 'acronym watcher', I cannot understand articles like those in the October issue by Robert Ilson and John Haycraft . . . As for effusions like that of Miss Cheshire in the first issue, they are more suited for a journal of psychology, and in general your writers seem more concerned with chronicling changes and neologisms rather than with defending the purity of our native tongue. How does one combat errors such as PRONOUNCIATION which one hears almost daily on radio and television, except through journals such as yours: but what are you doing about it?

Jack Conrad, a fellow of the Institute of Linguists, writes from London with a comparable anxiety about corruption:

> I am very concerned at the way the English language has been rapidly deteriorating during the past few years, even when spoken and written by people who should know better, including authors and journalists. I have exchanged correspondence with the BBC and newspaper editors about the growing use of slipshod English but

still it goes on. For example, such expressions as 'between you and I', 'never ever', 'hopefully' and dozens more are now in common use and the process of deterioration has become a landslide.

Heather O'Dare adds from Bath:

> People who use ugly English, including for example the singular 'they', do not inspire respect and pleasure. When I read or listen, I admire those who can use the language correctly and beautifully. Our language is a precious heritage. One cannot respect professional communicators who cannot use the tools of their trade expertly. If I opened a novel and read, 'the average person has *their* own ideas,' I should close the book in disgust. As a matter of great interest to me, is there a book entirely without faulty English?

I do not know of any that would measure up, because there is quite simply no way of assessing the candidates for such a literary role. Shakespeare's 'most unkindest cut of all' would disqualify him on grammatical grounds, and his 'make the multitudinous seas incarnadine' would do badly in a Plain English test. Every single one of us has a private yardstick—however cleverly or crudely worked out—relating to the grammar and the aesthetics of the standard language. As I read the angrier letters that arrive in the post, I wonder who or what the variously distressed correspondents *could* accept as a final arbiter of such things as usage, spelling, and punctuation.

The anger often has a shape as well as a target. Bertram Lippman, a retired professor of English living in New York, identifies both when he writes: 'William Safire in the *New York Times* appears to take the view that in pronunciation, and ultimately in usage, when enough of us are wrong, we're right.' Here, William Safire, whom many people appear to regard as a final arbiter of usage (or at least as someone who seeks to hold back the barbarians at the gates), represents the media, while the general evil is statistical—the *mobile vulgus* at work contaminating the language. Professor Lippman adds that he finds the dictum he attributes to Safire 'not only offensive but linguistically noxious. There is an assumption that correctness is an unattainable goal.' Lippman also makes the point that some permissivists who tolerate individual neologisms and abuses will become as puristic as the next man if neologism is piled on neologism and abuse upon abuse. To illustrate his point he offers an intriguing 'synthetic paragraph' of his pet dislikes:

> Let me give you some advice for free, it is not too important, but anyhow . . . If you're buying a home, even if it's not finished yet, is when you have to be real careful to get the true facts, they may turn out to be fortuitous for you and whoever you are buying it with. For one thing, you may be able to work the sales agent for something extra, say a chaise lounge or maybe a casket for somebody's internment. I wish you get there before it gets real late, so you don't miss nothing. Those agents seldom or ever miss out on a chance to put one over on you. I could care less what you do, but why not get the best deal for your money? It just makes me livid with rage to think you might lay down tonight with a bad conscience.

There seem to be three problems with a passage like this, excellent as it might be as a collage of complaint. Firstly, it is socially discriminatory, marked by judgements about education, class background, sloppy thinking, dialect, dialect differences, and in certain circumstances race and religion as well (although these may not be specifically built into *this* collage). They could, however, appear in somebody else's chamber of horrors. Secondly, it falls foul of Howard's problem: how, when, where, and why do you draw your line between the approved and the disapproved, the standard and the 'other'? Thirdly, what do you do when a skilled writer or speaker deliberately blends the standard and the rest, for artistic and communicative purposes? Lippman's collage serves Lippman's purpose. What about all sorts of other collages serving all sorts of other purposes—and still in the end being 'standard' enough to grasp?

Some people do, however, appear to want legislation in the style of the French academy. Others want the language professionals to clean up their act, so that they can then serve as exemplars for the rest of us—and particularly for the mob, when it opens its collective mouth or picks up its collective pen. It is hard, however, to legislate for something so/as vast and protean as present-day English. It is altogether too large for crusades. It currently defies the efforts of the most dedicated and sophisticated scholars—as witness Robert Burchfield's observations in *ET*5 about the new grammar produced by Randolph Quirk and his colleagues. Most people consider the Quirk grammar dauntingly large; Burchfield sees it as 'deliciously small', and not at all sufficient for the task of describing the grammar of English. There is, however, no doubting the sincere anguish of people who have over long and productive lives cared greatly about the state of the language. As Jack Conrad says, in closing his letter:

> What can be done? I have long been of the opinion that the decline of our language is part and parcel of our permissive and decaying society. Some years ago, in despair, I thought of forming an association for the defence of English, but I am afraid that my age—I am 73—and my physical and mental vigour are against me. Anyway, I hope that you and your new journal will help to repair some of the damage. All power to your elbow.

It is tempting and touching when the mantle of saviour descends, but it is, I suspect, risky for all concerned. The magazine that I am privileged to edit is called *English Today*, warts and all—not *Good English Today*, with the implication of better English tomorrow. It is equipped neither with easy solutions nor a big linguistic stick.

At the same time one cannot and would not want to abdicate entirely. It is possible to want—and to try to use—well-composed standard English at the same time as one looks dispassionately or humorously or critically or intently or casually or linguistically or sociologically or indeed puristically at all the goings-on in English today. There is plenty to do, and we hope people will write well while they are doing it. But contributors will make mistakes and eagle-eyed readers will spot those slips, or object to errors as they perceive them. The present issue is replete with examples of this, as for instance where Bill Broughton rebukes Bill Beavis on page 3 and Laurence Urdang has something to say about Robert Ilson and American English on page 5. This is the kaleidoscope of the language and people's reactions to other people's language and ideas. We can learn from it all, all of us. Sybil Sarel puts it as follows, in an elegant blend of purism and optimistic tolerance:

> An English friend living in Calgary (Alberta) is appalled by the standard of English used by her son's teacher of English, the latest example she sent me being: 'I don't got any problem'. Her husband has spotted numerous spelling mistakes on classroom blackboards, exclusive of the British and American/Canadian differences mentioned in Robert Ilson's very interesting article in *ET*4. Parents' evenings at this Calgary school are consequently lively, to say the least! Considering that much of youngsters' reading, in Britain today, is of American style and spelling, should our teachers—and those in America and Canada—not draw attention to the differences, and so avoid confusion over what *is* a spelling mistake and what isn't? I used to do this, and it made interesting talking points. I must confess that, depending on how many books I'd marked and how tired I was, I would sometimes comment acidly, in red, 'Re-write, in ENGLISH!'

May I be forgiven . . . My mind has since broadened by reading your excellent publication; alas, too late for me, but not for those still teaching, to enrich English lessons. Perhaps *ET* should be regulation issue to all schools using English? And in fairness to the Canadian teacher, it should be said that English teachers' mistakes are not unknown in Britain.

Or anywhere else the language is used . . . . It is a seductive thought, a mandatory copy of *ET* in every English-using school. We would love to see copies of the magazine in every institution in any way concerned with the language, but not by diktat. If a government, ministry, or board chose to buy *ET* in bulk for all its schools, that would be fine—as long as the people in those schools had the fullest possible freedom to make up their own minds about what was in the magazine, or to abstain from looking at it at all.

At the end of the day or the article, however, the fear and fury are still there, and are hard to exorcize. They are part of the kaleidoscope too. Bertram Lippman quotes Bertrand Russell, from *Human Knowledge*, where he says:

> This brings me to a fundamental divergence between me and many philosophers. . . . They are persuaded that common speech is good enough, not only for daily life, but also for philosophy. I, on the contrary, am persuaded that common speech is full of vagueness and inaccuracy, and that any attempt to be precise and accurate requires modification of common speech both as regards vocabulary and as regards syntax.

Quoting Russell in a context of standard and non-standard language implies a strong desire for a specialized 'uncommon speech'. Such an element is certainly part of the evolution of Europe's standard languages, the scholarly strand that mingles with the courtly strand, with the translations of the Bible, with the invention of the printing press, with middle-class aspirations, with ideas of a 'classically pure' literary language, with canons of 'good taste', and with the overriding needs of centralized governments. It is this *un*common speech that purists defend. As Peter Strevens put it in his article in *ET*2, however, that special core is alive and well, and living in every English-using country in the world. It is a demanding medium to use, and can be used well or badly, but it is highly likely that more people are nowadays using it consistently well than have ever done in any generation in the past.

On editing *English Today*

Let me start by repeating part of the opening to 'Smoothing out the wrinkles', my editorial comment in *ET*8 (October 1986), in which George Racz, a subscriber in London, took the magazine to task:

> My impression from what I have seen so far is that you are holding up a mirror to the English language, so that we can see all the wrinkles in it—but I have not found advice on how to smooth them out. I am concerned with the lack of uniformity in English: Different spellings, pronunciations, constructions are heard and/or seen and there is noone [sic] who has the authority to say which is right, *inquire* or *enquire, dispatch* or *despatch, different from* or *different to* . . . Until someone is authorised to rule on these matters the language will continue to lack uniformity and one day will become unteacheable [sic].

There it is, in a nutshell, a theme in many of the letters that come to *ET*, and a particular theme among those correspondents—all of them older males living in or linked with England—who have announced that they are not renewing their subscriptions or at best have been giving *ET* one more year to get it right. And getting it right appears to mean appointing ourselves as the arbiters at least of the standard language if not crusaders for the standardization of *all* 'deviant' forms of English wherever they are. The gist of the complaint is that *ET* has not been set up as the new Académie Anglaise, and should have been so set up. While this is a relatively rare response, it does represent in a more extreme form the hope expressed by other—usually enthusiastic—readers that *ET* should offer guidance about a wide range of usage issues.

Not long after the publication of *ET*8, Paul Thompson of Shrewsbury in England wrote:

> I always feel that it is a little unfair of editors to add 'sic' after obvious slips of the pen in correspondents' letters, as if to say: 'Get a load of the live one we've got here!' Doubly so in the case of the quotations from George Racz's letter . . . as the letter is a plea for uniformity in English!'

Quite so. In my own experience, when editors use 'sic' it is largely defensive, so that *other* writers won't accuse them of perpetrating the offences in question. It is a distancing technique as much as a highlighting technique. In this particular instance, it was necessarily both. As editor of *ET*, I walk a fine line between leaving contributors to be themselves in their idiosyncrasies and applying an editorial yardstick. To get the language in the raw, one would simply photocopy what came in and print it like that (We have the technology). Few people, however, would be likely to buy the inelegant and inconsistent mass that would result.

So there is an enormous amount of standardizing in a magazine like this: the kind of uniformity that George Racz asks for. The trouble is that he asks for it all the way, right through to the bone. And what editor exists who has the right or the ability to do that to contributors, to lecture the world, and still be editor of a magazine called 'the international review of the English language'? At about the same time that Paul Thompson commented on my rare use of 'sic', F.H.G. Percy of the Whitgift School in South Croydon, England, wrote in with seven pages of magisterial comment. In them, he enumerated *thirty-two* faults of grammar, style, and culture in 'Linguicidal tendencies?', the editorial of *ET*6 (April 1986), and ended: 'Dr McArthur, *why* do you have these linguicidal tendencies?'

Clearly, an editor with such tendencies is in no position to reorganize (and debauch?) the writings of others, beyond perhaps the nicety of a comma added here, a spelling slip amended there. Indeed, such an editor needs an editor, and behind that another editor, in an infinite regress of editors. . . .

All of which originally related not just to George Racz and the question of good usage, but my invitation in *ET*8 to readers for constructive suggestions about how we could develop the discussion and help offered in the magazine on matters of confusing and disputed usage. Is it more or less sufficient, and if not how can it be improved? David Crystal [the Consulting Editor at the time] and I had no idea of the quality and quantity of the responses that might come in as a result of that invitation. As it happened, in relation to the large mail that comes to *ET* from all over the world, there was almost no response at all. Ten letters came in relating to the invitation (often among other things); of these, nine came from addresses in the United Kingdom, and one from a Briton in Germany. Of these, only *one* contained a practical suggestion for the magazine. This, out of the 10,000-plus people who read *ET* each quarter. One in a thousand.

It is clear, however, from these and other letters that the editorial style of *ET*, and the techniques as well as the messages in its features, interest readers just as much as usage at large. In fact, the one cannot be separated from the other, because *ET* is part of the phenomenon (or the problem, if you believe the language *is* going to the dogs, and that linguistic scholars have shares in dog-food). *ET* is part of the media, and the media notoriously do/does not escape censure. Although it is broadcasting that bears the brunt of angry comment (I regularly receive material castigating both British and American broadcasters for their accents, their mispronunciations, their abuse of fine old words, and very nearly their qualities as human beings), books and periodicals are in the front-line too. And rightly so. Being an Aunt Sally goes with the territory.

As regards attitudes to English, Paul Thompson went on in his letter: 'Good English is that which does efficiently its job as a medium of communication and self-expression. To do this it must be clear, unambiguous, comprehensive, and expressive. This is most evident where there is a certain level of education, which in turn is most evident in places which are prosperous.' He goes on to argue that 'snobs' end up condemning anything else as 'ignorant', 'lower-class', or 'bad English'; 'their snobbishness cannot be condoned, however it is an uncomfortable fact that they are right! Good Lord I sound pompous!'

We often do sound pompous when we argue for standards and find that there is elitism historically built into the argument. And we often do feel guilty when a defence of excellence in language flows into what looks like a defence of the class status quo or of scholarly superiority. It is a problem built into the dichotomy of the popular Englishes and Standard English that I have discussed in the preceding article. Many of us are indeed anxious that the world of our literate peers shall perceive us as literate too. This centrality of literacy comes out clearly in reminiscences sent in by Sybil Sarel, a retired teacher of English living in Orkney:

> 'What made *you* good at English?' I asked myself, thinking about *ET* articles and the current agonisings over the teaching of English. In the first place, before school-days, I had learned to read from *Chick's Own* comics, which had the words under the pictures split into syllables. I learnt to write cursively, before I learnt to print. My mother taught me. I was fascinated by printing on specially-lined pages, when I went to school at five, and saved my 'other writing' for home use. I was bored by the cards matching pictures, because I could already read well. At Prep. school we learnt Grammar, and lots of poetry-by-heart. I loved that, being a quick memoriser. Repetition of well-strung words is very beneficial. There was plenty of written work in other subjects, including French, which was taught the traditional way, even to 9/10-year-olds, verbs, etc. Only very good, educated speech by our teachers, with plenty of old-fashioned courtesy and discipline. *No bad thing.*

Certainly this is a description of the adventure of language, but it is other and more than that. With its depiction of a world in which sound and letters are interlaced, with emphasis on the letters, it is also an apologia for a certain kind of civilization. The language is not just a language; it is a vehicle of high culture, a protection against Outer Darkness. We all need such protections, and it would be as well to appreciate how deeply the idea of a 'standard' language is linked with the idea of a bearable life. Here, Sandra Slade from Sussex in England adds:

> George Racz's Orwellian vision of total uniformity I find very unattractive, a sort of linguistic equivalent to everyone being forced to wear Chairman Mao suits. One of the most fascinating things about our language is its diversity. An English deprived of its dialect words, local pronunciations, and regional differences would be an English deprived of its vitality. Unfortunately for the supporters of an Académie Anglaise, Britons do not all belong to the educated upper middle or upper classes, nor do we all live somewhere in the South East of England. A language is a living thing; no self-appointed arbiters will have any effect on its development. Bad spelling of the 'Krankies Elektronik Komik' kind, deliberately perpetrated by those who know better, is deplorable. The efforts of Plain English campaigners to simplify otherwise nonsensical official jargon are to be commended. But heaven forbid that we should reach the stage of trying to dictate to people the way they should use their native tongue. What's wrong with a bit of individuality anyway?

Fred Parrott, also of Sussex, adds:

> Much of what used to incense and now incenses purists is marginal to effective language. The obstacles to good communication lie much deeper and require for their removal the kinds of self-knowledge and language sensitivity which are not obtained by focussing on lists of common errors. What is fascinating about the common-errors lists which I as an English teacher purveyed in the 1950s (having adopted them from my own teachers in the 1930s) is not that forty years later a few elderly people are excessively bothered by certain kinds of 'abusage', but that so many expressions which were condemned authoritatively as proven errors have since gone from strength to strength in general usage.

What, finally, of the single practical suggestion for an international review with limited resources but considerable reach? It comes from Mrs M.F. Cannell in Midlothian in Scotland:

LANGUAGE

Have a look, if you will, at the *Anna* knitting and needlecrafts magazine (Verlag Aenna Burda, West Germany). No, I'm not suggesting you take up knitting instead of writing about English, but in there you will find in the centre a course for a particular craft. Could you not do the same thing in *ET*, and use a middle section like that (four pages or so) to give the latest position on English usage? These pages could be lifted out of the main magazine without damaging it and could be collected to form a kind of 'reference work' for those who use English and encounter practical problems. The problems I am thinking of are, for example, the use of the apostrophe, where to close quotation marks (before or after the full stop), breaking words at the end of lines, American and English spelling, etc., etc.

Now *that* is a practical suggestion: a serialized usage book. It is, alas, unlikely that the economics and current production techniques of *ET* would allow such a procedure, and we would also have problems in finding the 'right' people to cover the 'right' topics in the 'right' way, but the suggestion is stimulating. We believe that as it stands *ET* as a whole is just such an on-going guide, but in a less specific do-this/do-that kind of way. If any other readers have further stimulating suggestions, I will [sic] always be happy to entertain them.

9

The pedigree of Plain English

[A plenary address to the Second (International) Conference of Plain English Campaign (PEC) held at the Queen Elizabeth Conference Centre, Westminster, London, May 1993. An earlier version was given at the First (National) Conference held at Maddingley Hall, Cambridge, in 1990, a revised and extended version of which was published in *English Today*, 27, July 1991. The differences between the versions arose out of further study and reflection. The organizers of PEC tell me that they have issued thousands of copies of the *ET* article as a background document for the PE movement.]

In the course of compiling the *Oxford Companion to the English Language*, I had to decide what the term *plain English* means, how old it is, and how it has been used. My conclusion was that it has in fact three basic 'dictionary' senses.

One of these is 'blunt, no-nonsense language', as in this example from a US government report in 1868: 'If we double the thickness, the outside will be but one twenty-fifth as useful, or in plain English, nearly useless'. Another sense is 'strong or foul language', as in the *Observer* of 3 September 1989, where Princess Anne was said 'to express herself in plain English when she found herself upside down in a water jump', surrounded by press photographers. The third sense, however, is the oldest and commonest, dating from at least the sixteenth century. It is 'English that is straightforward and easy to understand', and my favourite early citation comes from the title page of the first ever English dictionary, *The Table Alphabeticall*, published in 1604 by the schoolmaster Robert Cawdrey. The rather lengthy title to this book runs:

LANGUAGE

> A Table Alphabeticall: Conteyning and teaching the true vvriting, and vnderstanding of hard vsuall English wordes, borrowed from the Hebrew, Greeke, Latine, or French. &c. With the interpretation thereof by plaine English words, gathered for the benefit & helpe of Ladies, Gentlewomen, or any other vnskilfull persons.

At the end of the twentieth century this sounds about as politically incorrect as you can get, but it was a progressive statement at the time, about a year after the death of Queen Elizabeth the First, when Shakespeare was at the height of his career. Cawdrey was aware of the extent to which women were cut off from the commanding heights of language. If they belonged to well-to-do families they might receive instruction from a private tutor, but the grammar schools, which were usually linked to the Church, were closed to them. In such schools, Latin was the language of education for boys from privileged backgrounds and the English used in them was therefore heavily Latinized. Middle- and upper-class women had no easy way of absorbing the layer of Latin words and usage that had formed, as it were, along the top of English, creating an 'aureate diction': that is, a gilded vocabulary and style that was often far from plain.

Most upper- and middle-class women (and all lower-class women and men) were not at ease in this high golden English, but some women were on the borderline: they were 'unskilful' not by being illiterate but because their literacy did not extend to classical borrowings—to what Cawdrey called the 'hard usual words' of English. With his emphasis on 'plaine English words' Cawdrey tried to do something about it—and Plain English Campaign is still trying to do something about it for all those still left out in the linguistic cold 400 years later.

Plain language

The idea of plain language, however, is much older than Shakespeare's time. John Wyclif, for example, first translator of the New Testament from Latin into English, wrote in the fourteenth century that 'this gospel tellith a playen storie', and at about the same time, in Chaucer's *Canterbury Tales*, the pilgrims' Host turns to the most academic person in the group, the Clerke of Oxenforde (the Oxford don, as it were), and says to him:

THE PEDIGREE OF PLAIN ENGLISH

Original
Telle us som mery thing of aventures;—
Your termes, your colours, and your figures,
Kepe hem in stoor till so be ye endyte
Heigh style, as whan that men to kinges wryte.
Speketh so pleyn at this tyme, I yow preye,
That we may understonde what ye seye.

My translation
Tell us an amusing adventure story;—
But all your colourful rhetorical figures,
Keep them in reserve for when you use
High style, the kind that men to monarchs write.
Speak so plain this time, I pray,
That we can follow what you say.

The two styles, the high and the plain, were well established in Chaucer's time, and the Host's words chime well with a statement made by James Dayananda, a plain-English campaigner in the United States, writing in 1986: 'A considerable body of information—central to the idea of plain English and derived from empirical research—has shown how a plain-English document stands out in sharp contrast to a fancy or rhetorical document'. People have been contrasting plain language and kinds of gobbledygook for a very long time.

In Chaucer's day, English was a hybrid that had only just regained its pre-Norman status as the national language of England. For some 200 years it had had third-class status in its own home. Before a new official English developed there was official French, the language of government and law, and above that was Latin, used internationally by the Roman Catholic Church and by all writers who wanted a wide readership. To be literate in England in those days meant being trilingual, much as it does in present-day India, Singapore, or Nigeria.

It took a long time for the status of English to rise. Between Chaucer's and Shakespeare's times French and Latin receded greatly, but left behind a residue of thousands of words and phrases in the underdeveloped English of law, government, religion and education. Generations of trilingual hybridizers transferred elements of their 'high' languages into 'low' English until there emerged in the seventeenth century not a smooth grammar and vocabulary (we still don't have those), but a complex layering of elements from several languages, to be used differently on different occasions.

The three rhetorical styles

However, the idea of plainness in language goes back much further than Chaucer and Wyclif. The very adjective *plain* comes from Latin: from *planus*, 'flat, even, low, clear, intelligible'. It was a technical term in a three-part scheme used by orators in ancient Rome. The first and most prestigious of the three styles in this scheme was the *grand* or *high style*, then the *middle*, then the *plain* or *low* style, and each was said to have its virtues and its vices.

The grand style (as Chaucer's Host indicates) was suited to royal courts and aristocrats. Remote from everyday life, it ran the risk of being inflated and pompous when used in the wrong settings. The middle style was suited to the world of learning, instruction, and the professions, but it risked becoming technical and pedantic. And the plain low style was suited to the mass of the people, but risked becoming coarse and vulgar or being used by scholars, lawyers, and the like to talk down to common folk, who simultaneously respected and suspected all book learning.

During the Renaissance and Reformation the middle style fared badly in English, in the struggle between conservatives and radicals. Styles tended to polarize between the high, classical, ornate, and often pretentious on the one hand, and the low, popular, vernacular, plain, straightforward, and often crude on the other. This polarization was central to the language of religious dispute. For example, Protestants in 'the Low Church' (alongside Dissenters and Nonconformists) favoured what was called *Puritan plain style*, while 'the High Church' with its Roman (or 'Popish') echoes, and high society generally, preferred a Latinate or Frenchified style.

The Royal Society of London, founded in 1660, is the oldest scientific society in the world. It began largely as a Puritan venture and therefore received little royal patronage or state support. As a result it enjoyed great freedom of expression and action, and in its early years showed an inclination to 'improve the English tongue, particularly for philosophic purposes', setting up in 1664 a committee with that end in view among whose members was the poet John Dryden.

The committee achieved nothing, but one member, Bishop Thomas Sprat, kept the discussion going. In his book *History of the Royal Society* (1667), he argued that the Society should require of its members 'a close, naked, natural way of speaking; positive expressions; clear senses; a native easiness; bringing all things as near the mathematical plainness as they can; and preferring the language of artisans, countrymen, and merchants, before that of wits and scholars'. With this radical proposal Bishop Sprat became in effect the founder of the plain-language movement.

The middle style only began to gain ground as schools were opened whose medium of instruction was English and not Latin. It became more common in the later eighteenth century, evidently because teachers in such schools favoured a way of speaking and writing that was neither too fancy nor too bare. By and large, modern English prose is the outcome of a long attempt to mediate—in such schools, in newspapers and elsewhere—between the low vernacular and high classical poles of the language.

The middle style is—by and large—the one I am using now. I am not using plain English. My style here may be plain quite often, but not uniformly so, because there are things I want to say and effects I want to produce that cannot be achieved in plain style. But I'm not declaiming grandiloquently to the assembled multitude either, except maybe here and there—for effect. In fact, public speakers and writers can and do play the styles like a piano, and have for centuries been expected to do such things and do them well. Generally, though, I'm talking to a Plain English Conference mainly in the middle style because I'm professionally comfortable in it, and to make the point that there is no one style in which everything can be done, on all occasions, for all purposes. To hope for such a state of affairs—whatever the style concerned—is to try to put the language in a straitjacket.

Saxon English

In the middle of the nineteenth century, William Barnes, a Dorset clergyman who was also a teacher and dialect poet, worried about the extremes of English. The few who remember Barnes today usually think of him as an eccentric who wanted to strip English of its Latin words and use Saxon synonyms instead. There was, however, more to it than that. Barnes considered it wrong-headed for scholars and teachers to expect people to jump from Saxon to Latin English. He proposed instead to remove the problem by removing the invasive words, for example replacing *medicine* with 'leechcraft', *lunatic* with 'moonmad', *cygnet* with 'swanling', and *omnibus* with 'folkwain'.

Some of the Saxonisms proposed by Barnes and his sympathizers were adopted into general usage, such as 'foreword' beside *preface*, and 'handbook' beside *manual*, but most have not survived. Some were so outlandish that they damaged his case: for example, 'breaksome' for *fragile* and 'etheldom' for *aristocracy*. His experiment in pure and plain

LANGUAGE

Germanic English failed, but in our own century there has been at least one instance of it, and that with a racist tinge. This style, called 'Blue-eyed English', was developed by the Australian composer Percy Grainger, who tried to remove all non-Germanic elements from his own usage. An example runs:

Original
It is wrong for a tone-wright to put his puzzle-wifty scores within the reach of know-nothing-y keyed-hammer-string players. . . . Allowing keyed-hammer-string dish-ups of my tone works . . . has wrecked my whole job-path as a tone-wright. (quoted in John Bird, *Percy Grainger*, Melbourne, 1977:141).

My translation
It is wrong for a composer to put his complex scores within reach of ignorant pianists. . . . Permitting piano performances of my compositions . . . has wrecked my whole career as a composer.

Grainger spent a lot of time on a 'Blue-eyed Dictionary' that, as far as I know, was never completed. But whatever he sought, we can hardly call it plain.

Basic English

Some years before Grainger carried linguistic nativism about as far as it can go, a Cambridge philosopher of language, C.K. Ogden, created something called Basic English. He developed it in the 1920s with the help of the literary critic I.A. Richards, and described it in a book of the same name in 1930. Ogden used the term *basic* both in its everyday sense and as an acronym for British American Scientific International Commercial.

Basic uses 850 key words taken from the general vocabulary of English. Most are vernacular words like *box, house,* and *work,* but some are Latin-in-English, such as *apparatus.* He used active sentences only (a model for which was the sentence *I will put the record on the machine now*), a simplified grammar with 18 'operators' (verbs like *get* and *put*), and phrasal verbs instead of Latinisms, as with *go away* and not 'depart', and *make up* instead of 'invent'. Basic was meant to be all things to all people: a world language, a vehicle through which foreigners could learn standard English, and 'a means of indicating to the English-speaking world the virtues of plain English'.

It had wide support into the 1940s, but was intensely controversial.

Winston Churchill persuaded Franklin Roosevelt that it was worth serious consideration, but leading teachers of English as a foreign language, such as Michael West and Harold Palmer, were against it, arguing that Ogden tried to make Basic serve too many ends and that he ended up with a kind of second-class artificial pidgin English. When Churchill asked Palmer to adapt and extend Basic, so as to make it more natural, the resulting proposals turned it from a stripped-down and closed logical system into a list of words and structures of the kind that Palmer, West, and others had been using for some years for textbooks, graded readers, and dictionaries.

Interest in Basic declined after about 1950, and in recent years it is only a vague public memory. However, the years when Ogden, Palmer, West, and others worked on simplifying the language for teaching purposes were seminal for TEFL (Teaching English as a Foreign Language) and TESL (Teaching English as a Second Language). Campaigners for plain English today might well look at the books for foreign learners written in simplified and graded English in an unbroken tradition since the 1930s, and consider how the principles of vocabulary and structure control developed for them could be used to serve the English-using public as a whole. The 'bank' of graded lists and structures used by English-language publishers and teachers is a major contribution to the idea of a straightforward, functional standard English.

Top-down and bottom-up

In recent decades there have been significant campaigns promoting plain English in the UK, the US, Australia, Canada, and increasingly elsewhere. In the 1970s, people on both sides of the Atlantic began to be interested in plain usage not in terms of rhetoric or separating the Germanic from the Latinate, but of how officialdom and business organizations should communicate with their publics—avoiding unnecessary jargon, technical language, and convoluted syntax when addressing wide and varied audiences and readerships.

It is only towards the end of the twentieth century that people have wanted, and have begun, to *institutionalize* the idea of plain English. For example, Plain English Campaign (PEC, without the definite article), the UK organization that hosts this conference, has a headquarters, publications and courses, annual awards, media packs, and campaign slogans, and there are other such organizations elsewhere, often with a commercial as well as a campaigning side to them. This novel development has slowly grown up over the last three decades or so within a double framework consisting of a top-down and a bottom-up approach to plain dealing in language.

In the *top-down approach*, institutions such as governments, professional bodies, or commercial organizations take the initiative. This is the way that things have generally gone in the United States, as for example when, in 1978, a New York state law required business contracts to be written in plain language (a law since matched by a number of other states). Another example is the National Council of Teachers of English, which in 1974 presented its first annual Doublespeak Awards. The Awards have since become a national event, in which the NCTE condemns particularly horrific examples of evasive and/or obscurantist language used especially by people in power. Hundreds of samples of such usage across the nation are recorded in the NCTE's on-going periodical *The Doublespeak Quarterly*.

In the *bottom-up approach*, grassroots movements put pressure on governments and other organizations to make changes. This is the way that things have generally gone in the UK, as for example with the founding of PEC in 1979, when some extraordinary 'ordinary' people shredded official forms in front of the Houses of Parliament in London. The organization gained the attention of the media and in 1982 began to bring out, in association with the National Consumer Council, the Plain English Awards, which have become annual national events. In addition, PEC has launched the Crystal Mark scheme, as far as I know the first public seal of approval regarding the use of language to take root in all the centuries of English.

Both approaches have proved effective and appear to have encouraged co-operation among all concerned, as witness this gathering today.

The lexical bar

All of this is admirable and highly desirable, and I have only one more point to add. In 1950, Victor Grove wrote a book about education and the English language, with the title *The Language Bar* (on the analogy of 'the colour bar'). It dealt with what he saw as a social and educational barrier, on one side of which lies the everyday vernacular language and on the other the usage of higher education—largely classical in origin and style. In 1985, David Corson wrote another book that developed the same theme, and called it *The Lexical Bar*. Both writers maintain—and it is a position I endorse—that many young people in schools around the English-speaking world, at about the ages ten to thirteen, fail to make the transition across this seldom-mentioned bar into fluent and fully fledged standard English.

This is an issue that organizers and teachers of a national curriculum for English (in England or anywhere else) ought to take seriously. It is also one that must some day be addressed by plain English campaigners, because it is not enough to keep things simple. Things cannot always be simple. There is an on-going obligation to open wide the doors of communication and let as many people through as possible. A large part of the problem is the ancient gulf between the vernacular that everybody knows and the relatively 'gilded' and Latinate language used by the educationally and socially secure. This style—despite the gobbledygook and obfuscation often associated with it—is remarkably stable, and has proved enduringly useful for professional and technical purposes. It is a key constituent of the international print standard of English. The need to teach it well cannot be ignored in the drive for greater compassion and clarity that animates all plain English campaigns.

10

The printed word in the English-speaking world

[The closing plenary paper at the conference Style Council 96, held as part of the Adelaide Festival, Australia, in March 1996, published in the proceedings of that conference, and printed with some small changes in *English Today*, 49, January 1997.]

This paper addresses the role of print, rather than of speech or writing, in defining and sustaining standard English, not only in particular territories but on an international scale. The discussion opens with observations by Samuel Daniel and Sir Francis Bacon in England at the turn of the sixteenth and seventeenth centuries, then considers the English-speaking world at the close of the twentieth century, in terms of the categories ENL (English as a native language), ESL (English as a second language) and EFL (English as a foreign language). International Standard English (ISE), a variety available to people belonging to all three categories, is seen as made up of at least five linked elements, each a standard in its own right: a print standard; a media standard; an administrative, governmental, and legal standard; a commercial and technological standard; and an educational standard. The last of these, because it serves as a sociocultural foundation for the other four, has long been the focus of a vigorous and emotional debate stemming in the main from a conviction among many people that Standard English is a threatened medium which has for some time been declining from a former state of grace. I argue, however, that ISE is—because of its powerful print base—a remarkably healthy high-level lingua franca, given the vast complexity of English as a whole.

THE PRINTED WORD IN THE ENGLISH-SPEAKING WORLD

Introduction

In 1620, Sir Francis Bacon—English courtier, littérateur, philosopher, and scientific investigator—made the following observation in his influential but nowadays little-known work the *Novum Organon Scientiarum* (New Instrument of the Sciences, i.e. the scientific method):

Original
Vim et virtutem et consequentias rerum inventarum notare juvat; quae non in aliis manifestius occurrunt, quam in illis tribus quae antiquis incognitae, et quarum primordia, licet recentia, obscura et ingloria sunt: Artis nimirum Imprimendi, Pulveris Tormentarii, et Acus Nauticae. Haec enim tria rerum faciem et statum in orbe terrarum mutaverunt.

My translation
It is worth noting the power, significance and effect of inventions, nowhere more easily seen than in three which were unknown to the ancients and, despite their newness, have obscure and humble origins: the Art of Printing, Artillery Dust (gunpowder), and the Mariner's Needle (the magnetic compass). These three have changed the face and form of things throughout the world.

It is also worth noting that Bacon, a contemporary of Shakespeare's, wrote this book in Latin because he wished it to be read by his peers throughout Western Christendom. There would have been no international readership if he had written in English, an offshore tongue with far less prominence or promise than Italian, French, and Spanish. Nowadays, however, few people educated to university level anywhere in the world know Latin (well or at all), and it is ironic that, if the *Novum Organon* is to be widely understood today, it must be re-cast in the mother tongue that Bacon chose not to use.

His above remarks are relevant in our time not only because of their content but also because the subsequent fate of Latin should make us cautious about what can happen to prestige languages. Bacon was an optimist about his 'new instrument' but a pessimist, or at least a realist, about circulating his views in the most effective language available: English could not outshine Latin, even though it had already—in the wake of Portuguese and Spanish—gone round Africa to Asia, and crossed the Oceanus Atlanticus to the Novus Mundus. He might also have guessed that, if the mysterious Terra Australis really existed, English would get there too, but such an awareness of its recent adventures did not tie in with his traditional learning, which told him—reasonably enough, but wrongly—that the language which named all these exotic places was a grander and more polished medium than his own tongue would ever be.

It was left to a less well-known contemporary to dream dreams about the future of English: the now almost forgotten poet Samuel Daniel, who published in 1599 a long poetic work with the Latin title *Musophilus* (Lover of the Muses, i.e. the Arts) and the English subtitle 'Containing a general Defense of Learning'. The book, written resolutely in English, contains the following question:

> And who in time knowes whither we may vent
> The treasure of our tongue, to what strange shores
> This gaine of our best glorie shal be sent,
> T'enrich vnknowing Nations with our stores?

These lines, with their prophetic and oddly triumphalist ring, have been prominently quoted in at least three late twentieth-century publications:

- *English as a World Language*, a collection of papers edited by Richard W. Bailey (of the University of Michigan) and Manfred Görlach (of the University of Köln, Germany), and published in 1982

- 'The idea of World English', an article by Richard Bailey in the first issue of the journal *English Today*, in 1985

- *The Story of English*, a book by Robert McCrum (a British author and publisher), William Cran (a British TV producer and journalist working in Canada and the US), and Robert MacNeil (a Canadian broadcaster working in the US), partnering the ground-breaking television series of the same name, in 1986.

For these writers, Daniel's lines constitute a kind of charter statement for everything that has happened to the language since his time: a prescient vision (even if it is couched as a question) at a point when a world role for this vernacular was hard to imagine and hardly guaranteed.

Neither Bacon nor Daniel foresaw the long sunset of Latin, or the conditions in which English would achieve a wider distribution and a greater influence than the language of caesars and popes. The three inventions that Bacon refers to have all been involved in its progress: probably more has been printed in English than in any other language, while explosives and the compass played a major part in building an empire that stretched from Glasgow in Scotland, where I was born, to Adelaide in Australia, where an earlier version of this paper was presented in the only kind of publication that the Romans ever knew—one's handwritten thoughts made public by reading them out loud in a forum.

The power of technology

Four centuries after *Musophilus*, there is a vast but indeterminate concourse of users of English on every continent and in every ocean, whose styles of language range from the virtually identical (such as British, American, and Australian standard usage) to the mutually unintelligible (as with Scots in Europe, Jamaican Patwa in the Americas, and Tok Pisin in Asia-Pacific). We do not know precisely who all the users—consumers?—of English are these days, but we do know that the non-natives now outnumber the natives and that well over 500 million and probably more than a billion people are engaged with this language in some form or other: from interacting on the Internet in the first world to begging on the streets of the third. McCrum *et al.* in *The Story of English* (Second Edition, 1992) put the matter as follows:

> The English language surrounds us like a sea, and like the waters of the deep it is full of mysteries. Until the invention of the gramophone and the tape-recorder there was no reliable way of examining everyday speech. . . . The music of our language eludes transcription. Similarly, written English has always been the preserve of the educated minority, and gives us tantalizingly few clues about the English of earlier centuries. English is—and always has been—in a state of ungovernable change.

The writers' maritime metaphor—English as mysterious sea—sits well with Bacon's allusion to mariners and their needles, and mention of the gramophone and the tape recorder reminds us of the printing press. Technological change has an enormous impact on language: how we use it, perceive it, and report on it. This year, for example, the personal computer has allowed me first of all to produce and then print out lecture notes which I could develop by hand on the plane from London and in my Adelaide hotel, then in due course send a final version in electronic and printed formats from Cambridge to Sydney, to be incorporated by further electronic manipulations into the proceedings of Style Council.

McCrum and his colleagues observe, above, that written English has always been the preserve of an educated minority with great influence over everyone else, and that is true. But within that minority there has for five centuries been a further minority—the gatekeepers of print—who since Gutenberg's day, and as Bacon implies, have held immense power over all other users of English or indeed any 'modern' language. Although the printed word is generally subsumed under the written word, the matter is not so simple. The power of the gatekeepers goes far beyond a capacity to write with a pen or tap something out on a typewriter or keyboard. As Elizabeth Eisenstein has argued in her seminal work, *The Printing Press as an Agent of Change* (1979), and as I have maintained in *Worlds of Reference* (1986), print is more—and other—than writing. It is a step beyond it, just as writing was a step beyond speech, and just as today electronic text is a step beyond traditional print.

To be 'modern' in language terms means to be typographically validated: not by the typographers themselves (who by and large have simply done as they were told), but by the publishers and editors who decide on the 'printworthiness' of ideas, reports, stories, and the like, then give the typographers and binders the go-ahead. The paradox is that such lords of print have seldom themselves been able to run the presses, or even in recent times been able to type, but they have nonetheless supervised the processes by which mental, spoken, and written language has been transformed—?elevated—into print. Once upon a time, for a language to be writable was enough but, increasingly over 500 years, this has been a necessary but not a sufficient condition for true sociolinguistic power and prestige.

Serious literacy—together with the standardization of 'high' languages—has long since gone beyond handwriting into such filtering and polishing processes as the editing and reviewing of text (initially hand- or type-written), these processes conducted largely within publishing-cum-printing houses whose cultural and commercial hierarchy ranges from sidestreet publishers of limited means to the collegiate prestige of Oxford and Cambridge University Presses, on the one hand, and the social potency of such large-scale commercial operators as Time-Life and HarperCollins, nowadays increasingly tied in with TV, radio, and other media networks, on the other.

Today, the computer keyboard and the laser printer (among other devices) are amending this entrenched procedure in various radical, even paradoxical ways. On the one hand, the new technological developments extend—and to some degree democratize—the membership, nature, and power of the print élite in ways that were unimaginable even twenty years ago, making the directly printed products of typing-cum-keyboarding ever more like finished text of a publishable standard. On the other hand, however, these developments have let loose an anarchy of prose styles along the information superhighway (and elsewhere) which bears little resemblance to the demure business of traditional typing and printing.

Even so, however, despite the contradictions and confusions, to be *post*modern in the 1990s means that people must be electronically literate global villagers: a McLuhanesque state of affairs that puts pressure on all printable languages.

The globalization of English

Although there is nothing simple about the nature and growth of English around the world, one fairly economical and straightforward set of categories has served linguists and teachers well in the last quarter of a century: a tripartite model first described in print, as far as I know, in 1970 by Barbara Strang, Professor of English Language and General Linguistics at the University of Newcastle upon Tyne in England:

> At the present time, English is spoken by perhaps 350 to 400m people who have it as their mother tongue. These people are scattered over the earth, in far-ranging communities of divergent status, history, cultural traditions and local affinities. I shall call them A-speakers, because they are the principal kind we think of in trying to choose a variety of English as a basis for description. The principal communities of A-speakers are those of the UK, the USA, Canada, Australia, New Zealand and South Africa. There are many millions more for whom English may not be quite the mother tongue, but who learnt it in early childhood, and who lived in communities in which English has a special status (whether or not as an official national language) as a, or the, language for advanced academic work and for participation in the affairs of men at the international, and possibly even the national level. These are the B-speakers, found extensively in Asia (especially India) and Africa (especially the former colonial territories). Then there are those throughout the world for whom English is a foreign language, its study required, often as the first foreign language, as part of their country's educational curriculum, though the language has no official, or even traditional, standing in that country. These are the C-speakers. 1970:17–18).

A more influential variant of Strang's classification was published two years later by Randolph Quirk and Sidney Greenbaum (of University College London), Geoffrey Leech (of the University of Lancaster, England), and Jan Svartvik (of the University of Lund, Sweden), the four editors of *A Grammar of Contemporary English* (1972). They put the matter as follows, but without using letters of the alphabet and with a lower estimate of the world's population of native English-speakers:

> English is the world's most widely used language. It is useful to distinguish three primary categories of use: as a *native* language, as a *second* language, and as a *foreign* language. English is spoken as a native language by nearly three hundred million people (1972:3).

The tripartite model was widely adopted by English-language professionals, in the course of whose work the categories have become known as *English as a Native Language (*contracted to *ENL), English as a Second Language (ESL),* and *English as a Foreign Language (EFL).* Commentators since then have usually referred to ENL, ESL, and EFL *countries,* but my own preference is *territories,* because it permits the inclusion of localities that, while not necessarily politically independent, are nonetheless linguistically significant and may indeed often be self-governing, such as Gibraltar (a British colony) and Puerto Rico (a commonwealth in association with the United States).

Because, however, each territory has its own unique language profile, the tripartite model—despite its rule-of-thumb usefulness—is not delicate enough to handle the sheer variety of English. There are, for example, many ESL/EFL users in the ENL territories, and vice versa, and it is often not easy to decide whether native speakers of the more opaque dialects, creoles, and nativized foreign varieties are 'really' speakers of English in the sense that many foreign learners—used to highly standardized materials—are not able (and perhaps cannot be prepared) to cope with them. In addition, a vast range of usage, while resembling the models of English offered in carefully constructed texts and tapes, etc., to learners of all kinds, differs from them to greater or less degrees, as for example the myriad usages of such cities as London and New York. All such varieties, however valid they may be within their own communities, are seldom closely attuned to the internationally viable norms which people everywhere—speakers of dialects, creoles, nativized varieties, and regional mainstream forms alike—regard as 'real', high-class English: in effect the usage of a relatively small and often highly trained minority often employed in the communication and education industries.

International standard English

In the 1990s, this 'real' English is a global phenomenon, used or sought after in universities, corporate headquarters, media outlets, and such institutions as the United Nations Organization. It is not owned by any one ENL territory, tied to any one accent, or subject to any single code of practices, but it manifestly exists, and can for convenience be called 'international standard English' (ISE). It is not possible here to go into detail about what exactly present-day 'standard English' consists of at its various local, national, and international levels and in its spoken, written, and printed aspects, or to discuss just how the term, the concept, and the reality came into existence over the last four centuries, but it may be useful here to point to three key aspects of this complex and difficult subject.

(1) *The term standard*
This term as it applies to language is not very old. It is the present-day version of a medieval Latin-cum-French-cum-English word which at first referred to such things as flags and weights and measures and later, in the eighteenth century, to language. The phrase *standard English* (with or without an initial capital *s*) dates at least from the Industrial Revolution (c.1830), when 'good' language began to be compared to such things as the regularized gauges of railway tracks, yardsticks, industrial and scientific units, and the like, as in *standard gauge, standard yard,* and *standard atmosphere.* The term *standard English* did not become common until the early twentieth century, and the concept which it enshrines continues to be hotly discussed by scholars, educationists, politicians, and others.

(2) *Standard languages and print*
It is difficult—perhaps impossible—to conceive of a standard language without bringing in the process of printing, which by the end of the nineteenth century was a fully industrialized activity available to all the languages of the world, many of them with their own ancient scribal heritages. Sanskrit, Latin, Arabic, Mandarin Chinese and other classical-cum-literary languages have had orthographies and canonical forms for centuries, even millennia, but these were not rigorously systematized and standardized until the move from chirography to typography took place.

(3) *Validation through print*
The standard forms of modern languages are taught not so much through speech or even writing (although that is important) as through textbooks, dictionaries, and other print products. The norms of present-day literacy radiate from such materials, and as a result—regardless of television and telecommunications—such standard usage continues to find its most

approved and even revered form in print alone. An example is this 'paper', which was first read out—and orally embroidered—at Style Council in Adelaide, then 'fixed' (to use a term popular in the eighteenth century) or 'validated' (to use a post-modernist term) through its appearance in a printed volume called a 'proceedings'.

Indeed, Style Council itself might lack validation if no print version emerged from its annual incarnations, and some of its speakers might not be sure about taking part if they did not get a listable 'publication' at the end. Finally, if there were no officially published outcome, some presenters (feeling that a printed end-product was desirable for their careers or for some other reason) would look for an outlet elsewhere, in a journal or newsletter.

A less immediately obvious but more potent example of the power of print is what the British phonetician David Abercrombie in 1959 called *spoken prose:* prose that is presented as speech, as when an actor utters memorized lines from a play, or someone gives a public address, or presenters use scripts on stage, screen, radio, and television. This term distinguishes all such speech from spontaneous, unscripted conversation. Abercrombie puts it as follows:

> Prose is essentially language organized for *visual* presentation. . . . Most people believe that *spoken prose* . . . is at least not far removed, when well done, from the conversation of real life. . . . But the truth is that nobody speaks at all like the characters in any novel, play or film. Life would be intolerable if they did; and novels, plays or films would be intolerable if the characters spoke as people do in life. Spoken prose is far more different from conversation than is usually realized. (1965: 3–4).

Spoken prose derives from drama, lectures, and disputation, the recitation of more or less memorized poetry, and the arguments of lawyers and orators (whose rhetorical craft originated in ancient Greece). Although conversation is distinct from it, spoken prose influences educated and formal spoken usage. Speakers often use the same devices whether they are speaking spontaneously, using a script, or working from notes, and a great deal of what passes for speech on radio and especially television (with the use of teleprompts) is print being read aloud, or writing and print that has been memorized (at least in part)—or *ex tempore* speech that, through years of practice, is structured in much the same way as printed text.

The sentences I used in the *ex tempore* parts of my delivery in Adelaide were more relaxed than those I read out, but by and large they had the same 'high' syntactic style and social flavour, and belonged to the same academic register. Indeed, a great deal of oral academic output is spoken prose, in the sense that it relates to the innumerable printed works that scholars have variously assimilated over the years.

Five standards

There appear to be several distinct strands to the complex rope of standardness, whether it is at the local, national, regional, or global level. Thus, one can create a model of such standardness which consists of at least five overlapping and inter-operating sociolinguistic elements, each of which can be called a standard in its own right. These are: a print standard; a media standard, with a continuum of print, print-derived speech ('spoken prose'), and relaxed spontaneous speech; a governmental, administrative, and legal standard; a commercial and technological standard; and an educational standard. We can take them each in turn.

(1) *The international print standard*
This has slowly emerged over some four centuries, from such works as the King James Bible and Shakespeare's First Folio in early seventeenth-century England. This form has in the process changed greatly, both as regards grammar and lexis and in terms of the conventions of typography, spelling, punctuation, and page layout. It is currently a composite of several national print standards, of which England (from c.1603), the United Kingdom and Ireland (from c.1707), and the United States (from c.1783) have been the trend-setters and arbiters. The UK and the US continue to be the bedrock influences, primacy passing after the Second World War from the UK to the US in terms of sociopolitical power and population size, but not in terms of the quantity of printed materials produced, in which the UK still leads. Towards the close of the century, however, other centres of actual and potential autonomy have been emerging: pre-eminently Australia, with its dictionaries, style manuals, and Style Council, then Canada, New Zealand, and South Africa, with stirrings in India, Singapore, and the Caribbean (notably in the media and linguistic and in lexicographical description). Despite such diversity and occasional adjustments in the international pecking order, the worldwide norms for print are remarkably uniform.

(2) *The international media standard*
For my purposes here, this term covers not only journalism, broadcasting, and the cinema, etc., but also publishing of every kind. The media standard exploits print both massively, in the press and publishing, and in smaller ways in television and the cinema, as with credit lists and scripted voiceovers. It also exploits those forms of regional speech (primarily on radio and television, and in the cinema) that are more or less internationally transparent, such as US Southern States usage, and Irish and Scottish usage. Some regional forms have long been considered standard by linguists and others (as for example *Received Pronunciation* or *RP* in England, whose centre of gravity is the upper and middle classes of southern England), but views on good spoken usage are currently much less *dirigiste* than earlier in the centrury, and the concept 'standard' is less and less applied to RP in the UK or to its supposed equivalent in the US, *General American* (many US linguists insisting that there is no such thing). A major feature of any kind of speech on radio and television, and in the cinema, is spoken prose and its correlates (as discussed above).

(3) *The international governmental, administrative, and legal standard*
This is the form which pervades large, usually centralized organizations of any kind, but especially governmental, administrative, and legal institutions. It is in the main territorial, being the range of formal usage associated with the management of those nation-states in which English is a *de facto* or *de jure* official language, but is also significantly international in for example the work of the United Nations, the International Monetary Fund, and the European Union. It has its own traditions and quirks, as for example with the English of the UN, in which for historical reasons (beginning with the League of Nations) the orthographic style of the UK predominates. US documents within this framework retain their own conventions, but any UN printed commentary on them follows UK conventions.

(4) *The international commercial and technological standard*
This is a less tightly ordered area, in which the administration for example of large multinational organizations (whether ENL-based or not) may follow mainly US or UK norms, or engage in a judicious mix of the two (depending on where they operate in the world). By and large, business executives, academics, and leading technologists comfortably engage in what might—with tongue only slightly in cheek—be called 'MBA English'. Two considerable exceptions to uniformity do, however, exist: first, the vast array of ESL/EFL businesspeople who used 'fractured' or

'approximate' or 'offshore' Englishes to negotiate and clinch their deals; second, the *laissez-faire* usage associated with computer technology and especially special-interest bulletin boards and other outlets on the Internet.

(5) *The international educational standard*
This last exists predominantly for the young, but also contains its own professional and other registers. It draws on the others and in turn feeds them as fresh generations emerge from schools and colleges to engage with the wider world. Because the educational standard is expected in this way to carry the other standard strands to the highest possible level of literacy and fluency among the largest possible number of young people, it bears a heavy burden of social expectation. As a result, it evokes an emotional debate that is often heavily politicized. Educational course books and institutional and other style manuals provide the more or less authoritative forms, recommendations, and suggestions that help sustain the whole dynamic structure.

There is plenty of this five-strand standard English around, but it is dwarfed by the innumerable non-standard varieties of the language, whether they are dialects (as in Yorkshire) or creoles (as in Guyana), or colloquial and slang usage generally, or nativized versions of what were formerly non-native varieties (as in Singapore). It is also at the same time and to an increasing extent continuous with all kinds of approximations to standard usage in ENL, ESL, and EFL communities alike, which is one source of the alarm felt by defenders of the standard faith. Arguing for the safeguarding of a core standard English around the world, Randolph Quirk observed in 1983:

> The English language works pretty well in its global context today: certainly the globe has at present no plausible substitute. But let me underline my main point by giving four examples of English working best in the global context. They are the BBC World Service of London; All India Radio of Delhi; the *Straits Times* of Singapore; and the *Japan Times* of Tokyo. They represent oral and printed media, and they represent ENL, ESL, and EFL countries. And there are several outstanding features in common to these and to the scores of analogous examples that might have been selected. They all use a form of English that is both understood and respected in every corner of the globe where any knowledge of any variety of English exists. They adhere to forms of English familiarly produced by only a minority of English speakers in any of the four countries concerned.

> And—mere accent alone apart—they observe as uniform a standard as that manifest in any language on earth. (p.6)

Quirk highlights the success of English-language print and broadcast media worldwide. What he says is true and will continue indefinitely to be true, just as Latin continued indefinitely to be the most effective international vehicle for people like Bacon for many years after he wrote the *Novum organon*. Despite all the argument and emotion surrounding the issue of maintaining standards in English, the international language, with its print base, is at the end of the twentieth century a marked success, serving all humankind as the first high-level global lingua franca. If such an entity did not already exist, the global village would have to invent it.

Part 3: Lexicography

11

The background and nature of ELT learners' dictionaries

[Based on a paper commissioned for and published in *Learners' Dictionaries: State of the Art*, edited by Makhan L. Tickoo, Anthology Series 23, SEAMEO Regional Language Centre (RELC P360-89), Singapore, 1989: up-dated here to the mid-1990s.]

Unilingual dictionaries for the use of foreign learners are curious objects. It is not inherently obvious that a learner of a language needs a dictionary *of* that language entirely *in* that language: the case for a bilingual dictionary followed in due course by the kind of dictionary available to native speakers would seem to be overwhelming, yet this curious bridging genre flourishes like the green bay tree. Such dictionaries were pioneered in and for English just when it was becoming the lingua franca of the planet. Although there are unilingual learners' dictionaries for some other languages, English retains pride of place, and for much of this century it was the only language for which such books were compiled. In addition, the pioneering was confined to British English and the genre continues to be largely a UK concern. Worldwide commercial competition is almost entirely among five British publishers: Longman, Oxford University Press, Collins, Chambers, and Cambridge University Press (listed in the order in which they have entered the fray).

The following review has three aims: to sketch the sociohistorical background to such dictionaries; to describe their salient features; and to provide a basis for the discussion of present and prospective works.

The lexicographical background

Although learners' dictionaries are products of the twentieth century, their pedigree goes back at least to the Renaissance, when the vernacular languages of Europe began to emerge from the shadow of Latin, the classical Western European language of culture, religion, and scholarship. Where dictionaries and other works of reference had previously been part of the teaching of Latin as an international language, the genre became available for speakers of such vernaculars as French and English, to help them understand and use their own languages. And where dictionaries had largely been unidirectional and bilingual (most commonly Latin words explained through glosses in the mother tongue), there were now also unilingual works for home consumption.

The first dictionary of English, the *Table Alphabeticall* of 1604, compiled by the schoolmaster Robert Cawdrey, was also the first English learner's dictionary. It was a small book of 3,000 entries 'conteyning and teaching the true writing, and vnderstanding of hard vsuall English wordes, borrowed from the Hebrew, Greeke, Latine, or French, &c. With the interpretation thereof by plaine English wordes, gathered for the benefit & helpe of Ladies, Gentlewomen, or any other unskilfull persons'.

The idea that 'hard usual' foreignisms could be explained by easy 'plain' words proved popular with the literate middle classes, most of whom had little or no classical learning. The dictionaries of Robert Cawdrey, John Bullokar, Henry Cockeram, Thomas Blount, and Edward Phillips have become known as 'the hard-word dictionaries' and flourished for a century, slowly evolving into the more general and normative works of such eighteenth-century compilers as Nathaniel Bailey and Samuel Johnson, whose *Dictionary of the English Language* (1755) was a significant milestone in establishing the spelling of standard English and was compiled with foreign learners as well as native users in mind.

Elocution was at that time an important issue in 'polite society' and many compilers of dictionaries were as concerned with *orthoepy* (proper speech) as with *orthography* (proper writing). Thus, Thomas Dyche, in *A Guide to the English Tongue* (1709) and *The Spelling Dictionary* (1723), provided help with word stress by placing a mark after the stressed syllable of a polysyllabic word (as in *di'nner* and *di'ocese*). Johnson adopted this convention, which survives in many general dictionaries today, although in some general and all learners' dictionaries the mark is now placed *before* the stressed syllable. In the decades after Johnson, at least five pronouncing dictionaries appeared, the works of James Buchanan, William Kenrick, William Perry, Thomas Sheridan, and John Walker. Kenrick marked separate syllables with numbers which referred readers to a table of pronunciation, while Walker, in *A Critical*

THE BACKGROUND OF ELT LEARNERS' DICTIONARIES

Pronouncing Dictionary of the English Language (1791), used superscript numbers indicating the 'powers' of the various written vowels. This method proved so popular that a number of books appeared which claimed to blend the definitions of Johnson with the pronunciations of Walker, but the superscripts died out in the mid-nineteenth century, probably because they were difficult to set as well as to read and use (and to my knowledge remained dormant in this role until the publication of the *Collins COBUILD Dictionary* in 1987).

Compilers of these dictionaries were not only English (Kenrick and Walker) but Irish (Sheridan) and Scottish (Buchanan and Perry). In his preface, Walker lectured not only the Cockneys and other miscreants at home but also the Scots and Irish abroad for not measuring up to the standards of 'refined' London usage. His dictionary offered a metropolitan standard of spelling and speech for both the native English and their more or less foreign neighbours within the British Isles. The works produced by the Irish and Scots conformed to much the same standard in grammar and vocabulary, but were marked by pronunciation values that were more typical of 'polite' Dublin and Edinburgh than refined London. Meanwhile, in the United States, Noah Webster rebelled against linguistic colonialism and published in 1828 his *American Dictionary of the English Language*, a powerful contribution to the establishment of a second national standard for the language. By and large, all such works catered as much to linguistic insecurity as to the disinterested spread of information: people felt they needed unequivocal help in using standard ('correct') language, and such dictionaries sought to provide it, particularly for the orthography but also as far as possible for the orthoepy.

In the nineteenth century, increased literacy prompted the production in both the United Kingdom and the United States of dictionaries for the population at large. Works like *Chambers's English Dictionary* (1872), published in Edinburgh, were intended with a crusade-like zeal for *everybody*; indeed, the Chambers brothers, William and Robert, promoted themselves as 'publishers for the people'. Such works were part of a drive for universal literacy: they were inexpensive, and so families and schools could afford to buy them in greater numbers than before. Along with their definitions, they provided help with pronunciation through a system of *re-spelling*, in which the values of vowels were given in a short list of words that served as touchstones for the rest. In Chambers, the values were in effect those of middle-class Edinburgh, but could be interpreted appropriately for any comparable group elsewhere in the English-speaking world. However, such books stood in sharp contrast to the vast scholarly works being prepared 'on historical principles' in several languages, the most prominent of which was James Murray's *New English Dictionary* (later renamed the *Oxford English Dictionary*).

Despite the steadily increasing range of activity, however, publishers did not usually give much thought to ease of consultation or whether the users of their books were native to some kind of English, were foreign immigrants to the UK or US, or were colonial subjects of the British Empire. A dictionary was a dictionary, and that was that. At this stage, it had also become a formidable array of conventions relating to layout, headword, pronunciation, grammatical label, definition, specimens of usage, pictorial illustration, punctuation, the arrangement of senses, and the presentation of derivatives, compounds, and idioms. By and large, these conventions were taken as given, much as the division of the Bible into chapter and verse was given: there were variations, but they were minor and occasional. And, by the end of the nineteenth century, it was implicitly established that to benefit from a dictionary one had to be literate in its use, a state of affairs which has been carried over into contemporary ELT learners' dictionaries. There was, however, little discussion of how anyone might reach that happy condition.

The educational background

Around 1880, a radical new 'method' of language teaching and learning emerged in Europe (and later the United States), whose pioneers wished to escape from what they saw as three negative aspects of Western language teaching and learning to date: (1) the weight of the classics, which persuaded many that modern languages were inferior to Latin and Greek; (2) a literary and textual bias in the study of modern as well as ancient languages; (3) the style of teaching now known as 'the grammar translation method', in which the structure of a language was learned through formal drill in memorizing and reciting established grammatical paradigms (such as the conjugations of regular and irregular verbs), accompanied by artificial sentences for translation and contrived exercises in composition, all of them formally corrected and often rewritten until perfection was achieved. And the emphasis throughout was on written rather than spoken usage.

The radicals wished instead to offer courses in everyday spoken language, conducted in a direct and 'natural' way, with a minimum dependence on texts and no translation at all. Wherever possible, the student should be immersed in the target language, so as to learn it by living it, and various new publications emerged extolling and embodying the new system as, for example, 'the Direct Method' and 'the Natural Method'. These pedagogical radicals included most notably Wilhelm Viëtor in Germany, Paul Passy in France, Otto Jespersen in Denmark, Henry Sweet in England, and Maximilian Berlitz in the United States.

By the beginning of the twentieth century, language teaching was in a ferment. Although the ELT learner's dictionary did not yet exist, the matrix from which it would emerge had been created and included: (1) an expansion of systems of education throughout the British Empire; (2) a growth in the publishing effort needed to sustain such an expansion; (3) a tradition of explaining harder words by easier words, often honoured in the breach; (4) a prescriptivist tradition of orthography and orthoepy (although the latter label had not been used for decades, having been largely replaced by such terms as 'pronunciation' and 'phonetics'); (5) a shift of attention away from classical formalism to a new and less rigid concern for the spoken, the direct, and the untranslated.

The phoneticians

The Phonetic Teachers' Association was founded in 1886 in France. Under the editorship of Paul Passy, a journal entitled *Dhi Fonètik Titcer* was started in the same year, to popularize a special alphabet for the description and teaching of the sounds of English. The journal's contents were printed entirely in that new alphabet. Membership of the Association became international and included most of the leaders of the reform movement. At the urging of Otto Jespersen, attention was also paid to the phonetic representation of languages other than English and a new phonetic alphabet was subjected to a process of development and modification which continues to this day. In 1897, the organization was renamed *L' Association phonétique internationale* (now more commonly referred to as the International Phonetic Association or IPA).

The science of phonetics grew in tandem with the concern for new and more natural methods of language teaching and the development of the Association. Many early phoneticians and members of the IPA were also ardent spelling reformers and some, like Jespersen, were Esperantists. They were interested in language at large and in international communication, and were pedagogical innovators, but, because of the centrality of print in Western civilization and the absence of high-quality audio-technology at that time, they worked with text rather than sound. Their advocacy of English spelling reform bore no fruit, but they made progress with their system of phonetic symbols both for transcribing all human language and as a pedagogical alphabet which began to run parallel to the alphabet as used for English.

This pedagogical aid, however, manifestly increases the learning load for students (when they can be persuaded to adopt it), and as a result there are now two sets of symbols for the dedicated foreign learner to master on the way to acceptable written and spoken English—double the load imposed on native speakers. For Western Europeans this has not been a major burden, since the phonetic alphabet is a child of the Roman alphabet, but for students who have learned to read and write in Arabic, Devanagari, Chinese, Japanese, and the like, the burden is considerable. Yet perfectionism and idealism were significant factors in the development of phonemic representation: indeed, it was widely supposed that an inventory could be so organized as to recreate on paper the 'true' sounds of any language. Thus, the booklet *The Principles of the International Phonetic Association* (1967) notes:

> The original International Phonetic Alphabet of 1888 contained quite a number of the special letters used today, but it was imperfect in various respects. The Council has accordingly, since 1889, worked unremittingly to remedy defects. . . . The result is that we now have a system which, though doubtless capable of still further improvement, is a very effective instrument for transcription on international lines, and one which can be used in 'broad' and in 'narrow' forms for the phonetic representation of all the principal languages of the world, and as a basis for orthographic reform for all languages needing it.

Daniel Jones and Received Pronunciation

From this background emerged in 1913 the *Phonetic Dictionary of the English Language*, by Daniel Jones. This pronunciation glossary was revised during the First World War as the *English Pronouncing Dictionary* (1917), which became one of the most influential ELT books ever published, running to fourteen editions by 1977, with a fifteenth by Cambridge University Press in 1997. Jones was a phonetician at the University of London and his work helped to establish that institution as a Vatican-like centre for the study of the phonetics of English. Both he and his immediate successor as editor of the *EPD*, the late A.C. Gimson, were professors there.

The *EPD* is a dictionary only in the sense that it is alphabetically ordered; there are no definitions. It lists a selection of English words (including well-known place and personal names) printed in traditional orthography, each followed by one or more phonemic transcriptions in what Jones in 1917 called *Public School Pronunciation (PSP)* and from 1926 onward *Received Pronunciation (RP)*. This was a prestigious accent, centred on south-eastern England, whose heyday was the inter-war years. RP apparently evolved during the later nineteenth century, more or less informally, in the major public (that is, private) schools of England, in comparable schools elsewhere in the British Isles and Empire, at the universities of Oxford and Cambridge, among the upper classes at large, and as the signature accent of the British Broadcasting Corporation, including notably the BBC World Service, from the 1920s. It has always been a minority accent, inspiring complex and often conflicting feelings in the United Kingdom at large, and foreign learners have seldom over the years been aware of the social implications of success in achieving the model offered to them.

Because of its social, imperial, and post-imperial standing, many people around the world have regarded RP as the only proper accent of English, either in general (a view which North Americans now massively reject) or in British English (a view which some Britons endorse and others reject). Many ELT practitioners have regarded it—and continue to regard it—as the only model which should be offered to foreign learners, although since c.1990 non-native teachers of English have become more alert to the implications of, and complications associated with, this model. Jones and Gimson, like the orthoepists of the eighteenth century, provided the accents of their own social and regional group as the universal norm, fully aware of the tensions involved. As a result, RP is the most described and transcribed accent of English and probably of any language, and is the classical model to which most British teachers and all British publishers of materials for foreign learners are currently committed. In the fifteenth edition of the *EPD* (Cambridge University Press), the editors, Peter Roach and James Hartman, have continued by and large with the standard RP model but have dropped the name, adopting instead the less contentious and better known but evasive label *BBC English*, and, like John C. Wells in his competing *Longman English Pronunciation Dictionary* (1990), have also included US forms in a transcription associated with the concepts 'General American' and 'Network English', which pose a range of sociolinguistic problems of their own.

Restricted vocabularies

Where Daniel Jones was interested in pronunciation, a colleague at the University of London was interested in vocabulary and usage. This was Harold E. Palmer, whose *The Scientific Study and Teaching of Languages* also came out in 1917. When Palmer went to Japan in 1922, to work for the Ministry of Education in Tokyo, he developed an approach that sought to complement the natural and direct approach to language learning with (among other things) a system of graded word lists, conceived as concentric groups of words radiating from an essential core. He considered that, by learning the key words of English in stages from around 300 to around 3,000, the student could be saved from floundering in a mass of ill-digested lexical information.

For Palmer, the circles of words could be judiciously ordered by means of an experienced teacher's (undefined) 'vocabulary sense'. This view was shared by Michael West, a fellow Englishman working in Bengal, whose lexically graded New Method Readers series was developed by Longmans Green in the 1930s. The subjective and pedagogical view of vocabulary control espoused by Palmer and West was not, however, the only school of thought at the time. It flourished alongside the objective and statistical approach of American word-counters, and in particular Edward L. Thorndike. Through frequency counts based on a range of widely used texts, Thorndike and his colleagues sought to establish the commonest words of English, usually organized in sets of thousands, from the first 1,000 most common to a point at which frequency of occurrence ceased to signify. In addition, C.K. Ogden in Cambridge created Basic English, an artificial language formed by limiting the grammar and vocabulary of Standard English according to principles of logical analysis. Ogden claimed that Basic, with its 850 core words and minimal grammar, had three functions: as an international lingua franca, a way into the standard language for foreign learners, and a cure for verbosity among users of English at large.

In the early 1930s, a feud developed between Ogden and West, who argued that Ogden had over-restricted Basic and created a crude and pernicious pidgin. Ogden as a result refused to attend the Carnegie Conference on vocabulary which took place in New York in 1934, leaving the field to the others. The New York meeting did not eliminate all the differences between the American objectivists and the British subjectivists, but considerable agreement led to the Carnegie *Interim Report on Vocabulary Selection and Control*, which served as the basis for Michael West's *General Service List of English Words* (1953). The appearance of this list with its 'Semantic Frequencies and a Supplementary Word-List for the Writing of Popular Science and Technology' set the seal on forty years of pre-electronic word-listing which contributed to the formula for the first proper learners' dictionaries the idea of a controlled defining vocabulary

The first learners' dictionaries

In 1935, there appeared the *New Method English Dictionary*, compiled by West and J. G. Endicott (Longmans Green). The work was complementary to the New Method Readers, which were written within levels or circles of a given number of words, from early beginner to relatively advanced. In this book, 20–30,000 items were defined within a vocabulary of less than 1,500 words. Ogden's *General Basic English Dictionary* appeared in 1940, under the copyright of his Orthological Institute in Cambridge. It used the 850 words of Basic to give 'more than 40,000 senses for over 20,000 words' and was intended both for the young mother-tongue user as well as the foreign learner. The preface asserted that the Basic words were 'naturally the *key* words for Dictionary purposes'. This work went through some twenty-four unrevised impressions before the decision was taken in 1988 by the publishers Bell & Hyman (inheriting the title from Evans) to discontinue publication.

Meanwhile, in Japan, three of Palmer's colleagues—A.S. Hornby, E.V. Gatenby, and H. Wakefield—had been working on a dictionary of English for the more competent foreign (and especially Japanese) learner, a work which would compactly combine lexical, idiomatic, and syntactic information. Begun in 1937, the dictionary was completed in 1940, when Japan entered the Second World War. In 1942, the Japanese publisher Kaitakusha brought it out in Tokyo as the *Idiomatic and Syntactic English Dictionary* (for the Institute for Research in English Teaching, the organization for which Palmer had started work in 1922). After the war the book was reprinted photographically by Oxford University Press and published in 1948 as *A Learner's Dictionary of Current English*, reprinting twelve times until a second edition came out in 1963 entitled *The Advanced Learner's Dictionary of Current English*, which in its turn had nineteen impressions until the third edition appeared in 1974 as the *Oxford Advanced Learner's Dictionary of Current English* (50,000 headwords and derivatives claimed), now by A.S. Hornby alone (as sole survivor of the three compilers), with editorial assistance from A.P. Cowie and phonetic assistance from J. Windsor Lewis.

By the 1960s, all the lexicographic elements available at the end of the

Second World War had become standard, and ELT learners' dictionaries were firmly established. The two leading publishers of the period, Oxford and Longman, brought out a variety of dictionaries for sub-groups of foreign learner, such as Michael West's *An International Reader's Dictionary* and A.S. Hornby and E.C. Parnwell's *An English-Reader's Dictionary*, establishing a staircase of such books from beginner through intermediate to advanced.

The new genre was marked by the alphabetic ordering of headwords, short compact entries, phonetic transcriptions, the identification of parts of speech, brief definitions for every identified sense, specimen phrases and sentences, and pictures where considered helpful. For the writing of definitions, either a strict 'defining vocabulary' was used (following West and Ogden), or a more relaxed 'carefully selected vocabulary' (following Hornby). In this, the ancient principle of easy words explaining hard words had been extended into a new area. For further pedagogical purposes, syntactic and other information was incorporated, as for example the set of numbered verb patterns in Hornby *et al.* For pronunciation, the phoneme inventory of RP, expressed by means of the alphabet of the IPA, was the sole model of the spoken language, the transcriptions usually developed with the help of a phonetician working in the Jones tradition. As time went on, the phoneticians and compilers were not necessarily themselves RP speakers, but proceeded as though they were, further idealizing a model which they might or might not possess or desire.

Advanced and specialized learners' dictionaries

The publication of *OALDCE* in 1974 set the standard for the rest of the decade, but equally important was a decision that Longman had made to challenge that standard. In the early 1970s, the publishers Tim Rix and Charles McGregor laid the foundation for a massive extension of Longman reference titles, whose centrepiece would be the *Longman Dictionary of Contemporary English* (*LDOCE*, 1978: over 55,000 entries claimed), edited by Paul Procter. Because they drew on a common inheritance from Jones, Palmer, West, and Hornby, the *OALDCE* and *LDOCE* were close cousins, characterized by similar entry, page, and even cover designs. Although the books differed in detail, the overall effect was similar and they seemed set to advance indefinitely along the same line, each adapting to the other, much like rival mother-tongue dictionaries in the United Kingdom and the United States.

Foremost among the features they shared was a revised position on models of pronunciation. The RP model was now accompanied by a second-order GA (General American) model. In an entry where transatlantic phonetic discrimination was considered necessary, an unlabelled British transcription came first, followed by its labelled American equivalent (given in full or in part). However, wherever possible there was no American entry, on the uncertain principle that the RP transcriptions were generally broad enough to serve both norms (and of course permit economies in typesetting and space). Foremost among the differences between the books were the use in *LDOCE* of a strict defining vocabulary of c.2,000 words (descended from West's *GSL*) and a system of grammatical codes based by Paul Procter on the seminal work of Randolph Quirk, Sidney Greenbaum, Geoffrey Leech, and Jan Svartvik on the grammar of the standard language (the work centring on University College London and being published by Longman: Quirk *et al.*, 1972).

In 1978, the Oxford monopoly at the advanced level was over. Although no other publisher could hope to approach the market share of the larger Oxford and smaller Longman giant, two contenders nonetheless emerged: the *Collins English Dictionary* (1974: over 30,000 words and phrases claimed), edited by David J. Carver, Michael J. Wallace, and John Cameron, intended for the EFL market alone, and the *Chambers Universal Learners' Dictionary* (1980: 54,000 'examples of modern English usage' claimed), edited by Elizabeth M. Kirkpatrick and with Tom McArthur as EFL adviser, available to all learners of the language.

Both titles were produced in Scotland, and differed from the English books in two respects: (1) where Oxford and Longman had pages packed with technically complex entries, Collins and Chambers were less intricate, more open to the eye, and avoided detailed and typographically complex coding; (2) where Oxford and Longman used specialized symbols in a narrow RP transcription, Collins kept to an older, broader, and simpler system, and Chambers (advised by the Edinburgh University phonetician David Abercrombie, a friend and colleague of Daniel Jones), adopted an 'extra-broad' transcription considered easier for students to read and representative of a wider range of speakers. With the major and minor differences among the various phonetic systems, the ELT field in 1980 resembled the orthoepic and geographic diversity of British lexicography in 1780.

The 1970s and early 1980s also saw the development of dictionaries for such specialized areas as phrasal verbs and idioms. These were: (1) the *Collins Dictionary of English Phrasal Verbs and Their Idioms*, edited by

Tom McArthur and Beryl T. Atkins (1974); (2) the *Oxford Dictionary of Current Idiomatic English, Vol. 1: Verbs with Prepositions & Particles*, edited by Anthony P. Cowie and Ronald Mackin (1975); (3) the *Longman Dictionary of English Idioms*, edited by Thomas H. Long (1979); (4) the *Oxford Dictionary of Current Idiomatic English, Vol. 2: Phrase, Clause & Sentence Idioms*, edited by A.P. Cowie, R. Mackin, and I.R. McCaig (1983); (5) the *Longman Dictionary of Phrasal Verbs*, edited by Rosemary Courtney (1983). The fact that such specialized books could be produced and sold while increasingly detailed information about such usages was also being added to the conventional works was—and remains—a testimony to the buoyancy of the ELT market, EFL lexicography, and worldwide interest in the language.

In addition to other pioneering developments at Longman, *LDOCE* pioneered the use of the computer in this field for lexicographic as well as typesetting purposes. ELT publishers were hesitant at the time to venture into such an area, and it is a mark of the swift evolution of hardware, software, ideas, and emotions that at the end of the 1980s it was unthinkable for any major work of reference in ELT or elsewhere to proceed without such an aid.

Innovations and adaptations

One lexicographical adventure of the 1970s spilled over into the new decade. It owed little directly to the tradition of the learners' dictionary, and a great deal to such works as Roget's Thesaurus, the Duden pictorial wordbooks, the research of John Lyons into structural semantics, and the work of the American cognitive anthropologists. It was an attempt to complement the alphabetic tradition with something thematic and closer to the everyday use of words. The idea of such a conceptual wordbook was first mooted to Longman by David Crystal, and subsequent discussions gave rise to two years' lexical research (1972–4) by Tom McArthur, who was then commissioned to compile what became the *Longman Lexicon of Contemporary English* (1981: over 15,000 defined words claimed).

Begun some time before the compilation of *LDOCE*, the *Lexicon* was integrated into the Longman development plan as a sister volume. It sought to cover the core words of the language in fourteen semantic fields, such as 'Life and Living Things', 'People and the Family', and 'Space and Time'. In turn, these fields divide into c.130 subfields and hundreds of lexical sets (identified by field letter and set number) in which synonyms, antonyms, and other associated words are defined and illustrated together. Access to the sets is through both the list of fields at the beginning of the book and an index of words and word senses at the back, the index doubling as an English-pronouncing dictionary. The *Lexicon* incorporated the defining vocabulary and grammatical codes of *LDOCE* and used many of its definitions as a basis for many of its own. Its aim was to display words in a somewhat more natural arrangement than the alphabet and to help students directly discriminate their meanings and uses, both for general purposes and for such specific tasks as writing in English.

The *Longman Active Study Dictionary of English* (1983: 38,000 words and phrases claimed), edited by Della Summers, was a cutdown of *LDOCE* with a simpler format and less complex grammatical codes. Where Longman and Oxford had produced workbooks to accompany their major dictionaries, a novel feature of *LASDE* was a workbook incorporated into the volume, as part of the guide to its use. However, because British ELT dictionaries did not sell significantly in the American ESL market, the two major publishers decided to create local adaptations for American teachers who perceived the originals as too British. The Americanized works appeared in 1983: (1) the *Longman Dictionary of American English* (38,000 words and phrases claimed), 'sponsoring editors' Arley Gray and Della Summers, a cutdown and adaptation of *LDOCE* with a close resemblance to *LASDE* (including a built-in workbook); (2) the *Oxford Student's Dictionary of AMERICAN English* (over 20,000 words and phrases claimed), under the editorial name of Hornby and with the 'American editors' Dolores Harris and William A. Stewart.

Both *LASDE* and the two US-oriented products had formats and styles closer in spirit to Collins and Chambers than to their originals. Both were major departures in terms of pronunciation models, their phonetic systems being exclusively American. With the publication of these books, UK publishers now offered the EFL/ESL world two asymmetrical pronunciation models: (1) a dual model for books published in the UK, in which RP is followed by GA, at least in part; (2) a single model for books published in the US, with GA only. Although this development received little attention at the time, it represented a significant social, psychological, and linguistic shift: the publishers had decided that in the American ESL market RP is irrelevant, while in the worldwide EFL/ESL market RP could no longer stand alone. Rather, it should be followed by a GA granted next-to-equal billing, but with the implication that the American model was in fact becoming the primary pronunciation model for standard international usage: that is, if books were to go on being sold, unequivocal adjustments had to be made in the direction of the United States.

Consolidation, competition, and revision

In the later 1980s and 1990s, the three themes have been consolidation, competition, and revision. Oxford followed some updatings of *OALDCE* with a fourth edition in 1989, edited by Anthony Cowie, and a fifth in 1995 by Jeremy Crowther, the broad tendency being towards a simpler look and greater user-friendliness, without significant innovation. In 1987 there was a double event when Longman brought out a second edition of *LDOCE* (56,000 words and phrases claimed), edited by Della Summers, at the same time as Collins radically replaced *CELD* with the *Collins COBUILD English Language Dictionary* (70,000 references claimed), edited by John Sinclair, the first dictionary in the field to be guided by word frequencies derived from an electronic text corpus.

Meanwhile, Chambers had created a joint reference imprint with Cambridge University Press, one aim of which was to bring out a distinctively international learners' dictionary to be called the *Cambridge International Dictionary of English* (*CIDE*), work on which began under the editorship of Tom McArthur in the later 1980s. The marriage was not a success, however, and in the 'divorce settlement' that followed the same basic *CIDE* material was kept by both separating partners. In 1995, having transferred the core of its lexicographical work to Cambridge, Cambridge University Press brought out a re-created *CIDE*, edited by Paul Procter. In the meantime, Chambers had been bought by the French publishing house Larousse, which had also recently acquired the London reference publisher Harrap. It hyphenated its British acquisitions as Chambers-Harrap, a combine that brought out, also in 1995, the *Harrap's Essential English Dictionary*, not an advanced learners' dictionary but an intermediate level work edited by Elaine Higgleton and Anne Seaton.

Novel strands were now developing in various ways in the various traditions. *LDOCE2* followed the direction taken by *LASDE* and its American cousin, slimming down Paul Procter's original grammatical codes and simplifying the layout and conventions of the pages and entries. *COBUILD* took the idea of simplicity and user-friendliness further than the competition by using whole-sentence definitions: for example, where for the first sense of the verb *hunt LDOCE* has 'to chase in order to catch and kill (animals and birds), either for food or for sport', *COBUILD* has 'When people or animals *hunt*, they chase wild animals in order to kill them, either for food or as a form of sport'. Where Longman was compact and spartan, Collins was expansive and even amiable, leading however to a more expensive and larger product that covered fewer items.

COBUILD's slim 'extra column'—a unique feature—was also a move towards greater simplicity and clearer, less cluttered entries, moving complex and even intimidating grammatical and semantic codes out of the entries proper into their right margins. In its pronunciations, however, the phonetician David Brazil reversed the trend towards simpler presentation and greater accessibility with a narrow notation for an RP described as 'a special type of Southern British English'. Included in this intricate notation are both Walker-like superscript numbers for certain vowels and nasals (relating to the centralizing and reduction of certain full vowels and diphthongs), and both heavy type and underlining for vowels in stressed syllables. The result was probably the most intricate system publicly offered to foreign learners in the 101 years since the IPA was formed. No American transcriptions were provided.

Where *LDOCE* has emphasized its internationalism, *COBUILD* has appeared resolutely British (describing its subject matter as '*real* English', perhaps on the analogy of 'real ale'). Both publications stress the importance of the electronic corpora lying behind their entries and specimens of usage, the Collins claim of 'real English' resting on the work of *COBUILD* itself, an acronym for the *COLLINS Birmingham University International Language Database*. Unique in several ways, the Collins dictionary also stands alone in having an academic work devoted to how it came into existence (Sinclair, 1987). This work implies that such a learners' dictionary is more than just a product and a service: it is a project in which significant publishable linguistic research can be developed and made available to the public rather than kept in the protected archives of commercial publishing. While true and commendable for its openness, this approach points up the uneasy relationship throughout the tradition of the learners' dictionary between, on the one hand, language academics (phoneticians, grammarians, and others), and on the other, language teachers and their students. It does not follow, for example, that a complex notation for the pronunciation, stress, and intonation of RP (however brilliant and accurate it may be in phonetic terms) is the best and most practical service that may be provided in a learners' dictionary.

The EFL/ESL dictionary industry is a phenomenon of the twentieth century of which the general public worldwide is largely unaware. Something new occurs in this complex on-going subject virtually every year, in terms of commercial competition, publishing takeovers, the starting up and closing down of ventures, the creation of new editions and spin-off products, and the application of new technologies and linguistic and pedagogical theories. However, neither that industry nor its products appeared out of nowhere or operate in a vacuum. Rather, as I have tried to show here, they have a long, complex, and very human history and have been operated on by a variety of social and academic forces. To provide an overview of this history, I have concentrated on the evolution of the main features of learners' dictionaries rather than on the detail of any particular book or books, in an attempt to provide as comprehensive a statement as possible of such a successful undertaking. It seems likely that such unusual unilingual works only make economic, educational, and lexicographic sense if the language to be learned is not simply international but close to universal. It is certainly only in such a context that the genre has so far flourished.

12

Thematic lexicography

[A paper given at the seminar 'The History of Lexicography', held under the auspices of the Dictionary Research Centre of the University of Exeter, March 1986, and published in its proceedings of the same name, edited by R.R.K. Hartmann, in the series Amsterdam Studies in the Theory and History of Linguistic Science, John Benjamins, Amsterdam & Philadelphia.]

There is more to the story of lexicography than dictionaries, if by 'dictionaries' one means no more and no less than alphabetically organized books that list words and their definitions. Nowadays, most people think of wordbooks in terms of ABC ordering, and by and large most lexicographers see themselves as engaged in the creation of such books. Both of these related views of what lexicographers do, however, may be a limited perspective on what lexicography in fact is.

Generally speaking, the historians of lexicography have tended to buttress these views, in which one can contrast 'monolingual' with 'bilingual' dictionaries, 'unabridged' with 'concise' dictionaries, and 'academic' with 'popular' or 'commercial' dictionaries. Murray in 1900, Mathews in 1933, Hulbert in 1955, Whitehall in 1985, Matoré in 1968, Read in 1976, and others have all tended to see lexicography—their area of reference technology and taxonomy—as essentially covering the invention and evolution of the alphabetic wordbook. It is only the occasional maverick like Starnes in 1946 who has sought to extend our attention beyond this rather closed-off view of things.

My argument here is that there is a 'micro-lexicography' in which the positions of Murray and the others can be justified, but that there is also a 'macro-lexicography' in which lexical reference materials can look rather different. Certainly, if one deals only with standard dictionaries and looks only at *their* history, it is easy to argue that they alone matter. This, however, is to select from the data of history only that material which supports a position already (explicitly or implicitly) held. A more panoramic examination of the history of reference technology and taxonomy suggests that lexicography—the art and craft of marshalling and relating words, etc.—consists of not one strong tradition-cum-format plus occasionally fascinating fragments of other approaches, but *two* distinct and complementary traditions.

These traditions are *alphabetic lexicography* on the one side and *thematic lexicography* on the other. As a format, the alphabetic mode was practised rather haphazardly and hesitantly until the invention of the printing press in the fifteenth century, but thereafter—and particularly from around 1600—it consolidated itself [in the West and in Westernized cultures elsewhere] into the dominant tradition, in a line of development that has been well delineated by such historians as those mentioned above. The thematic mode, however, is the older, broader tradition, with its roots in the classical traditions of Plato, Aristotle, and Pliny, and with strong foundations in the world of medieval Scholasticism. It is hardly a spent force today. Indeed, it is a covert influence on much of current reference-book practice, and is enjoying a modest overt renaissance among 'print' dictionaries, and could also have a useful future as lexicography moves into the electronic era.

My detailed review of the nature of thematic lexicography, and its relationship with alphabetic lexicography, set within a broad framework of reference materials through some five millennia of human history, can be found in *Worlds of Reference* (1986). I do not wish to duplicate that review here, but the core argument is worth a summary: lexicography is part—and an important part—of that interplay of technology and taxonomy which has helped our species to find means of storing information beyond the brain, our first and for an enormous length of time our only container of knowledge. The invention of writing systems and adequate writing surfaces, the development of storage and presentational systems, the growth of techniques for classification (etc.) have all combined to provide us with a wide range of options in the kind of product or artifact we create, the kinds of layout that will animate them, the kinds of formats available for use, and the kinds of information poured into those formats. Crudely—in terms of the macro-lexicography of secular reference books—the broad options can be shown by means of the accompanying device, which I would like to call 'the reference rectangle'.

THEMATIC LEXICOGRAPHY

the 'encyclopedic' option
producing artifacts that
handle 'things in the world'
marshalled for 'easy'
reference

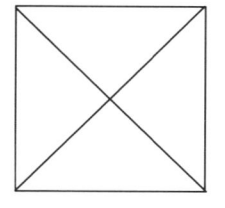

the 'wordbook' option
producing artifacts that
handle 'words', etc.,
marshalled for 'easy'
reference

the thematic option
formats which present
information of any kind
via themes, classes, topics,
contents list, menus, etc.

the alphabetic option
formats which present
information of any kind
via the alphabet as an
invariant series

The six lines in the diagram bring the four points of the rectangle together in various combinations, within which many further minor permutations are possible [including the use of two further organizational options: *the graphic* (with pictures and the like) and *the numeric* (with numbers used in various ways]. They cover, for example, alphabetic encyclopedias like the traditional *Encyclopaedia Britannica*, thematic encyclopedias like the *Cambridge Encyclopedia of Archaeology*, conventional dictionaries like the *Oxford English Dictionary*, the *Concise Oxford Dictionary*, *Webster's Collegiate Dictionary*, *Chambers 20th Century Dictionary*, and so forth, thematic wordbooks such as *Roget's Thesaurus*, a pictorial *Duden*, or my own *Longman Lexicon of Contemporary English*, and an indefinite range of mixed alphabetic-cum-thematic compilations such as the *Reader's Digest Great Illustrated Dictionary* and the Petit Robert *Dictionnaire universel des noms propres*, which also mix the ideas (or genres) of 'dictionary' and 'encyclopedia' in interesting ways. There is in fact very little in the world of reference materials—including library catalogues and telephone directories—which does not fit comfortably into the model as shown.

It is necessary to stress, however, that the model is independent of such words as 'encyclopedia' and 'dictionary'. Such words are historically and culturally volatile; there may be a broad consensus of what they can and should mean, but in practice that consensus tends constantly to be violated. Thus, in the eighteenth century such encyclopedists as Ephraim

LEXICOGRAPHY

Chambers, Denis Diderot, and the Edinburgh Society of Gentlemen who created the *Britannica* called their works 'dictionaries'. Many a work that is called a 'dictionary' could just as easily be called an 'encyclopedia'—the Petit Robert title mentioned above, for example, or a Penguin 'Dictionary of Saints'. In Tudor times, John Withals brought out a 'dictionarie' for young students of Latin which was entirely thematic in layout, while at the present time my own *Lexicon* is often loosely referred to by its publisher Longman as a 'semantic dictionary'. Roget's original *Thesaurus* was entirely thematic—without even an index—but nowadays there are many works which call themselves thesauruses and are entirely alphabetic. The key generic terms of macro-lexicography are therefore inherently fuzzy in strict referential terms, and should be accepted as such; they have been referentially fuzzy since they first came into use in the Middle Ages. This is one reason I prefer to talk about 'wordbooks' for generic purposes, rather than 'dictionaries'.

With the macro-lexicographic perspective, however, one can place books—whatever their names may be—somewhere in the reference rectangle; that is, one can see where they are located in terms of the historically and culturally significant interaction among the genres and formats available to us. And this is as true of the French, German, and other traditions as it is true of English-language lexicography (wherever practised). Indeed, using such a model as the rectangle, one can talk about where the French tradition tends to locate itself, and show for example how the Scottish lexicographical tradition differs from the English, and where the American differs from the British as a whole. Without such a model, one's statements may tend to remain diffuse and unfocused. Within such a model, it may be possible to demonstrate succinctly ways in which the French tend towards encyclopedic dictionaries and crypto-thematic 'analogical' presentations of words, while in the Anglophone world the tradition centred on the *Concise Oxford Dictionary* resists anything encyclopedic at the same time as the Merriam-Webster tradition embraces it in a typically American way (with an emphasis on thematic appendices of all kinds to the main alphabetic list).

Despite all this, however, it is true to say that in the immediate world of wordbooks people do not readily think of thematic works. If invited to do so, they will probably bring in Roget, shortly followed, perhaps, by comments on the arcane and idiosyncratic quality of his conceptual scheme (if they have in fact ever looked at it). Roget was first published by Longman in 1852, and the work has been one of the great publishing successes of the English-using world. But its taxonomy is highly Latinate

THEMATIC LEXICOGRAPHY

and academic, and most of the people who use the book get to its lists via the index. Additionally, as I have indicated above, there have been many re-castings of Roget in straight alphabetic form, and both these points—the index and the re-casting—inevitably suggest the primacy of alphabetization over thematization.

At first sight this looks daunting, but I would suggest that it conceals one of a number of pseudo-problems that arise in minds conditioned to think alphabetically about lexis. The core of the problem is the assumption that a thematic layout promotes a compiler's eccentricity while an alphabetic layout inhibits it. The thematic compiler is seen as having one idiosyncratic view of the world, foregrounded for all to see by his or her conceptual schema, and users are seen as having *their* own schemata, inevitably at odds with the compiler's. In quasi-Whorfian terms, it may not be possible to map any one schema on to any other, or in broad philosophical terms there may not exist any Platonic 'true' list from which a non-eccentric thematic work could be derived.

I belong among those who consider that it *is* impossible to find an ultimate true schema for ordering things and words in the world; in Popperian terms there can only be better or worse schemata for any purpose, whether it is Roget's plan or the Yellow Pages. Even where such schemata are created by committee or consensus rather than by one compiler, they will still be culture-bound, period-bound, place-bound, and (say) Anglocentric or Francocentric. And this is where the pseudo-ness of the problem comes in: all this is just as true of alphabetic wordbooks, except that the alphabet helps shuffle the material in such a way that the limitations, relativity, and idiosyncrasy of such books are not immediately or panoramically obvious. However, as one retreats in time and style from such non-thematic books, the 'failings' of time, place, culture, and personality increasingly display themselves. This is amply demonstrated, for example, by looking at commentaries on the idiosyncrasies of the great alphabeticist himself, Samuel Johnson in 1755, every bit as eccentric in his own way as the great thematicist Peter Mark Roget a century later. It could therefore be said that a thematic format has the virtue of being more patently limited than an equally—but covertly—limited alphabetic format.

Additionally, to judge thematic compilations in terms of one such work, *Roget's Thesaurus*, is no more an argument against the genres involved than would be a judgement against dictionaries because of deficiencies in—well, choose the present-day dictionary that you like least. Once we look beyond the limits imposed by an alphabet-centred view of lexicography, it becomes apparent that there are many kinds of thematic presentation in which the thematic tradition flourishes, as for example:

- travellers' phrase books, such as those published by Berlitz, Collins, and Harrap

- pictorial wordbooks, of which the Duden *Biltwörterbücher* in Germany and the Oxford Duden collaborations in the UK are leading examples

- specialized vocabulary lists topically arranged, included in a wide range of standard language textbooks (both unilingual and bilingual)

- sets of appendices in conventional dictionaries

- sets of two or more subdictionaries within a single volume, arranged topically

- individual innovative works in this century, such as *What's What: A Visual Glossary of the Physical World* (Fisher & Bregonier, Hammond, NJ, 1981), an American cousin of the Duden approach

- as already touched on, elements in or behind alphabetic works which are either overtly or covertly thematic. Overt examples are grouped appendices of various kinds in many standard works, or whole volumes of classified glossaries, as for example Don Ethan Miller's *The Book of Jargon* (Macmillan, New York, 1981), divided into six themes with a total of twenty-four subtheme glossaries, and my own *Lexicon*. Covert examples are legion, among them the analogical background to the varied listings of related words in the *Dictionnaire Le Petit Robert*.

Behind all of these recent works lies a traceable tradition going back at least to the Scholastics, if not to classical and remoter times. One could draw attention to a variety of conceptual schemata for presenting the entire cosmos in thematic form: for some examples of these, see *Worlds of Reference*. I shall content myself here, however, with noting that such orderings do indeed vary with the personality of the compiler and the time and place in which the compiling was done, while also containing a surprisingly consistent 'core' of thematic ideas which—if not culturally universal—is evidence of the shared interests of all literate communities

THEMATIC LEXICOGRAPHY

and also of a continuous tradition. To illustrate this point let me juxtapose two such orderings. The first is a condensed version of an eleventh-century list from England (based on the work of Aelfric, Abbot of Eynsham near Oxford); the second is the list used in my *Lexicon*.

Aelfric (eleventh century)	*Tom McArthur (1981)*
1 God, heaven, angels, sun, moon, earth, and sea	1 Life and living things
2 Man, woman, parts of the body	2 The body, its functions and welfare
3 Kinship, professional and tradespeople; diseases	3 People and the family
4 Abstract terms	4 Buildings, houses, the home, clothes, belongings, and personal care
5 Times of the year, the seasons, the weather	5 Food, drink, and farming
6 Colours	6 Feelings, emotions, attitudes, and sensations
7 Birds, fishes, beasts, herbs, trees	7 Thought and communication, language and grammar
8 House furnishings, kitchen and cooking utensils, weapons	8 Substances, materials, objects, and equipment
9 Parts of the city	9 Arts and crafts, science and technology, industry and education
10 Metals and precious stones	10 Numbers, measurement, money, and commerce
11 General terms, both concrete and abstract	11 Entertainment, sports, and games
	12 Space and time

13 Movement, location, travel, and transport

14 General and abstract terms

Aelfric's list could have been cut up differently; it is by no means as neat as the above groupings suggest. By the time I finalized my own set of themes for the *Lexicon*, I was aware of Aelfric's and a variety of other lists, but was hardly likely to base a twentieth-century compendium for foreign learners of English upon a *vocabularium* of Latin and Anglo-Saxon terms a thousand years earlier. It is, however, worth noting that the two pedagogues in question have produced markedly similar schemes, and also that my twentieth-century needs have dictated a set of themes closer to the medieval than to the nineteenth-century erudition of Roget.

Aelfric's schema is representative of his time. The Schoolmen were well disposed towards the idea of classifying the cosmos, of catching the *omne scibile* ('all that is knowable') in a thematic net. Aelfric's is the tradition of the *vocabularium*, the (usually bilingual) word list by means of which the young cleric could acquire Latin, his passport to religious and cultural elevation. That tradition remains fundamental to the growth of thematic reference materials, but is only one of two powerful medieval trends in this direction. The other relates to the proto-encyclopedic inclinations of such theologians and scholars as Thomas Aquinas with his *Summa theologiae* (uncompleted when he died in 1274) and Vincent de Beauvais with his *Speculum triplex* of 1244. These were philosopher-compilers, each with a three-fold conceptual frame for the universe running from God and his angels through to the broad and nefarious doings of 'man'.

All such medieval views were hierarchical and hyponymic, with the higher subsuming the lower until all 'nature' was included. Although grounded in theology and Catholic Christian dogma, they were also fed with a rationalism derived through the seven liberal arts from the secular tradition of ancient Greece. They possessed as a consequence an inner tension between faith and reason, which became tenser still with the advent of first the Renaissance and then the Reformation. Both the pedagogic tradition typified by Aelfric and the philosophical tradition typified by Aquinas continued through this turbulent period into the early seventeenth century, the time when alphabetic wordbooks were establishing themselves in Western Europe. This was also a period of seminal activity for the thematic mode, initiated by two key figures, the first a pedagogue, the second a philosopher.

The pedagogue was the Irish Jesuit William Bathe who, in 1611, brought out his thematic *Ianua Linguarum*, a Latin-to-Spanish manual that in 1615 acquired in London its Latin-to-English equivalent. This 'Gate of Tongues' was religiously orientated, had twelve great themes, and some 5,000 items accompanied by 1,200 illustrative sentences. It was in the Aelfric tradition, a straightforward vocabulary-builder, and was a commercial success.

The philosopher was Sir Francis Bacon, who at about the same time in his *Instauratio Magna* ('Great Renewal') created a taxonomy of knowledge descended from the work of the Scholastics but defined in secular and proto-scientific terms. It was also tripartite, but its divisions covered first nature, then 'man', then man acting upon nature. Within the schema the great areas had sub-areas, and the sub-areas sub-sub-areas until—it was assumed—everything worth talking about could be covered. It was both the basis for an encyclopedic compilation that was never written and a blueprint for the scientific revolution, in which power to change our circumstances was given into the hands of human beings. This taxonomy (cf. McArthur, 1986:111) has had a profound and fully acknowledged influence on many taxonomists since, including the encyclopedists Diderot in France in the eighteenth century and Samuel Taylor Coleridge in England in the nineteenth.

There were, however, more immediate repercussions than these, in the work of Bishop John Wilkins of the Royal Society of London, and of John Comenius, the Moravian bishop and educator. Wilkins in 1668 produced an erudite work—another master plan for scientists and logicians—entitled *Towards a Real Character and a Philosophical Language*. This contained, among other things, a conceptual scheme for the organization of words which has links with the tradition of Aelfric and Bathe as well as of Aquinas and Bacon. Meanwhile, in 1631, Comenius brought out his wryly entitled *Ianua Linguarum Reserata* ('The Gate of Tongues Unlocked'), intent on improving upon the system offered by Bathe—a Protestant improving upon a Catholic and a Jesuit. This was followed by his radical *Orbis Sensualium Pictus* ('The Illustrated World of Things we Can Feel') in 1657, which was not only also thematic, but made use of vivid pictorial aids in which numbers linked elements of the pictures with words on the printed page.

These men either knew each other or knew of each other. For example, when Comenius studied in Heidelberg he read the works of Bacon, and (in the words of the commentator John Sadler, 1976) 'returned home convinced that the millennium could be obtained with the aid of science'. Additionally, the influence of these men on later thematic compilers is as traceable as, say, the influence of Nathaniel Bailey on Samuel Johnson and of Samuel Johnson on Noah Webster in the complementary alphabetic tradition. Bishop Wilkins was, for example, a founder of the Royal Society. Peter Mark Roget in the nineteenth century was for twenty-two years secretary of that society and acknowledges the influence of Wilkins in the introduction to his *Thesaurus*. Furthermore, in his younger days Roget wrote articles for the short-lived *Encyclopaedia Metropolitana*, planned and started by Coleridge who in his turn had been influenced by Bacon's *Instauratio*.

These then are some of the historical elements in the development of thematic lexicography, which has until now lacked nothing as a lexicographical tradition except a label. Like most people who have found themselves working in this field, I have to confess both a pedagogical and a philosophical interest in the format, plus a more modern linguistic-cum-semantic interest which arises directly from the work of Ferdinand de Saussure, Edward Sapir, Benjamin Lee Whorf, the structural semantics of John Lyons, and the cognitive anthropology of Stephen Tyler and Harold Conklin. Separately, and apparently with little or no knowledge of the history of the thematic mode, modern linguists with interests in lexis and ethnology have proposed that alternatives to the alphabet be sought out as a means of usefully handling the systemic aspects of the vocabularies of the world's languages (cf. in particular Tyler, 1969).

Indeed, it was influence of Lyons's description of structural semantics in 1968 together with the enthusiasm of David Crystal for the potential of 'conceptual wordbooks' that conspired to launch me into this area, when I became the researcher for Longman in the early 1970s whose spadework in due course became the *Lexicon*. The group which commissioned me to explore this area was not in the least interested at the time in my diggings into the history of the subject (which also became part of my doctoral research); they were focused on modern linguistics, not ancient Scholastics and Restoration 'scientists'. In my own view, however, having spent quite a lot of time in the area subsequently, I feel that the two cannot reasonably be separated and, if anything, I owe more to the ancient tradition in which by chance I found myself than to the relatively programmatic developments in the modern sciences of linguistics and anthropology.

Effectively, however, they fuse in the late twentieth century into one organically developing tradition. That tradition—which I have elected to call 'thematic lexicography'—has great potential in the electronic era, either on its own or in combination with the currently more powerful alphabetic tradition. My own expectation is that lexicographers with alphabetic bents will steadily—almost willy-nilly—be nudged into looking at the thematic options available to all of us, particularly because of the exigencies of computerized lexicography. This hardly seems pernicious, allowing for all sorts of judicious blends of the two formats, enriching the profession in the process.

The two modes need not be seen as rivals, but as complementary approaches to the same deeply intractable material—the lexis of any natural language. It is possible to foresee compilations in the not-too-far-distant future where material from the same data core (however arranged there) will be presented to the user (on demand by means of a monitor or a printout) in either of the formats—a service that may well help make the mass of material less intractable. I look forward to that possibility.

13

Reference materials and their formats

[The opening paper at the conference 'Die Welt in einer Liste von Worten/The World in a List of Words', held at the University-GH-Essen, Germany, in 1992, and published in its proceedings of the same name in the series Lexicographica Maior, Niemeyer.]

Over the last twenty years I have been trying to look behind the rather confusing words that people use when talking about works of reference: behind, for example, both everyday terms like *dictionary* and *thesaurus* and specialist terms such as *onomasiological* and *semasiological*. As a compiler, consultant, and commentator in this field, my aim has been to determine (as far as I could) what has actually been going on in both traditional and contemporary reference publishing, regardless of the titles that people give to finished products and the terms that are generally employed to discuss and describe them.

I have long felt that many terms common in general and academic use fit only loosely over the realities of creating and describing reference materials. Most terms in current use are in some sense relevant and helpful, and few are likely to go away, but some widespread usages do not penetrate to the heart of the enterprise. Rather, they constitute a kind of shopfront behind which significant processes are at work that often lack specific names.

Take, for example, the apparently key terms *dictionary* and *thesaurus*. Down the centuries, as many have pointed out, the applications of these words have been varied and even contradictory. The term *dictionary* has at times been a coverall for just about any kind of reference book, including encyclopedias; at other times it has been used to contrast with *encyclopedia* for some purposes (while excluding *thesaurus*) and with *thesaurus* for other purposes (while excluding *encyclopedia*). In addition, a book of a particular type can be called a *dictionary of synonyms* by one publisher while for another it is a *thesaurus*, and for a third the two lie comfortably side by side, as in the *Oxford Thesaurus: An A–Z Dictionary of Synonyms* (Laurence Urdang, 1991).

Even so, however, many people would say that, although this is all true, a dictionary does—'in general terms'—list words in alphabetical order, each word being defined in some way, while a thesaurus lists them taxonomically and in clusters, without definitions and generally without any other kind of discrimination. This is also true enough, yet it is a shaky basis on which to build a firm theoretical description of works of lexical reference. I can cite, for example, the case of my own *Longman Lexicon of Contemporary English* (1981). In order to describe it to someone who has never seen it, various people have run the gamut of possibilities with *dictionary* and *thesaurus*, calling it (among other things) a 'kind of non-alphabetical dictionary', a 'conceptual dictionary', a 'semantic dictionary', a 'new kind of thesaurus', a 'thesaurus with definitions', and 'a combination of dictionary and thesaurus'.

All of these are, yet again, true enough in rough-and-ready ways, yet none indicates in any real way what the *Lexicon* is and does—and the term *lexicon* is not much help either. By their very variety the descriptions emphasize the fuzziness and fluidity of the terms we employ for reference genres. In fact, they tell us more about the nature of words and reference at large than they do about works of reference. I know of only one pragmatic way out of this terminological predicament: to start by talking contrastively about 'the dictionary as conventionally understood' on the one hand and 'the thesaurus as conventionally understood' on the other, before pointing out that the titles given to many lexical reference books do not have much to do with this assumed dichotomy.

There are also problems with the strictly academic terms mentioned above, *onomasiological* and *semasiological*, terms used more or less exclusively by people who write monographs and attend metalexicographical conferences. They are seldom if ever employed by actual makers of reference books, at least in the English-speaking world. Practising lexicographers and their publishers have not taken to them with the readiness they have shown towards, for example, *macrostructure* and *microstructure*, terms which seem to me to be among the most valuable late-twentieth century neologisms in the field. I have not myself found *onomasiological* and *semasiological* useful, but I accept that others have, especially in Continental European circles. These terms arose separately in the Western European philological tradition and do not seem to me to be natural opposites:

(1) According to the *Oxford English Dictionary* (Second Edition, 1989), *onomasiology* is 'the study of the principles of nomenclature', while *semasiology* is 'that branch of philology which deals with the meanings of words, sense-development and the like'.

(2) According to the *Random House Dictionary* (Second Edition, 1987), *onomasiology* is 'the study of the means of expressing a given concept', while *semasiology* is 'semantics, esp. the study of semantic change'.

(3) The *Collins English Dictionary* (Second Edition, 1986) has two senses of *onomasiology*, the first presenting it as a synonym of *onomastics*, the second as 'the branch of semantics concerned with the meanings of and meaning relations between individual words'. *Semasiology* is 'another name for semantics'.

These definitions do not tally, but even so they make it clear that in the mainstream of English lexical usage the two nouns do not provide a safe base for adjectives used to label a contrast in the classification of lexical reference works. Yet the contrast is eminently worth making: between works that seek to move, as it were, from concept to word, and works that seek to move from word to concept (whatever we may understand by *word* or, worse, by *concept*). The adjectives may be the best terms at present for labelling this contrast, virtually by default, but they ought not to be pushed too far, and are too erudite to become fashionable beyond university seminars and papers. There may be nuances at work in the use of such terms in languages other than English, such as French and German; these may have encouraged their use in this way in English, and I may have failed to note them. But even if that is so, the problem is, I believe, present as much at the international level as in English, and will not go away.

The most important issue for me, however, is that regardless of the serviceability of these terms to mark a significant contrast, they do not relate to the format of reference books any more directly than the terms *dictionary* and *thesaurus*. There is no *a priori* requirement that an 'onomasiological' book should be thematic in format while a 'semasiological' book is alphabetic. Onomasiological works can equally well be alphabetic, as with dictionaries of names and A-to-Z thesauruses (which deal in 'concepts' just as much as thematic thesauruses do).

Similarly, avowedly semasiological works can be wholly or partly thematic, as with *The Reader's Digest Great Encyclopedic Dictionary* (1972), which has two conventional 'dictionary' volumes plus a volume of thematically arranged alphabetic glossaries. The *Longman Lexicon* is clearly semasiological (in terms of both semantics and semiotics), and is described on the cover as 'the new vocabulary source book', yet many observers see it as primarily onomasiological, like *Roget* ('a thesaurus, not a dictionary').

It seems to me crucial not to confuse the conceptual/lexical dichotomy to which the terms *onomasiological* and *semasiological* apparently refer with the alphabetic/thematic dichotomy transparently marked by the terms *alphabetic* and *thematic* and referring to classificatory style. No matter what we call the products of lexicography and related activities, whether we see them as moving from word to word, concept to concept, word to concept, or concept to word, whether we call them dictionaries, encyclopedias, thesauruses, lexicons, directories, or anything else, the alphabet/theme contrast marks a truly basic option in shaping delivery systems: from the original taxonomic and hierarchical *Roget* to the many alphabetical *Rogets*.

The alphabetic format is of course currently dominant in lexicography, if that craft is narrowly defined as 'the making of conventional dictionaries', for reasons that I discuss in *Worlds of Reference* (1986). The thematic format is a minor player on this field, but a major player elsewhere in the structuring of textbooks, magazines, newspapers, amd many encyclopedic works, all of them topic-driven and some of them hierarchical.

I have previously underlined the ancient structural opposition between these two 'classic' formats by contrasting *alphabetic lexicography* with *thematic lexicography*, seen as either distinct crafts or as major divisions in the same craft. I did this because, until the late 1980s, many lexicographers, publishers, and academic commentators seemed to have been virtually set in alphabetic concrete, unable to consider thematic formats as serious options, complements, or supplements. They often cavalierly dismissed the idea of two modes of compilation, except for such traditional and very minor forms as the thematically listed appendices at the ends of their A–Z books.

This resistance is weaker now, as witness the convening of this conference and the number of works being published which are either overtly thematic (as for example the *Random House Word Menu*, 1992) or make use of 'deep' thematic lists in the preparation of 'surface' A–Z lists (increasingly a standard procedure), or that lace thematic elements into their main alphabetic arrangement (as with the special-interest sections in recent editions of EFL learners' dictionaries), rather than bundling them up as appendices at the end. A major factor in this change of attitude stems from unavoidable technological development: the use of electronic aids to compilation and delivery, including menu-driven software, that are in effect a new incarnation of ancient thematic hierarchies. As a result, I now feel free to downplay the idea of two 'rival' kinds of lexicography and place my stress instead on all the options available to a more generous and inclusive lexicography. With this freedom, one can see that alphabetic and thematic formats are not the only players on the field: a third option is the *numeric format* of the chronology, and a fourth is the *graphic format* of traditional atlases.

When one begins to think in these terms, the essential hybridity of format in many works of reference leaps into focus: for example, how the pictorial Duden tradition and such works as *What's What: A Visual Glossary of the Physical World* (Hammond, 1981) combine the thematic, the numeric, and the graphic, and how conventional A–Z dictionaries often have thematic appendices, are numeric in the marking of their sense divisions, and are graphic in their use of diagrams and pictures. Everybody has always known this, of course, but we have not necessarily given much attention to formalizing what we know.

My first graphic attempt to model formats and options was the *reference rectangle* (in 'Thematic lexicography', a paper in *The History of Lexicography*, ed. Reinhard Hartmann: John Benjamins, 1986 [see p. 151]. This diagram links the thematic and alphabetic formats to the genres of encyclopedia and *wordbook* (a term in English that has a traditionally negative tinge to it but can be used, as in this instance, as a neutral and more comprehensive term than 'dictionary'). The six lines in this diagram serve both as links among genres and formats and as continua along which one may move, nearer to one node or another, to 'generate' thematic or alphabetic encyclopedias, thematic and alphabetic encyclopedias, comparable wordbooks, encyclopedic dictionaries, or dictionary-thesauruses, and so forth. A similar rectangle can be framed to serve the four options, variously blending or separating alphabet, themes, numbers and graphics.

The practical application of the format options can be demonstrated in many ways, but I thought that the most useful procedure here would be to survey two of my own compilations: the *Longman Lexicon of Contemporary English* (1981), a wordbook that is primarily thematic but with alphabetic, numeric, and graphic elements, and the *Oxford Com-*

panion to the English Language (1992), an encyclopedia that is primarily alphabetic with thematic, numeric, and graphic elements.

The *Lexicon* is aimed at upper intermediate to advanced learners of English as a second or foreign language, as a means of extending one's vocabulary and sense of word relationships, and improving one's reading and writing skills. Its structural features are described in the following list and displayed in Reproductions 1, 2, 3 (mainly for its macrostructure) and 4, 5 (mainly for its microstructure):

(1) *Semantic fields.* The core of the book is a set of fourteen semantic fields, each identified by a letter and a title, and consisting of further titled subfields (without identifying letters) and, within them, many titled lexical sets introduced by both a letter and a number. Field letters and set numbers serve to locate the sets and also (through the opening sets of each subfield) the subfields themselves. By doing without a middle level of letters and/or numbers, three hierarchical levels are economically labelled for retrieval purposes by means of only two identifying elements. Thus, the letter *B* introduces the semantic field *The body: its functions and welfare* and the letter and number *B1* correlate with both the opening lexical set in the field, *The body itself*, and by contiguity with the title of the subfield *The body generally*. Compare Reps 2 and 4.

(2) *Cross-referencing.* In addition to fields, subfields, and lexical sets, arrowed cross-references operate across all levels. For example, in the lexical set *B1: The body itself*, senses in the entry *body* cross-refer variously to *H116: Frames and structures, C324: Souls, spirits and ghosts, G1: Mind, thought and reason*, and *L2: Planets, suns and stars*. See Rep 4.

(3) *Index.* In addition to access by means of fields and sets, it is possible to enter the system through an index, which, in addition to including a self-contained glossary of IPA pronunciation for each word listed, points to one or more senses for each word. For each sense there is a prompt word or phrase and one or more identifying letters and numbers. See Rep 3. Thus, the entry for *body*, near the end of the first column, provides five distinct senses: the body 'generally', in *B1*; the body 'when alive', in three separate sets, *A120, B3*, and *B130*; a body meaning a 'group', in *C76*; a body meaning a 'structure', in *H116*; and the body 'of a vehicle', in *M100*.

(4) *Set content.* Each set is linked semantically to any immediately preceding and subsequent sets. Thus, *B1* contains nouns relating to the body proper, *B2* contains four adjectives with the same role, *B3* contains nouns referring to kinds of dead bodies, and *B5* contains nouns referring to substances of the body. See Rep 4. Each entry in each set normally consists of a headword, one or more definitions, and one or more specimens of usage. In addition, a grammatical code is usually appended to a set title or an individual entry, and its elements are explained on a table of grammatical codes on the inside back cover of the book.

(5) *Illustrations.* Some sets consist of, contain, or relate to tables, diagrams, and drawings [applying the graphic option]. For example, set *B10* (not shown here) relates to the full-page annotated drawings of a man and a woman shown in Rep 5, while set *B11* (also not shown here) contains, along with several normal entries, the annotated drawing of a skeleton.

The *Companion* differs greatly from the *Lexicon*. It is intended for anyone interested in a high-level description and discussion of the English language. It follows the typical A–Z format of the long-established Oxford Companion series. Its distinctive structural features are shown in the following list and displayed in Reproductions 6 to 8 (mainly the macrostructure) and 9 (the microstructure):

(6) *The circle of English.* Although the core structure of the *Companion* is an A–Z list, it derives from a set of twenty-two themes represented diagrammatically in the introduction as making up a 'circle of English'. The text was compiled in alphabetic sections under the theme headings there displayed. See Rep 6.

(7) *Cross-references.* Each theme allows for cross-references across all entries: major, mid-length and minor, all such cross-references being printed in small capitals and usually set in short lists at the ends of entries. To form the master list, the themes, themselves alphabetically ordered, were shuffled into one overall A–Z format, their contents being preserved for reference as theme lists (in alphabetical order and small caps) following each 'theme entry'. See Rep 7 for the Americas theme, which follows the entry *America*.

(8) *Index.* The index, which is non-numeric, lists only persons mentioned in entries in the *Companion*, followed by the titles of the entries in which they appear. See Rep 8.

(9) *Entry order and content.* Entry structures employ a range of contrastive presentational devices, including: etymologies in square brackets at the beginning of entries; section subheadings within longer entries; dictionary-like definitions (sometimes numbered for subsenses), as appropriate; italicized specimen expressions; short quotations within standard paragraphs, long quotations in paragraphs of their own (and reduced type size). There are occasional illustrative diagrams.

There are no presentational devices in either of these books that have not appeared in innumerable other works of reference, but in each case the options inherent in the four formats and other well-tested referential techniques have been exploited in novel ways. A different format dominates each, and is buttressed in unique ways by the other three—and these arrangements proceed regardless of what the final product might have been called: dictionary, thesaurus, lexicon, companion, guide, and onomasiological or semasiological. The *Lexicon* might well have been called the *Longman Thesaurus of Contemporary English*, except that we liked the alliteration and wanted to stress the lexical bent. The *Companion* might have been called the *Oxford Encyclopedia of the English Language*, except that it was conceived as sister to the already established *Oxford Companion to English Literature*, and companions sound more user-friendly than encyclopedias. [NOTE: A comparable but primarily thematic work by David Crystal came out in 1995 with the title the *Cambridge Encyclopedia of the English Language*.]

The proportions in which format options are blended (the degree to which alphabet or themes dominate, the presence or absence of graphics, the ways in which numbers are put to use, and so forth) are key elements in shaping our understanding and appreciation of the genre to which we assign a work of reference, however crudely, in functional terms. The titles they are given have no necessary relationship with the blend: lexicons are usually fully alphabetic, and companions can be thematic and hierarchical. This has been so for centuries and will continue to be so, even in vistas that as yet have hardly entered the awareness of lexicographers. Such vistas include multimedia, hypertext, and virtual reality, in whose domains all the formats that one can already imagine —and some that one cannot—will go on working snugly together for conceptual, lexical, encyclopedic and even cybernetic purposes.

This and the following four pages demonstrate the main features of the *Longman Lexicon of Contemporary English*

Contents

	page
Pronunciation Table	inside front cover
Short forms used in the Lexicon	
Acknowledgments	iv
Preface	vi
List of Sets	vii

How to use the Lexicon	xii
Guide to the Lexicon	xiv

THE LEXICON

A	Life and Living Things	1
B	The Body; its Functions and Welfare	39
C	People and the Family	79
D	Buildings, Houses, the Home, Clothes	169
E	Food, Drink, and Farming	213
F	Feelings, Emotions, Attitudes, and Sensations	237
G	Thought and Communication, Language and Grammar	297
H	Substances, Materials, Objects, and Equipment	381
I	Arts and Crafts, Science and Technology, Industry and Education	429
J	Numbers, Measurement, Money, and Commerce	457
K	Entertainment, Sports, and Games	505
L	Space and Time	545
M	Movement, Location, Travel, and Transport	603
N	General and Abstract Terms	679
The Index		785
Grammar Table		912

168

List of Sets

Set titles are shown in **bold type**, with major cross-references listed underneath

A Life and Living Things

A1 Life and Living Things
- C1 People
- C20 Courting, Sex, and Marriage
- C50 Death and Burial
- I74 The Life Sciences
- L200 Old, New, and Young
- N1 Being, Becoming, and Happening

A30 Living Creatures Generally
- B1 The Body Generally
- E Food, Drink, and Farming

A50 Animals/Mammals
- C1 People
- E31 Meat

A70 Birds
- M19 Moving
- E31 Meat

A90 Reptiles and Amphibians

A100 Fish and Other Water Creatures
- L86 Areas of Water
- E31 Meat
- M19 Moving

A110 Insects and Similar Creatures

A120 Parts of Animals
- E34 Cuts of Meat

A130 Kinds and Parts of Plants
- E30 Food

A150 Plants Generally

B The Body: its Functions and Welfare

B1 The Body Generally
- C324 Souls, Spirits, and Ghosts
- E30 Food
- H1 Substances and Materials Generally
- G1 Mind, Thought, and Reason

B10 The Body: Overall
- A120 Parts of Animals
- A130 Kinds and Parts of Plants

B20 The Head and the Face
- F240 Actions of the Face Related to Feelings
- G1 Thinking, Judging, and Remembering

B30 The Trunk, Arms, and Legs
- E30 Food

B50 The Skin, the Complexion, and the Hair
- A120 Parts of Animals
- D170 Cleaning and Personal Care
- L20 Light and Colour

B60 Fluids and Waste Products of the Body
- D40 The Bathroom
- D42 Plumbing and Pipes
- H13 Rubbish and Waste

B80 Bodily States and Associated Activities
- F1 Feeling and Behaviour Generally
- F260 Senses and Sensations

B110 Bodily Conditions Relating to Health, Sickness, and Disability
- F260 Senses and Sensations

B140 Diseases and Ailments
- E80 Cigarettes and Drugs

B160 Medicine and General Medical Care
- I170 Science and Technology

C People and the Family

C1 People
- A1 Life and Living Things
- A50 Animals/Mammals
- C212 Inheriting and Bequeathing
- D60 Residence
- D130 Clothes and Personal Belongings

C20 Courting, Sex, and Marriage
- A1 Life and Living Things

C40 Friendship and Enmity
- C270 Fighting, War, and Peace
- F140 Admiration, Pride, Contempt, and Abuse
- F170 Kindness and Unkindness
- F190 Honesty, Loyalty, Trickery, and Deceit

C50 Death and Burial
- A1 Life and Living Things

INDEX

n D140
blue whale /ˌ·ˈ·/
  n A58
blunt /blʌnt/
  rude *adj* F194
  general *adj*, *v* H159
blurb /blɜːb‖ blɜrb/
  n G163
blush /blʌʃ/
  v, *n* L38
boa constrictor /ˈbəʊə
  kənˌstrɪktəʳ/
  n A90
boar /bɔː/
  n A55
board /bɔːd‖ bɔrd/
  live *v* D60
  living *n* D66
  wood *n*, *v* H39
  company *n* J231
  in games *n* K136
  enter *v* M9
-board
  comb form H39
board & lodging
  /ˌ·ˈ··/
  n D66
boarder /ˈbɔːdəʳ‖ ˈbɔr-/
  n D63
boardinghouse
  /ˈbɔːdɪŋhaʊs‖ ˈbɔr-/
  -houses /ˌhaʊzɪz/
  n M79
board out
  v D60
board up
  v H39
boast /bəʊst/
  v, *n* F136
boastful /ˈbəʊstfəl/
  F 136
boat /bəʊt/
  n M150
boatman /ˈbəʊtmən/
  -men /mən/
  n M163
boatswain, bosun
  /ˈbəʊsən/
  n M164
bob /bɒb‖ bɑb/ **-bb-**
  v hair B52
  action M42
bob
  n hair B52
  money J84
  action M42
bobbin /ˈbɒbɪn‖ ˈbɑ-/
  n I58
bobby /ˈbɒbi‖ ˈbɑbi/
  n C221
bodily /ˈbɒdɪli‖ ˈbɑ-/
  adj B2
body /ˈbɒdi‖ ˈbɑdi/
  n generally B1
  when alive A120, B3,
    B130
  group C76
  structure H116
  of a vehicle M100
bodyguard /ˈbɒdigɑːd‖
  ˈbɑdigɑrd/
  n C223
bodywork /ˈbɒdiwɜːk‖

ˈbɑdiwɜrk/
  n M100
bog /bɒg‖ bɑg, bɔg/
  n toilet D41
  ground L109
bogus /ˈbəʊgəs/
  adj I13
boil /bɔɪl/
  n B126
  v E100
boiler /ˈbɔɪləʳ/
  n M157
boiler room /ˈ··ˌ·/
  n M157
boilersuit /ˈbɔɪləˌsuːt,
  -sjuːt‖ ˈbɔɪlərsuːt/
  n D160
boiling point /ˈ··ˌ·/
  n L43
bold /bəʊld/
  adj brave F129
  shameless F154
bollocks /ˈbɒləks‖ ˈbɑ-/
  n B40
bolster /ˈbəʊlstəʳ/
  n D115
bolt /bəʊlt/
  eat *v* E7
  bar *n* H38
  cloth *n* H47
  fastening *n*, *v* H148
  run *v* M25
  close *v* M64
bomb /bɒm‖ bɑm/
  v C279, H247
  n H246
bombard /bɒmˈbɑːd‖
  bɑmˈbɑrd/
  v C279
bombardier
  /ˌbɒmbəˈdɪəʳ‖
  ˌbɑmbər-/
  n C307
bombardment
  /bɒmˈbɑːdmənt‖
  bɑmˈbɑrd-/
  n C276
bomber /ˈbɒməʳ‖ ˈbɑ-/
  n plane H250
  person H252
bond /bɒnd‖ bɑnd/
  money *n* J114, 160
  as an action *v* N326
  as an action *n* N327
bondage /ˈbɒndɪdʒ‖
  ˈbɑn-/
  n C164
bonded warehouse
  /ˌ··ˈ··/
  n M160
bonds /bɒndz‖ bɑndz/
  n C250
bondsman /ˈbɒndzmən‖
  ˈbɑndz-/
  n C163
bond(s)woman
  /ˈbɒnd(z)ˌwʊmən‖
  ˈbɑnd(z)-/
  n C163
bone /bəʊn/
  n B4
  v E102
bonnet /ˈbɒnɪt‖ ˈbɑ-/

n hat D146
  car M100
bony /ˈbəʊni/
  adj B106
boob /buːb/
  breast *n* B31
  mistake *n*, *v* N219
booby-trap /ˈ··ˌ·/
  n H246
  v H247
book /bʊk/
  charge *v* C226
  general *n* G162, 163
    (picture)
  drawing *n* I47
  order *v* M82
bookie /ˈbʊki/
  n K124
booking /ˈbʊkɪŋ/
  n M83
book-keeping
  /ˈbʊkˌkiːpɪŋ/
  n J222
booklet /ˈbʊklɪt/
  n G164
bookmaker
  /ˈbʊkˌmeɪkəʳ/
  n K124
books
  n J222
bookseller /ˈbʊkˌseləʳ/
  n G176, 177, J194
bookshop /ˈbʊkʃɒp‖
  -ʃɑp/
  n G177, J194
bookstall /ˈbʊkstɔːl/
  n G177
boor /bʊəʳ/
  n C169
boorish /ˈbʊərɪʃ/
  adj C168
boot /buːt/
  n shoe D156, K199
  of a car M100
booth /buːð/
  n J181
bootlace /ˈbuːtleɪs/
  n D156
booty /ˈbuːti/
  n C238
booze /buːz/
  n, *v* E63
bordello /bɔːˈdeləʊ‖
  bɔr-/
  n C38
border /ˈbɔːdəʳ‖ ˈbɔr-/
  n, *v* M122
borderline /ˈbɔːdəlaɪn‖
  ˈbɔrdər-/
  n, *adj* M122
border on
  v M122
bore /bɔːʳ‖ bɔr/
  not interesting *v*, *n*
    F230
  dig *v* I114
-bore /bɔːʳ‖ bɔr/
  comb form H238
bored /bɔːd‖ bɔrd/
  adj F81
boredom /ˈbɔːdəm‖
  bɔr-/
  n F232

boring /ˈbɔːrɪŋ‖ bɔr-/
  adj F231
born /bɔːn‖ bɔrn/
  adj A6, A7
borough /ˈbʌrə‖ -rəʊ/
  n C82
borrow /ˈbɒrəʊ‖ ˈbɑ-,
  ˈbɔ-/
  v J100
bosom /ˈbʊzəm/
  n B31
bosomy /ˈbʊzəmi/
  adj B104
boss /bɒs‖ bɔs/
  leader *n* C160
  order *v* G115
  employer *n* I117, J228
bossy /ˈbɒsi‖ ˈbɔsi/
  adj C160, G115
bosun /ˈbəʊsən/
  n M164
botanical /bəˈtænɪkəl/
  adj I74
botanist /ˈbɒtənɪst‖ ˈbɑ-/
  n I74
botany /ˈbɒtəni‖ ˈbɑ-/
  n I74
both /bəʊθ/
  det N101
bother /ˈbɒðəʳ‖ ˈbɑ-/
  v F89
  n F91
bottle /ˈbɒtl‖ ˈbɑtl/
  n H170
  v H187
bottleful /ˈbɒtlfʊl/
  n H170
bottom /ˈbɒtəm‖ ˈbɑ-/
  n of the body B33
  of gears M111
  of a boat M157
  of the sea M168 **go to
    the bottom** M169
  position M201
boulder /ˈbəʊldəʳ/
  n H60
bounce /baʊns/
  v, *n* M42
bound /baʊnd/
  adj books G163
  certain N34
  tied N326
  be bound for M74
boundary /ˈbaʊndəri/
  n M122
bounds /baʊndz/
  n M122
bountiful /ˈbaʊntɪfəl/
  adj N103
bounty /ˈbaʊnti/
  n N104
bourbon /ˈbʊəbən‖ ˈbɜr-/
  n E65
bourgeois /ˈbʊəʒwɑː‖
  bʊərˈʒwɑ/
  adj, *n* C166
bourgeoisie
  /ˌbʊəʒwɑːˈziː‖ -ər-/
  n C153
bout /baʊt/
  n K103

B

The body, its functions and welfare

The body generally

B1 nouns : the body itself

body [C] **1** the whole of a person or animal, esp as opposed to the soul or mind: *The body is the physical structure* [⇨ H116] *of any living thing. We know that the body exists but·we cannot prove that the soul exists.* [⇨ C324 SOUL, ⇨ G1 MIND] **2** this without the head or limbs: *He was wounded in the leg, not the body.* **3** (*fig*) a large number or amount : *a body of men/water/information* **4** (*fig*) an object: *The sun and moon are heavenly bodies.* [⇨ L2]
physique [C] the form and character of a human body: *That man has a powerful physique; look at his muscles. Her physique is excellent for her age.*
build [C; U] the way in which a body, esp of a man, is built; the shape and size, esp of the human body: *That young man has a very good build. We are both of the same build.*
constitution [C] the general condition of the body, esp a person's ability to keep off disease or tiredness: *He has a healthy constitution; he should live for many years yet.*
figure [C] the human form, esp in its general appearance and what it suggests: *That girl has a beautiful figure. He is a fine figure of a man. They saw some dark figures among the trees. She says she has lost her figure since having her second child* (= lost the shape which she liked best).
person [C; *of* U] a living human body or its outward appearance: *He put his person between the little girl and the mad dog. The dead man had no money on his person. She was small and neat of person.* **in person** bodily, physically: *I can't attend the meeting in person* (= myself, personally), *but I am sending someone to speak for me.*

B2 adjectives : the body itself [Wa5]

bodily 1 [A] of or in the (human) body: *They supply all our bodily needs. He was the victim of violent bodily assault.* **2** [adv] in a body; as a whole: *He lifted her bodily out of the car.*
physical [B] of or concerning the body: *He is a man of great physical strength. Food is one of our physical needs.* **non-** [neg] **-ly** [adv]

constitutional [B] of or concerning the human constitution **-ly** [adv]
organic [B] **1** of an organ or organs [⇨ B4] of the body: *The wound is in the flesh only; there is no organic damage.* **2** having bodily organs: *All organic creatures need oxygen in order to live.* **3** of, concerning, or obtained from living creatures: *Organic chemistry deals with the nature and products of animal and plant bodies.* **in-** [neg] **-ally** [adv]

B3 nouns : kinds of dead bodies

body [C] a dead person: *There was a body lying in the hall, the body of a middle-aged man. Bodies lay all over the battlefield.*
corpse [C] the dead body of a human being, usu stiff or dead for some time: *A corpse lay uncovered on the hospital table. The corpse of a child was found on the beach this morning.*
cadaver [C] a corpse, esp as used in medical experiments **cadaverous** [B] like a cadaver: *He had a thin, cadaverous face.*
carcass, carcase [C] **1** the dead body of an animal, esp one prepared for cutting up as meat: *Several sheep carcasses hung up in the butcher's shop.* **2** *deprec often humor* a human body: *Come on, move your carcass, you lazy devil!*
remains [P] *often fml* the decaying corpse or bones of a human being or animal: *His remains lie in a local churchyard. They found the remains of a man and some animals in that cave.*
carrion [U] dead and decaying flesh: *Birds such as crows eat carrion.*

B4 nouns : substances of the body

flesh [U] **1** the soft material which covers the bones of human beings and animals, including fat and muscle: *The lion had eaten the flesh off the dead animal's leg. He had a flesh wound; no organs were damaged.* **2** any similar material in parts of fruit, nuts, etc
meat [U] *infml often humor* flesh: *Poor man,*

head

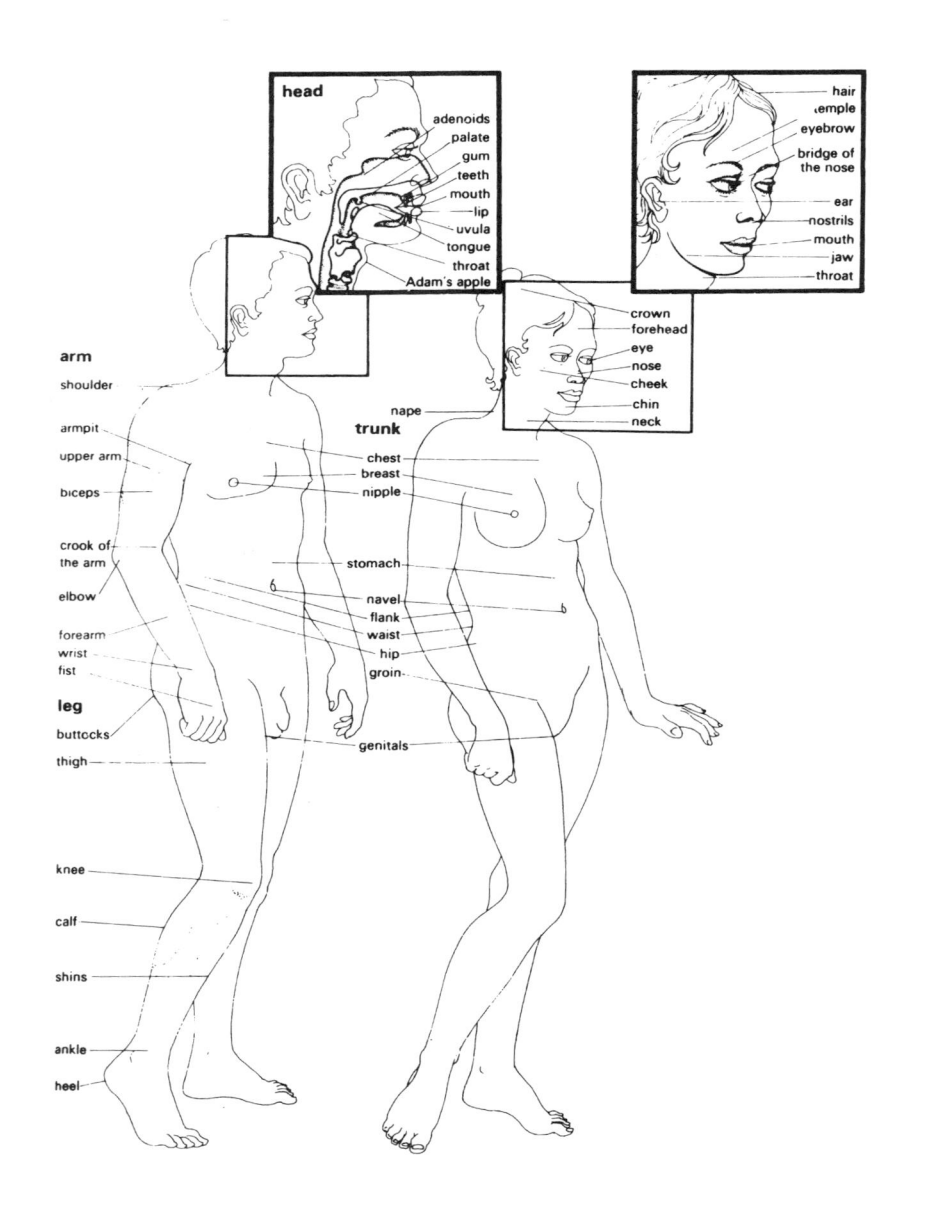

- adenoids
- palate
- gum
- teeth
- mouth
- lip
- uvula
- tongue
- throat
- Adam's apple

- hair
- temple
- eyebrow
- bridge of the nose
- ear
- nostrils
- mouth
- jaw
- throat

- crown
- forehead
- eye
- nose
- cheek
- chin
- neck
- nape

arm
- shoulder
- armpit
- upper arm
- biceps
- crook of the arm
- elbow
- forearm
- wrist
- fist

trunk
- chest
- breast
- nipple
- stomach
- navel
- flank
- waist
- hip
- groin
- genitals

leg
- buttocks
- thigh
- knee
- calf
- shins
- ankle
- heel

This and the following three pages show the main features of the *Oxford Companion to the English Language*

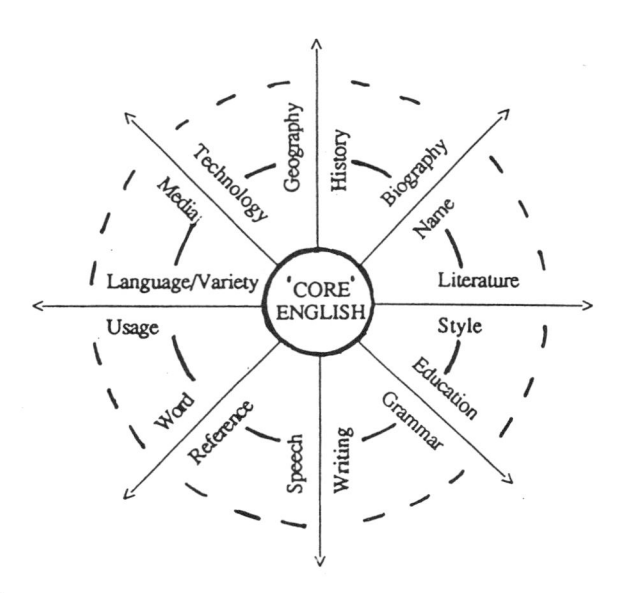

Fig. 3

- *Africa*, with entries such as *African English, Bantu, Flytaal, Krio, Ngugi wa Thiong'o, South African broadcasting*, and *Zambia*. Theme list p. 19.
- *Americas*, with entries such as *American English, Black English Vernacular, Dictionary of Bahamian English, New Orleans, Quebec*, and *Rasta Talk*. Theme list p. 34.
- *Asia*, with entries such as *Babu English, Filipino literature in English, Gairaigo, Hobson-Jobson, Indianism, Pacific Rim*, and *Taglish*. Theme list p. 85.
- *Europe*, with entries such as *Black Irish, English in England, European Community, Germanic languages, Latin[1], Jespersen, Malta, Norn*, and *Shakespeare*. Theme list p. 389.
- *Oceania* (treated here as including Australasia), with entries such as *Australian English, Godzone, Hawaii Pidgin English, Kriol, Maori English, New Zealand literature*, and *Tok Pisin*. Theme list p. 721.

History. Entries for events, conditions, concepts, institutions, persons, and works considered significant in the development of the language, such as *Anglo-Saxon Chronicle, Bible, Defoe (Daniel), etymology, Great Vowel Shift, Indo-European roots, Library of Congress, Renaissance*, and *Royal Society*. Theme list p. 475.

Biography. Capsule reviews of the careers, activities, and views (often with quotations) of individuals influential in the use and study of the language, such as the American lexicographer *Barnhart (Clarence L.)*, the Scottish

34 AMERICA

Beirut was murdered because he was the symbol of America' (*International Herald Tribune*, 9 May 1984). However, the term is open to uncertainties: the name *The American Heritage Publishing Company* (New York) refers to the US alone; in the company's publication *The Golden Book of America* (1974), a children's book about the US, the first chapter asks 'Did Columbus Discover America?', without making it clear that a different sense of the word is needed when discussing Columbus. [AMERICAS, GEOGRAPHY, HISTORY, NAME].   T.MCA.

The Americas theme

A. AFRICAN-AMERICAN, AFRO-SEMINOLE, ALBION, ALEXANDER (H.), ALLIANCE QUEBEC, AM-, AMER, AMERENGLISH, AMERICA, AMERICAN[1], AMERICAN[2], AMERICAN BLACK ENGLISH, AMERICAN BROADCASTING, AMERICAN DIALECT SOCIETY, AMERICAN ENGLISH, AMERICAN ENGLISH AND BRITISH ENGLISH, AMERICANESE, AMERICAN HERITAGE DICTIONARY, AMERICANISM, AMERICANISTICS, AMERICAN LANGUAGE, AMERICAN LANGUAGE (THE), AMERICAN LANGUAGES, AMERICAN LITERATURE, AMERICAN NAME SOCIETY, AMERICAN PLACE-NAMES, AMERICAN PRESS, AMERICAN PUBLISHING, AMERICAN SIGN LANGUAGE, AMERICAN SPEECH, AMERICO-, AMESLAN, ANGLO-, ANGLO-AMERICAN, ANGLO-CANADIAN, ANGLO ENGLISH, ANGLO-IRISH, ANGLOPHONE, ANGUILLA, ANTIGUA AND BARBUDA, ANTILLES, APPALACHIAN ENGLISH, ARGENTINA, ASSIMILATION, ATLANTIC, ATLANTIC CREOLES, AVIS.

B–C. BADIAN, BAHAMAS, BAILEY (B.), BAJAN, BARBADOS, BARNHART, BAY ISLANDS, BELIZE, BERLITZ, BERMUDA, BIERCE, BLACK, BLACK ENGLISH, BLACK ENGLISH VERNACULAR, BLACK IRISH, BLOOMFIELD, BOLINGER, BONEHEAD ENGLISH, BOSTON, BRATHWAITE, BROOKLYNESE, BURGESSISM, BUSH, CAJUN, CAN-, CANADA, CANADIAN, CANADIAN BROADCASTING, CANADIAN DICTIONARIES IN ENGLISH, CANADIAN ENGLISH, CANADIANISM, CANADIAN LANGUAGE ORGANIZATIONS, CANADIAN LANGUAGES, CANADIAN LITERATURE IN ENGLISH, CANADIAN PLACE-NAMES, CANADIAN PRESS, CANADIAN PUBLISHING, CANADIAN STYLE GUIDES, CARIBBEAN, CARIBBEAN ENGLISH, CARIBBEAN ENGLISH CREOLE, CARIBBEAN EXAMINATIONS COUNCIL, CARIBBEAN LANGUAGES, CARIBBEAN LITERATURE IN ENGLISH, CASSIDY, CAYMAN ISLANDS, CENTRAL AMERICA, CHICANO, CHICANO ENGLISH, CHINOOK JARGON, CHOMSKY, CLASSICAL LANGUAGE, COLLEGE ENGLISH ASSOCIATION, COLONIAL, COMMONWEALTH, COMMONWEALTH CARIBBEAN, COMMONWEALTH LITERATURE, CONTINENT, CRAIGIE, CULTURA, CURME.

D–H. DIALECT IN AMERICA, DIALECT IN CANADA, DICKINSON, DICTIONARY OF AMERICANISMS, DICTIONARY OF AMERICAN REGIONAL ENGLISH, DICTIONARY OF BAHAMIAN ENGLISH, DICTIONARY OF CANADIANISMS, DICTIONARY OF JAMAICAN ENGLISH, DICTIONARY OF NEWFOUNDLAND ENGLISH, DICTIONARY OF PRINCE EDWARD ISLAND ENGLISH, DICTIONARY SOCIETY OF NORTH AMERICA, DIXIE, DOMINICA, DUB, DUTCH, EDUCATIONAL TESTING SERVICE, ELEMENTS OF STYLE (THE), ELIOT, ENGLISH, ENGLISH CANADA, ENGLISH CANADIAN, ENGLISH LANGUAGE AMENDMENT, ENGLISH LITERATURE, ENGLISH-SPEAKING UNION, ENGLISH TEACHING FORUM, ETHNIC NAME, EXAMINING IN ENGLISH, FALKLAND ISLANDS, FRANCIZATION, FRANGLAIS, FRENCH, FRIES, FUNK, FUNK & WAGNALLS, GEECHEE, GEISEL, GENERAL AMERICAN, GENERAL AMERICAN ENGLISH, GRENADA, GRINGO, GULLAH, GUYANA, HALLIDAY, HANLEY, HAWAII, HAWAIIAN, HAWAIIAN ENGLISH, HAWAII CREOLE ENGLISH, HAWAII PIDGIN ENGLISH, HEMPL, HERITAGE LANGUAGE, HILLBILLY, HILL SOUTHERN, HISPANIC, HONDURAS, HOUSE STYLE.

I–M. INDIA, INDIAN, INDIAN ENGLISH[2], INDIES, INNIS, INTERNATIONAL LINGUISTIC ASSOCIATION, INUIT, JAMAICA, JAMAICAN CREOLE, JAMAICAN ENGLISH, JIVE (TALK), KRAPP, KUHN, KURATH, KWEYOL, LANGUAGE, LANGUAGE POLICE, LATIN[2], LATINO, LEACOCK, LEEWARD ISLANDS, LIBRARY OF CONGRESS, LIEBER, LINGUISTIC ASSOCIATION OF CANADA AND THE UNITED STATES, LINGUISTIC ATLAS, LINGUISTIC ATLAS OF THE UNITED STATES AND CANADA, LINGUISTIC SOCIETY OF AMERICA, MCDAVID, MCLUHAN, MCWORD, MAGAZINE, MALEDICTA, MARCH, MARITIME PROVINCES/MARITIMES, MARSH, MATHEWS, MELVILLE, MENCKEN, MERRIAM-WEBSTER, MESTIZO, MÉTIS, MID-ATLANTIC, MISKITO COAST CREOLE, MODERN LANGUAGE ASSOCIATION, MONTSERRAT, MOTION PICTURE, MOVIE, MULATTO, MULTICULTURALISM.

N–S. NAIPAUL, NATIONAL COUNCIL OF TEACHERS OF ENGLISH, NATION LANGUAGE, NATIVISM, NCTE, NETWORK STANDARD, NEW ENGLAND, NEWFIE JOKE, NEWFOUNDLAND, NEWFOUNDLAND ENGLISH, NEW ORLEANS, NEW YORK, NEW YORKER (THE), NEW YORKESE, NEW YORRICAN, NICARAGUAN ENGLISH, NORTH AMERICAN, NOVEL, OFFICIAL ENGLISH (MOVEMENT), OTTAWA VALLEY, OXFORD ENGLISH DICTIONARY, PACIFIC RIM, PANAMA, PATOIS, PENNSYLVANIA DUTCH, PLAIN ENGLISH, PLANTATION SOUTHERN, POLITICALLY CORRECT, PORTUGUESE, POUND (L.), PUERTO RICO, QUEBEC, RACISM, RANDOM HOUSE, RANDOM HOUSE DICTIONARY, RAP, RASTA TALK, READ, REGGAE, RICKERT, SAINT CHRISTOPHER AND NEVIS, SAINT LUCIA, SAINT VINCENT AND THE GRENADINES, SAMANA, SAPIR, SARAMACCAN, SCOTCH-IRISH, SOUTH, SOUTHERN ENGLISH, SOUTHRON, SPANGLISH, SPANISH, SRANAN, STANDARD AMERICAN, STANDARD AMERICAN ENGLISH, STANDARD BLACK ENGLISH, STANDARD CANADIAN ENGLISH, STRATHY LANGUAGE UNIT, SURINAM(E), SYNECDOCHE.

T–Z. TEFL, TEIL, TESD, TESL, TESL CANADA, TESOL, TEXAS, TEXIAN, TEX-MEX, THORNDIKE, TIME MAGAZINE, TIMESPEAK, TRIN(I)BAGONIAN, TRINIBAGIANESE, TRINIDAD AND TOBAGO, TURKS AND CAICOS ISLANDS, TURNER (L.), TWAIN, UNCLE SAM, UNITED STATES, UNITED STATES ENGLISH, URDANG, US, USA, US ENGLISH, USIA, USIS, VERBATIM, VIRGIN ISLANDS, VOICE OF AMERICA, WASP, WEBSTER, WEBSTERS, WEBSTER'S COLLEGIATE DICTIONARIES, WEBSTER'S DICTIONARY OF ENGLISH USAGE, WEBSTER'S NEW INTERNATIONAL DICTIONARY, WEBSTER'S NEW WORLD DICTIONARY, WEST INDIAN, WEST INDIES, WHITE, WHITE ENGLISH, WHITNEY, WHORF, WINDWARD ISLANDS, WORCESTER, YANK(EE), YIDDISH, YIDDISHISM, YINGLISH, Z.

AMERICAN[1] [16c]. A term that first referred to the entire western hemisphere, its peoples, animals, and plants, then to the British colonies which became the United States of America. In 1697, the Boston clergyman Cotton Mather applied the term as a noun to settlers from England, but the use was slow in spreading; when Joseph Addison noted (1711, *Spectator* 56) that 'the Americans believe that all things have souls', he was referring not to the colonists but to the indigenous peoples. As late as 1809, a traveller writing about the people of the ex-colonies as *the Americans* added: 'that

174

Index of Persons

An asterisk (*) prec[edes a] name indicates that the person concerned appears in the bibliography following that entry [but not in the] entry itself. Names mentioned in the *Chronology of English* are not listed.

Aarsleff, H.
  Oxford English Dictionary
Abad, G.
  Filipino literature in English
Abate, F.
  foreignism
Abbott, E.
  *Shakespeare
Abbott à Beckett, G.
  Punch
Abercrombie, D.
  Abercrombie, accent bar,
  Anglo-English, English, festschrift,
  learner's dictionary, *phonetics,
  Received Pronunciation, rhotic and
  non-rhotic, *Scottish English,
  Simplified Spelling Society, spelling
  reform, spoken prose
Abercrombie, L.
  Society for Pure English
Abrams, M.
  *English literature, *figurative
  language
Abruquah, J.
  Ghana
Achebe, C.
  Achebe, African English, African
  literature in English, contact
  variety, English literature,
  Heinemann, Nigeria, novel
Acheson, L.
  Reader's Digest
Achtert, W.
  house style
Adams, C.
  private language
Adams, D.
  Heinemann, science fiction
Adams, F.
  aptronym
Adams, H.
  *poetry
Adams, Howard
  Métis
Adams, J.
  Indian press
Adams, J. G.
  English literature, rhetoric
Adams, K.
  *English Language Amendment
Adams, P.
  quotation
Adams, R.
  enjambement
Adams, R. M.
  *English literature
Adams, V.
  *word-formation
Addams, C.
  New Yorker
Addison, J.
  Addison, American[1], article[2],

Addison, J.—*cont.*
  Augustan, book, Canadian
  literature in English, essay, history
  of English, journalism, lampoon,
  periodical, poetic justice, prose,
  pun, rebus, Steele, usage guidance
  and criticism
Adhelm
  Latin[1]
Adler, Betty
  *Mencken
Adler, Jerry
  simile
Aelfric
  Aelfric, Bible, language teaching,
  Latin[1], prose, sermon, Wessex
Aeschylus
  drama, Greek literature, tragedy,
  trilogy
Aesop
  allegory, fable
Aggarwal, N. K.
  *South Asian English
Aidoo, C. Ama Ata
  Ghana
Aig-Imoukhuede, Frank
  African literature in English,
  Nigeria
Aijmer, K.
  corpus
Aikin, John
  English literature
Aitchison, J.
  *linguistics, *psycholinguistics, *slip
  of the tongue, *terminology
Aitken, A. J.
  Aitken's Law, Aitken's vowel,
  English, *Scots, Scottish
  dictionaries, *Scottish English,
  Scottish vowel length rule, style
  drifting
Akimoto, M.
  *Survey of English Usage
Albee, Edward
  euphemism
Alcuin
  Latin[1], punctuation
Aldhelm
  Latin[1]
Aldington, R.
  free verse
Aleichem, S.
  Jewish languages
Alexander II of Scotland
  Isle of Man
Alexander, H.
  Alexander (H.), Avis, Canadian
  dictionaries
Alexander, L. G.
  Alexander (L.), ELT publishing,
  language teaching, Longman

Alexander, M.
  alliterative verse
Alexander, W.
  dialect in Scotland, Scots literature
Alexander of Aphrodisias
  logic
Alexander the Great
  alexandrine, analogy and anomaly,
  Greek
Alford, H.
  hymn, King's English, usage
  guidance and criticism
Alfred
  Alfred, Anglo-Saxon Chronicle,
  Bible, English Literature, Indian
  English[1], Latin[1], Wessex
Algarin, M.
  New Yorrican
Algeo, J.
  *American English, *American
  English and British English,
  American Speech, *history of
  English, *name, nice-nellyism,
  taboo
Alger, H.
  American publishing
Ali, A.
  Pakistani English
Allaby, M.
  encyclopaedia, scientific usage
Alladina, S.
  community language
Allen, D. E.
  Walian
Allen, F. Sturges
  *Webster's New International
  Dictionary*
Allen, H. B.
  General American, linguistic atlas,
  Linguistic Atlas of the United
  States and Canada
Allen, R. E.
  encyclopaedia, house style,
  *punctuation, usage guidance and
  criticism
Allen, Stannard
  BBC English[2]
Allen, W.
  *novel
Allen, W. S.
  accent
Alleyne, M.
  *Caribbean English
Allingham, M.
  proper
Allingham, W.
  Anglo-Irish literature
Alston, R.
  Early Modern English Dictionary
Altenberg, B.
  corpus, *Survey of English Usage

175

66 ANGLIKAANS

of immigrant and indigenous speakers of other languages' (Joshua A. Fishman, in Ferguson & Heath (eds.), *Language in the USA*, 1981). Compare the relationship between *Frenchify* and *Gallicize*. See ANGLICIZE. [EUROPE, VARIETY].
T.MCA.

ANGLIKAANS [Mid-20c: a blend of *Anglo* and *Afrikaans*]. An occasional informal term for a colloquial mixture of English and Afrikaans: 'In the popular press, the speech style combining English and Afrikaans elements is sometimes called *Anglikaans* in imitation of *franglais*. . . . Many literal translations from Afrikaans give this variety its typical flavor: *bell* "to telephone" (e.g. *I'll bell some of the chicks*)' (L. W. Lanham, 'English in South Africa', in Bailey & Görlach (eds.), *English as a World Language*, 1982). See AFRIKAANS ENGLISH, CODE-MIXING AND CODE-SWITCHING, SOUTH AFRICAN ENGLISH. [AFRICA, VARIETY].
T.MCA.

ANGLO [1830s: a free form of *Anglo-*]. (1) In and around the US Southwest, a clipping of Spanish *anglo-americano* and English *Anglo-American* standing, sometimes pejoratively, for a (white) speaker of English: 'Chicano norms always seem to be somewhat less formal than Anglo norms' (Fernando Peñalosa, *Chicano Sociolinguistics*, 1980). (2) In Canada and especially Quebec, a clipping of *anglophone*, standing for a speaker of English: *anglo rights*. It does not usually have a capital and may contrast with *franco*: see ALLIANCE QUEBEC, ANGLOPHONE. (3) In Scotland, a clipping of *Anglo-Scot*, standing for someone who is half-English, half-Scottish, a Scot who has been influenced by English ideas, mannerisms, etc., and a Scot who plays for an English soccer team. (4) In South Africa, a clipping of the company name *Anglo American Corporation*: 'He joined Anglo as a consultant.' [AFRICA, AMERICAS, EUROPE, NAME].
T.MCA.

ANGLO- [16c: from Latin *Anglus* English]. A combining form relating to: the Angles (*Anglo-Saxon culture*), England and the English (*Anglo-Welsh relations*) or Britain and the British (*the Anglo-Irish agreement*), location in England (*Anglo-Jewry* the Jews of England), and the English language (*Anglo-Danish pidgin*). In Northern Ireland, Scotland, and Wales, the use of the term to mean *Britain/British* is widely disliked. In Scotland, newspapers tend to avoid this sense of *Anglo-*, using instead such phrases as *the British-Irish agreement*. See ANGLO, ANGLO-SAXON, BRITISH-. [EUROPE, NAME].
T.MCA.

ANGLO-AMERICAN [Early 18c]. (1) Relating to England or Britain and the US: *Anglo-American trade talks*. (2) A citizen of the US born in England or of English origin. (3) An American who speaks English: compare ANGLO. (4) A term for the English language proposed by the British zoologist and amateur linguist Lancelot Hogben in *The Mother Tongue* (1964). (5) American English: 'Since the Second World War, the Nordic languages have taken over not only direct loans, but also calques and grammatical constructions from Anglo-American' (*Language International* 2: 2, 1990). [AMERICAS, EUROPE, NAME].
T.MCA.

ANGLO-ARGENTINE. See Argentina.

ANGLO-AUSTRALIAN. See ANGLO-CELTIC.

ANGLO-CANADIAN [19c]. (1) Relating to England or Britain and Canada: *Anglo-Canadian ties*. (2) Formerly, a citizen or resident of Canada born in England or of English origin. (3) Currently and especially in Quebec, an English-speaking or anglophone Canadian, usually without regard to ethnic background. See ANGLO, ANGLOPHONE. [AMERICAS, EUROPE, NAME].
T.MCA.

ANGLO-CELTIC [19c]. (1) Relating to the Angles, England, the English, or the English language on the one hand and the Celts (in Ireland, Scotland, Wales, the Isle of Man, or elsewhere) on the other: 'The relative importance of the formal rules of communication in Anglo-Celtic cultures as opposed to those of the German-speaking countries can be seen in the conduct of formal meetings' (Larry E. Smith, *Discourse Across Cultures: Strategies in World Englishes*, 1987). (2) By nature or in origin both English or British and Celtic, as used by the English physician and anthropologist John Beddoe (1823–1911) in an article comparing mortality rates in Britain and Australia. From the 1880s, the term acquired a special significance in Australia; unlike *Anglo-Australian* and *Anglo-colonial*, it recognized the Irish-Catholic section of the population. As Australia has become multicultural, *Anglo-Celtic* has been used to distinguish people of British and Irish descent from immigrants of European or Asian descent, and from the Aborigines. See ANGLO-, CELTIC. [EUROPE, NAME, OCEANIA].
T.MCA., W.S.R.

ANGLOCENTRIC [1880s]. Centred on England and the English (or Britain and the British), or on the English language: 'The Commonwealth has moved further and further away from being Anglocentric' (*The Economist*, 26 May 1962). See BRITOCENTRIC, CENTRICITY. [EUROPE, LANGUAGE, NAME].
T.MCA.

ANGLO-CHINESE SCHOOLS. See HONG KONG.

14

A mutually defining circle of words: some reflections on the making of the *Longman Lexicon of Contemporary English*

[A paper presented to 'Language Study and the Thesaurus in the World,' the Fifth International Symposium of the National Language Research Institute, Tokyo, Japan, 29 August 1997.]

You have kindly invited me to Tokyo to talk about a book of mine published sixteen years ago, in 1981. I actually finished work on the *Longman Lexicon of Contemporary English* in 1978, the publisher taking three further years to bring it out. Although I receive a percentage on all sales, the copyright of the *Lexicon* belongs wholly to Longman, and I have done no published work relating to it since 1980 (when I wrote the personal parts of the front matter). I am therefore talking to you today about a project which I completed nineteen years ago after some six years' work, and for which I therefore began the research *a quarter of a century ago*. So it was during the 1970s that I developed some of the fundamental concepts and techniques which I identified in the 1980s as part of an international tradition I called 'thematic lexicography' (in contrast to 'alphabetic lexicography').

I have undertaken many projects since finishing the *Lexicon*, as a result of which it has not been easy to think myself back to the 1970s. Longman has done little with the book since publication, apart from selling it, the key exceptions being a successful Chinese bilingualization by Longman Asia (Hong Kong, 1992) and a Japanese bilingualization that, regrettably, never materialized. There are no plans for a revised edition, nor is there now or likely to be in the future a published electronic version; indeed, to my knowledge, no electronic version of any kind exists, and recent direct developments of the *Lexicon* idea have been the work of other publishers. Although I have observed these with interest, I have not been involved in any of them; the potential for such products seems only to have become apparent to publishers recently, but I continue to be convinced that the *Lexicon* idea has great potential over the next few decades.

Origins

I became involved in lexicography in my early thirties, after some ten years of language teaching and administration. After graduating from Glasgow University in 1958, I was first an education officer in the British Army, then a teacher in a secondary school in Birmingham, then Head of English in Cathedral School, Bombay, as well as visiting professor at Bharatiya Vidya Bhavan, a constituent college of Bombay University. Some British Council officers in India drew my attention to the developing subject applied linguistics, and so when I returned to the UK in 1968 I enrolled at Edinburgh University first for the Diploma of Applied Linguistics, then for a Master of Letters in linguistics (subject, metaphor), and finally for a doctorate in lexicology (subject, the English word).

It was necessary to support my wife and family while studying, and to do this I first taught Latin part-time in a local school, then developed classes in English for foreign graduate students at the university, and began to work with EFL publishers. One of my early books was the *Collins Dictionary of Phrasal Verbs and Their Idioms* (1974), the first of the wide range of dictionaries of phrasal verbs now on the market. I compiled this work with Beryl Atkins, then the editor-in-chief of the *Collins English-French Dictionary*, whose brother John Sinclair later created the *COBUILD* dictionaries. The subject matter of our phrasal-verb dictionary was innovative and radical at that time, but its format was unexceptionally A-to-Z. The book is still in print, unrevised, despite massive competition, and a Japanese bilingualized version of it was published in 1976 by Sanseido International, but its glory days are long gone.

One of my teachers at Edinburgh was David Abercrombie, who had editorial ties with Longman and told me in 1971 that the company was looking for a lexicologist to undertake a year's research into the feasibility of what they were calling a 'conceptual dictionary', something that could go beyond traditional A-to-Z format and would (somehow) explicitly exhibit real relationships among words. I was duly interviewed in London by an advisory committee under the chairmanship of Randolph Quirk, when I learned that David Crystal, a member of the committee, had been inspired to suggest such a book by the theory of structural semantics proposed in 1968 by John Lyons (also of Edinburgh University) in his *Introduction to Theoretical Linguistics* (1968). Despite or because of a vigorous interview session, I got the job.

Some members of the Longman committee were consistently against the idea of such a project, but largely because of David Crystal's sustained interest one research year became two, after which I was contracted in 1973 to turn the research into a work of EFL reference. The early research was difficult and radical, and looking back I am surprised that the project got past the more negative advisers and executives. Certainly, even after the book came out, some Longman people appear not to have valued it, despite its commercial success. The *Lexicon* received relatively little promotion when published in 1981, yet it sold tens of thousands of copies within months, and has been in print ever since, with at least twenty paperback and twelve hardback impressions.

Theoretical and other influences

As I noted above, the theory of structural semantics outlined by John Lyons in 1968 was central to the project, leading me to think in terms of hundreds of distinctive 'lexical sets' based on such sense relations as *synonymy, antonymy, hyponymy, homonymy, polysemy*, and what later came to be called *meronymy*. Another recommended source was a US collection of papers entitled *Cognitive Anthropology*, edited by Stephen A. Tyler (1969). It offered such concepts as 'folk taxonomy' (a system through which communities avowedly structure their lexis), from which I developed some ideas for a pragmatic and relativistic list of semantic fields into which my Lyons-influenced lexical sets might fit. A third influence was Yorick Wilks's *Grammar, Meaning, and the Machine Analysis of Language* (1972), which proposed for its purposes that 'meaning is other words', another pragmatic approach that saved me a lot of semiotic heart-ache. As a result, the *Lexicon* is in essence a vast mutually defining circle of words.

To these three up-to-the-minute dimensions I added a fourth. The interests of most of Longman's advisers, like many linguists at the time, were synchronic, but I found that, in order to be both systematic and comprehensive about 'conceptual' or 'structural lexicography' (as I called it then), I also needed to be diachronic, in order to find out if there was a tradition to which my work belonged. My Longman paymasters were not linguistically doctrinaire; their impulses were primarily commercial, and they had after all since 1852 published many editions of the most successful non-alphabetic wordbook of all time, *Roget's Thesaurus*. They therefore had no problem with my interest in Roget (both man and book), despite the fact that many linguists and language teachers at the time regarded the book as a semantic dinosaur.

Consequently, blending ideas on lexical sets, semantic fields, and meaning-as-other-words with my examination of Roget, I was able to formulate what at the time I tentatively called 'index-to-system lexicography', but which in fact gets us to the lexical system of a language through two doors: (1) a thematic set of fields listed at the front of the volume; (2) an A-to-Z indexical list at the back. Roget created a massively erudite and hierarchical system of concepts-within-concepts-within-concepts, to which an index was added in the second edition because users could not easily get to the right word lists via his complex Latinate taxonomy. His index made the collection more user-friendly, but in essence the *Thesaurus* remains a massive list of categorized but undiscriminated words, whereas the *Lexicon* categorizes *and* discriminates, using contrastive definitions and illustrations (often providing collocational information) for the vast majority of its words and senses of words.

My historical studies established that *Roget's Thesaurus* had not appeared out of nowhere. Instead, there had been compilers of non-alphabetic reference works for centuries, all over the world; indeed, the further back I pushed the subject (which by then had become part of my doctoral research), the clearer it became to me that thematic formats had once been the primary means of managing lexical and encyclopedic information in *all* cultures, whether they used alphabetic, syllabic, ideographic, or hybrid writing systems. The worlds of reference were thematic long before they were alphabetic and might well become so again—as the development of menu-driven electronic procedures in the 1980s has amply demonstrated. It transpired, then, that I was not so much creating a new approach as using an old one in new ways. The *Lexicon* would be new, but it would also be old, paradoxically bringing together techniques from all over the world and across millennia. I in due course wrote about such matters in *Worlds of Reference: Language, Learning and Lexicography from the Clay Tablet to the Computer* (1986, with a Japanese translation, M. Mitsunobu, 1991).

Links with *LDOCE*

At about the time I was formulating the principles of the *Lexicon*, the Longman executive Charles McGregor offered me the editorship of a learner's dictionary intended to compete with the well-established *Oxford Advanced Learner's Dictionary* (*OALD*). This was the book that appeared in 1978 as the *Longman Dictionary of Contemporary English* (*LDOCE*), and in tandem with this work, he indicated, my current project would become the *Longman Lexicon of Contemporary English*. However, taking on this role would have meant moving the family from Longniddry near Edinburgh to Harlow near London, and my wife Feri and I did not want to do this. As a consequence, Paul Procter was appointed to the editorship of the dictionary, and he and I co-operated closely for a number of years in order to bring out the two books as sister products. Our co-operation included his sending me the bulk of *LDOCE* definitions to speed up compilation and harmonize the two works as much as possible, while I was free to use or not use this material, and if I used it to adapt it to my particular needs.

Because of the similarity of the titles and the co-operation, and also because the *Lexicon* came out later than *LDOCE*, many people have assumed that the *Lexicon* is a side-product of *LDOCE*. Thus, the American lexicographer and publisher Sidney Landau has stated that the *Lexicon* was 'produced automatically from a database for the ESL market' (1984:273). Computers were certainly used to store, display, and print *LDOCE*, but the 1970s were not the era of desktop computers and electronic spinoffs. The *Lexicon* project was prior to *LDOCE*, despite the fact that it did indeed look in the 1980s like a product of PCs and databases. But the reality was quite different: the lexicographers in Harlow wrote their definitions on paper pads, after which their work was keyed into the Longman mainframe, while in Longniddry I created the *Lexicon*'s fields and sets and my wife Feri created its index using paper, cards, pencils, pens, and a typewriter, plus endless heaps of (much-hated and often faint) yellow bottom copies of handwritten Longman definitions that arrived almost daily by post—by present-day standards a very low-tech operation indeed.

By 1977, the *Lexicon* was more or less what I wanted it to be, but I needed time to refine it, time which was in fact no longer available. Della Summers, who had replaced Charles McGregor at Longman, pressed me to bring the work to completion as quickly as possible, and I was very willing to do so, although I had to leave a number of ideas undeveloped. *LDOCE* was published in 1978, and I expected the *Lexicon* to follow it, probably in 1979, the year in which I took up the post of Associate Professor of English at the Université du Québec in Canada. But Longman, having pushed to finish the work quickly, for reasons still unclear to me held back publication of the *Lexicon* until 1981.

The snowflake principle and the rolling definition

Most features of the *Lexicon* are self-evident on inspection and require little further discussion here. They include: alphanumerically identified semantic fields, lexical sets, and cross-references; a set of differentiating style and other labels; a range of illustrative pictures, diagrams, and tables; definitions and usage specimens; and an index with lexical clues, alphanumeric references, and a built-in pronouncing dictionary. There are, however, other less immediately obvious features, two of which I would like to mention here, because they are not among the traditional inventory of devices available to the creators of reference materials. I call them the *snowflake principle* and the *rolling definition*.

The *snowflake principle* relates to nouns, verbs, and adjectives in a basic word list such as Michael West's *General Service List* (1953). To provide the wordstock of a work like the *Lexicon,* such items can be logically expanded along two lines: (1) a *morphological line,* through formational processes that include derivation, compounding, conversion, and abbreviation; (2) a *semantic line,* through the sense relations listed above. The systematic application of this principle produces for each base word a range of derivatives and senses, not all of which are necessarily relevant to the task in hand. In terms of such a principled expansion, each word is a snowflake, its morphosemantic pattern and potential distinct from all other words, because (as far as I can tell) no two words open up morphologically and semantically in precisely the same way.

By applying the snowflake principle, one can 'explode' a basic list of, say, 2,000 words into thousands of further words: in the case of the *Lexicon,* with appropriate pruning and refining, some 15,000 items, but in a future electronic *Lexicon* the number could be enormously increased. Certainly, because of the computer revolution, it is now easier for publishers and others to appreciate thematic formats than it was in the 1970s, when alphabetism reigned unchallenged.

My second feature, the *rolling definition,* occurs within a lexical set whose key member is a generic or superordinate term. Such a term logically comes first, its definition (buttressed by usage specimens) serving as the foundation for all succeeding definitions, which roll along to the end of the list with appropriate differentiations for each item. In an ideal set, the definition of each successive item proceeds from the preceding definition(s), so that, for example, an initial definition of *big* is followed by dependent definitions of *large, great, grand, immense, vast, huge,* and so forth (arranged in what I think of quite simply and unrepentantly as 'a pleasing sequence', because this is art as well as science). As with the snowflake principle, however, no set is ideal; each is unique, and requires appropriate adjustments to take in the special relationships that pertain among its various associated words.

The snowflake principle was built into the *Lexicon* from the start. I had, however, only begun to refine my rolling definitions when Longman required me to finish the book, and as a result that aspect of the work was incompletely realized. In many cases, in order to meet the deadline, I put words into sets in a fairly rough-and-ready way, minimally adapting the *LDOCE* definitions to achieve the kinds of subtlety of which a *Lexicon*-like work is capable. My best excuse (apart from pressure to finish) is that, because most sets are small, the reader can study their members side by side, largely regardless of order. Simply bringing such words together was service enough, given that this was a novel book and time was short. I still believe this to be true and satisfactory, but regret not having had time to refine a procedure which I believe has great practical virtues.

Offspring

For many years, although the *Lexicon* sold well and teachers worldwide spoke well of it (especially as a students' aid in composition), it attracted few reviews in ELT, linguistic, and lexicographical circles, nor were 'clones' produced by other publishers as they had rushed to do with dictionaries of phrasal verbs. Although the *Lexicon* was created to fit a niche in ELT reference, it has been consistently absent in reviews of intermediate and advanced ELT wordbooks, solely—it would appear—because it is not alphabetic. If one takes the view that only A-to-Z wordbooks can be tools for checking words and developing vocabulary, then sadly the *Lexicon* is irrelevant, but if one asks what works of reference are available to help learners check words and acquire vocabulary skills, then the *Lexicon* should be discussed alongside conventional dictionaries.

There is, it seems to me, a duty to discuss it, but by and large this discussion has not taken place. Instead, there has been a tendency either to note the book's existence in a single sentence and move on, or not to note it at all. However, there are at least two marked exceptions to this approach: (1) Howard Jackson's *Words and Their Meanings* (1988), which discusses 'McArthur's *Lexicon* and Roget's *Thesaurus*' together in some detail in his Chapter 14, entitled 'Not alphabetical', immediately followed by a subsection called 'Thematic lexicography'; (2) Leonhard Lipka's *An Outline of English Lexicology: Lexical Structure, Word Semantics and Word-Formation* (1992), which relates the *Lexicon* in some detail to developments in semantics and lexicology, but asserts that the book is 'based on the *LD[O]CE*'.

Relative neglect by linguists and publishers (though not by teachers and students) was the fate of the *Lexicon* for much of the 1980s, but in the 1990s there has been a change. Given that it takes years to get major wordbooks from initiation to publication, one can assume that awareness of the potential of *Lexicon*-type formats dates from c.1990, a decade after the book appeared. I can currently identify five [now six] books with a family resemblance: three non-alphabetic works and two [now three] that compromise between theme and alphabet (much as there are alphabetical *Roget*s). In addition, and importantly, I must mention a sixth thematic work which owes nothing to the *Lexicon* but illustrates the intermittent vigour of the non-alphabetic tradition. These works are:

- A set of at least three thematic and bilingual works under the general editorship of Michael McCarthy, published by Cambridge University Press as the Wordroutes series: for French, Greek, and Spanish learners of English. The example I am using here is from the *Cambridge Word Selector, Inglés-Español: Diccionario tematico del inglés contemporáneo*, Chief Editor Elizabeth Walter, 1995. We may note that this 'thematic dictionary' has a long numbered list of lexical sets and an index (but no semantic fields), and that the bilingualism is comparable to the Chinese bilingualization of the *Lexicon*. I have always considered that the format would be bilingually valuable, and am impressed by these books.

- The *Longman Language Activator: The World's First Production Dictionary*, Editorial Director Della Summers, Managing Editor Michael Rundell, 1993. This is an A-to-Z book, but in effect it superimposes sets that could have been separately organized, perhaps thematically (the larger sections), on what is in effect an index (the undefined and cross-referred words in the same list). This is apparently done to escape—or appear to be escaping—the two-stop problem presented by thematic works. One-stop alphabetic works appear to avoid this problem, but often in fact do not do so, because we often have to travel on from a particular entry to a second destination. In some ways the massive, radical, and adventurous *Activator* is Longman's successor to the *Lexicon*, but without semantic shape.

[NOTE In 1997, at the same time as this presentation was being given in Tokyo, the *Longman Essential Activator: Put Your Ideas Into Words* was published, Director Della Summers, Managing Editor Michael Rundell. This is a much more compact work (without being called a concise version) that retains the A–Z list for 750 'basic words' that serve as the titles for lexical sets, moving the equivalent of the original *Activator*'s undefined words to an index that indicates under which of the 750 headings they are dealt with. This moves the *Activator* concept closer to that of the *Lexicon*, without however introducing a conceptual framework.]

- The *Oxford Learner's Wordfinder Dictionary*, compiled by Hugh Trappes-Lomax, 1997. This is also an alphabetic book, whose single word-list performs the same double duty as the *Activator*'s. Among its features are whole-sentence definitions that echo COBUILD [see p. 146] but for me an intriguing innovation is the presentation of new lexical material through association with the headword(s) in question: thus, the set *hand/arm* has not only labelled anatomical diagrams of the parts of the hand and arm, but adds such reverse-defining statements as 'the top part of a finger: *fingertip*'. This handy practice is comparable to the rolling definition.

- The *Random House Word Menu*, compiled by Stephen Glazier (first edition 1992, second 1997), whose use of *menu* echoes computer terminology; the 1997 cover statement calls it 'The revolutionary reference book that organises language by subject matter, the way we understand it and use it'. The *Word Menu*, although compiled (as I checked with the publisher) without any knowledge of the *Lexicon*, has comparable semantic fields and lexical sets on one side and an index on the other. It differs from the *Lexicon*, however, in that its lexical sets are A-to-Z lists of words and definitions, without further semantic structuring. It is intended specifically for writers and generally for anyone interested in vocabulary, and flies the flag of thematic lexicography with panache.

This paper today has only scratched the surface of the *Lexicon* in particular and thematic lexicography in general. I hope, however, that it may stimulate discussion and experimentation in Japan, whose intricate and subtle orthographic tradition provides an excellent base for the development of conceptually-organized materials, especially electronically. It has been a pleasure and a privilege to address this gathering.

Appendix 1
A two-page display of main features of the *Cambridge Word Selector: Inglés-Español* (English/Spanish)

GRUPOS DE PALABRAS

sparkle *vi* centellear, destellar *Her eyes sparkled with delight.* Le brillaban los ojos de regocijo. *sparkling wine* vino espumoso

24.4 Cosas que proporcionan luz

light *sn* luz *to switch/turn the light on* encender la luz *to switch/turn the light off* apagar la luz

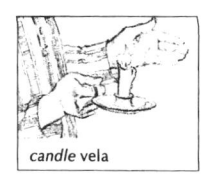

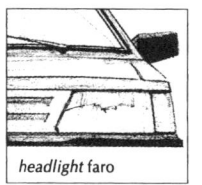

candle vela	*bulb* bombilla

table lamp lámpara de mesa	*bicycle lamp* faro de bicicleta	*headlight* faro	*torch* (*brit*), *flashlight* (*amer*) linterna

25 Calendar and Seasons Calendario y Estaciones

25.1 Días y semanas

USO

En inglés los días de la semana se escriben con mayúscula. Normalmente se usan con la preposición **on**: p.ej. *We play tennis on Thursdays.* (Jugamos al tenis los jueves.) No se usa la preposición **on** si vienen precedidos de palabras como **next**, **last** o **every**: p.ej. *John phoned last Monday.* (John telefoneó el lunes pasado.)

Monday (*abrev*. **Mon.**) lunes
Tuesday (*abrev*. **Tues.**) martes
Wednesday (*abrev*. **Wed.**) miércoles
Thursday (*abrev*. **Thurs.**) jueves
Friday (*abrev*. **Fri.**) viernes
Saturday (*abrev*. **Sat.**) sábado
Sunday (*abrev*. **Sun.**) domingo

day *sn* día *I go there every day.* Voy allí cada día. *How many days are you staying for?* ¿Cuántos días se va a quedar?
daily *adj* diario *a daily paper* un (periódico) diario **daily** *adv* a diario
tomorrow *adv & sn* mañana *the day after tomorrow* pasado mañana
yesterday *adv & sn* ayer *the day before yesterday* anteayer
date *sn* fecha *What's the date today?/What's today's date?* ¿A qué día estamos?
date *vt* poner fecha a, fechar *your letter dated March 16th* su carta con fecha del 16 de marzo
week *sn* semana *once a week* una vez por semana **weekly** *adv* semanalmente **weekly** *adj* semanal
weekday *sn* día laborable *They open on weekdays.* Abren entre semana.
weekend *sn* fin de semana *See you at the weekend* (*brit*)/*on the weekend* (*amer*). Hasta el fin de semana.
fortnight *sn* (*brit*) dos semanas

25.2 Meses y estaciones
ver también **L21 *Making arrangements***

spring primavera
summer verano
autumn (*esp. brit*), *fall* (*amer*) otoño
winter invierno

187

INDICE DE PALABRAS EN INGLÉS

tools /tuːlz/ **382.1** ☆
screwdriver /'skruːˌdraɪ·vɚ/ **382.1** ☆
scribble /'skrɪb·l̩/ **369.1**
script /skrɪpt/ **369.3**
scripture /'skrɪp·tʃɚ/ **232.7**
scrounge /skraʊndʒ/ **375.2**
scrub /skrʌb/ **187.2**
scrum /skrʌm/ **389.1** ☆
scrutinize /'skruː·tɪ·naɪz/ **91.3**
scrutiny /'skruː·tɪ·ni/ **91.3**
scuba /'skuː·bə/ **391**
sculpture /'skʌlp·tʃɚ/ **381.5**
sea /siː/ **13.4**
seagull /'siː·gʌl/ **9.2**
seal /siːl/ **10.3**
sealed /siːld/ **331.7**
sealed off **178**
sea lion /'siːˌlaɪən/ **10.3**
seam /siːm/ **381.6**
seaman /'siː·mən/
  war **248.3** □
  ships and boats **312.5**
search /sɜːtʃ/ **94**
seashore /'siːˌʃɔːr/ **13.5**
seaside /'siːˌsaɪd/ **13.5**
season /'siː·zᵊn/ **157.1**
seasoning /'siː·zᵊn·ɪŋ/ **157.1**
seat /siːt/ **308.1**
seat belt /'siːtˌbelt/ **308.1**
seaweed /'siːˌwiːd/
  fish and sea animals **10.1** ☆
  geography and geology **13.6**
secateurs /ˌsek·ə'tɜːz/ **384.1**
secondary modern /ˌsek·ən·dɚ·i ˈmɒd·ən/ **233** □
secondary school /ˌsek·ən·dɚ·iˌskuːl/ **233** □
second class /ˌsek·ənd 'klɑːs/ **340.2**
second-hand /ˌsek·ənd'hænd/ **200.2**
secret /'siː·krət/ **339.1**
secretarial /ˌsek·rə'teə·ri·əl/ **272.2**
secretary /'sek·rə·tᵊr·i/
  organisation **206.1**
  office **272.2**
secretary of state /ˌsek·rə·tə·tᵊr·i əv 'steɪt/ **227** □
section /'sek·ʃən/ **52**
secure /sɪ'kjʊər/ **253**
security /sɪ'kjʊə·rə·ti/ **253**
seduce /sɪ'djuːs/ **432**
seductive /sɪ'dʌk·tɪv/ **432**
see /siː/ **91**
seed /siːd/
  plants **11**
  fruit **152.6**
seek /siːk/ **94**
seem /siːm/ **37**
seemly /'siːm·li/ **420.1**
see-saw /'siːˌsɔː/ **385** ☆
see through **114**
seize /siːz/ **375.1**
seldom /'sel·dəm/ **444.2**
select /sɪ'lekt/ **73**
selection /sɪ'lek·ʃən/ **73**
self-control /ˌself·kən'trəʊl/ **151.3**
self-controlled /ˌself·kən'trəʊld/ **151.3**
selfish /'sel·fɪʃ/ **226**
self-respect /ˌself·rɪ'spekt/ **431**
self-service /ˌself'sɜː·vɪs/ **310**
sell /sel/ **263**
seller /'sel·ɚ/ **263**
sellotape /'sel·əʊ·teɪp/ **294.3**
semester /sɪ'mes·tɚ/ **233** □
semicolon /ˌsem·iˈkəʊ·lən/ **363**
semi-detached /ˌsem·i dɪ'tætʃt/ **174.1** ☆
senate /'sen·ɪt/ **227** □

senator /'sen·ə·tɚ/ **227** □
send /send/ **340.2**
senile /'siːˌnaɪl/ **129.2**
senior /'siː·ni·ɚ/
  old **200.1**
  superior **419**
sensational /sen'seɪ·ʃᵊn·əl/ **257.2**
sense /sents/
  sensible **238**
  meaning **364**
senseless /'sent·sləs/ **241.3**
sensible /'sent·sə·bl̩/ **238**
sensitive /'sent·sɪ·tɪv/ **151.2**
sentence /'sen·tənts/
  legal system **209.4**
  words **362.2**
separate *adj* /'sep·ᵊr·ət/ **295**
separate *v* /'sep·ᵊr·eɪt/
  social customs **195.3**
  separate **295**
September /sep'tem·bɚ/ **25.2**
Serbo-Croat /ˌsɜː·bəʊ'krəʊ·æt/ **361.1**
sergeant /'sɑː·dʒᵊnt/ **248.3** □
serial /'sɪə·ri·əl/ **378.1**
series /'sɪə·riːz/ **378.1**
serious /'sɪə·ri·əs/
  important **74**
  sensible **238.1**
  sad **447.2**
seriously /'sɪə·ri·ə·sli/
  important **74**
  sensible **238.1**
sermon /'sɜː·mən/ **232.6**
serrated /sɪ'reɪ·tɪd/ **61**
servant /'sɜː·vᵊnt/ **274.5**
serve /sɜːv/ **389.5**
service /'sɜː·vɪs/
  religion **232.6**
  ball sports **389.5**
service line /'sɜː·vɪsˌlaɪn/ **389.5** ☆
serving dish /'sɜː·vɪŋˌdɪʃ/ **170** ☆
set /set/
  put **289**
  ready **328**
  ball sports **389.5**
set down **289**
set off **32**
setsquare /'setˌskweɚ/ **297** ☆
settee /set'iː/ **180** ☆
setting /'set·ɪŋ/
  areas **14.2**
  put **289**
settle /'set·l̩/ **175.1**
settle for **73**
settlement /'set·l̩·mənt/ **175.1**
settler /'set·lɚ/ **175.1**
set up **293.2**
severe /sɪ'vɪər/ **229**
sew /səʊ/ **381.6**
sewing machine /'səʊ·ɪŋ məˌʃiːn/ **381.6** ☆
sex /seks/ **199**
sexism /'sek·sɪ·zᵊm/ **212**
sexual /'sek·ʃʊəl/ **199**
sexual intercourse /ˌsek·ʃʊəl 'ɪn·tə·kɔːs/ **199.2**
sexuality /ˌsek·ʃu'æl·ə·ti/ **199**
sexy /'sek·si/ **199.1**
shade /ʃeɪd/ **23**
shadow /'ʃæd·əʊ/
  dark **23**
  follow **409.2**
shadowy /'ʃæd·əʊ·i/ **23**
shady /'ʃeɪ·di/ **214**
shake /ʃeɪk/ **255.3**
shake hands **196**
shallow /'ʃæl·əʊ/ **40** ☆

shame /ʃeɪm/ **449**
shameful /'ʃeɪm·fᵊl/ **449**
shampoo /ʃæm'puː/ **184.2**
shandy /'ʃæn·di/ **166.5**
shape *n* /ʃeɪp/ **38**
shape *v* /ʃeɪp/ **39**
shapeless /'ʃeɪp·ləs/ **38.5**
share /ʃeɚ/
  finance **264.3**
  give **372.3**
shark /ʃɑːk/ **10.1**
sharp /ʃɑːp/
  cut **133.5**
  flavours **157.5**
  on time **327**
  music **379.8** ☆
shattered /'ʃæt·əd/ **182.3**
shaver /'ʃeɪ·vɚ/ **184.4**
shawl /ʃɔːl/ **192.2**
shear /ʃɪɚ/ **173.7**
shears /ʃɪəz/ **384.1**
shed /ʃed/ **174.5**
sheep /ʃiːp/
  wild animals **1.1** □
  farm animals **6**
sheet /ʃiːt/ **181.1**
shekel /'ʃek·l̩/ **265.1** □
shelf /ʃelf/ **180** ☆
shell /ʃel/
  fish and sea animals **10.2** ☆
  war **248.4**
shellfish /'ʃel·fɪʃ/ **10.2**
shelter /'ʃel·tɚ/ **254**
shepherd /'ʃep·əd/ **173.7**
sherry /'ʃer·i/ **166.6**
shield /ʃiːld/ **254**
shift /ʃɪft/ **411.1**
shimmer /'ʃɪm·ɚ/ **24.3**
shin /ʃɪn/ **86**
shine /ʃaɪn/ **24.2**
ship /ʃɪp/ **312**
shipbuilder /'ʃɪpˌbɪl·dɚ/ **312.5**
shipbuilding /'ʃɪpˌbɪl·dɪŋ/ **312.5**
shipwreck /'ʃɪp·rek/ **312.6**
shipyard /'ʃɪp·jɑːd/ **312.5**
shirk /ʃɜːk/ **324**
shirt /ʃɜːt/ **190.4**
shit /ʃɪt/ **102**
shiver /'ʃɪv·ɚ/ **19**
shock /ʃɒk/ **118.1**
shoddy /'ʃɒd·i/ **438**
shoe /ʃuː/ **191**
shoebrush /'ʃuːˌbrʌʃ/ **191** ☆
shoelace /'ʃuːˌleɪs/ **191** ☆
shoe polish /'ʃuːˌpɒl·ɪʃ/ **191** ☆
shoot /ʃuːt/
  kill **198.1**
  war **248.4**
shooting /'ʃuː·tɪŋ/ **394**
shop /ʃɒp/ **273**
shop assistant /'ʃɒp əˌsɪs·tᵊnt/ **273** ☆
shopkeeper /'ʃɒpˌkiː·pɚ/ **273** ☆
shoplifter /'ʃɒpˌlɪf·tɚ/ **220.1**
shopping /'ʃɒp·ɪŋ/ **273**
shopping centre /'ʃɒp·ɪŋ sent·ɚ/ **273**
shopping trolley /'ʃɒp·ɪŋ trɒl·i/ **273** ☆
shore /ʃɔːr/ **13.5**
short /ʃɔːt/ **44.1**
shorten /'ʃɔː·tᵊn/ **47**
shortly /'ʃɔːt·li/ **329**
shorts /ʃɔːts/ **190.3**
shortsighted /ˌʃɔːt'saɪ·tɪd/ **124.4**
shot /ʃɒt/
  cures **126.3**
  athletics **390.2**
shoulder /'ʃəʊl·dɚ/ **86**
shoulder blade /'ʃəʊl·də ˌbleɪd/

188

Appendix 2
One-page display of the main features of the *Longman Language Activator*

FINISH/USE ALL OF STH   503   **FIRE**

1 to use all of something so that there is none left
- finish
- use up
- exhaust
- run out of

finish /ˈfɪnɪʃ/ to eat or drink all of something so that there is none left [v T]
The kids have finished the ice-cream. | Terry finished all his drink in one gulp. | Don't open a new bottle until you've finished the old one.

use up /ˌjuːz ˈʌp/ to use all of something, especially something important such as a supply of food or money, and to have very little chance of getting any more [phr v T]
use up sth Some old people are left with a choice between using up the last of their fuel or freezing to death. | They've used up all their assets – now nothing can save them from bankruptcy. | **use sth/it/them up** "I wanted some of that green paint." "Too bad, I've used it all up."

exhaust /ɪɡˈzɔːst/ to use all of something, especially a natural supply of something such as coal, oil, or gas [v T]
There is the danger that, in time, the human race will exhaust the world's store of useful energy. | Over-intensive farming had exhausted the supply of nutrients in the soil. | After exhausting all her ready excuses, she could think of nothing left to say.

run out of /ˌrʌn ˈaʊt ɒv || -ɑːv/ to use all of something that you want or need so that you have to get some more [v T not in passive]
By the time they got to the camp they'd run out of water. | I've run out of cigarettes. Do you think you could go down to the store and get some?

2 ways of saying that all of something has been used so that there is none left
- be finished
- exhausted
- be used up
- be all gone
- none left/not any left
- run out

be finished /biː ˈfɪnɪʃt/ having used all of a supply of something, especially food [v phrase]
In this area, emergency food aid is likely to be finished within days. | When that can's finished, there won't be any fuel left. | Are all the vegetables finished yet?

exhausted /ɪɡˈzɔːstɪd/ a supply of something, or a place that produces something, that is **exhausted** is one in which all the materials, etc have been used so that there is nothing left [adj]
The oxygen supply would soon become exhausted. | All that's left are some barren hillsides and a couple of exhausted mines. | It's only a matter of time before the world's oil supplies are exhausted.

be used up /biː ˌjuːzd ˈʌp/ a supply of something, especially something important, that **is used up** has all been used [v phrase]
The logs are all used up – we don't have anything to make a fire with. | When the fertile elements in the soil are used up, the land becomes incapable of producing anything.

be all gone /biː ˌɔːl ˈɡɒn || -ˈɡɔːn/ an informal expression: if something **is all gone**, there is none of it left because it has all been used [v phrase]
My money's all gone. How the hell can I pay for anything? | "Are there any cookies left?" "No, they're all gone."

none left/not any left /ˌnʌn ˈleft, ˌnɒt eni ˈleft/ if there is **none left** or **not any left** of something, all of it has been used or sold [adj phrase]
There is none left/there are none left Don't eat any more cake or there will be none left for me. | **there isn't any left/ there aren't any left** I'm sorry but there aren't any dresses left in a size 12. | **there is no wine/milk etc left** There's no coffee left. Shall I go and get some more?

run out /ˌrʌn ˈaʊt/ if something, especially something you regularly need or use, **runs out**, all of it has ben used [phr v I]
Our supplies had run out and all we could do was wait. | If coal reserves run out, the situation will become critical. | It was a dreadful party: first the vodka ran out, then the beer, then the CD player packed up.

3 to not use all of something
- not finish
- leave

not finish /ˌnɒt ˈfɪnɪʃ/ [v T]
No you can't have another notepad – you haven't finished that one yet. | Try not to finish your food rations too quickly. We don't know when there will be more.

leave /liːv/ to not use or eat all of something, especially because you do not want to, or because you want to keep some [v T]
leave sth I think Tom may be sick – he left nearly all his dinner. | **leave sth for sb** They didn't use all the fuel supplies – they left some for us. | **leave sb sth** Move up, you lot. Leave me some space!

4 words for describing something that is never all used
- inexhaustible

inexhaustible /ˌɪnɪɡˈzɔːstɪbəl/ **inexhaustible supply/ source/list etc** (=one that is never finished because it is so big) [adj]
The enemy seemed to have an inexhaustible supply of ammunition. | I regarded my father as an inexhaustible source of cash and good will. | The list was inexhaustible.

finished   FINISH DOING STH **9**
finished: be finished   FINISH/USE ALL OF STH **2**
finishing touch: put the finishing touch/touches to   FINISH DOING STH **2**
finite   LIMIT **7**
fire   FIRE **1**, **2**, **3**, LEAVE A JOB OR ORGANIZATION **2**, SHOOT **2**
fire: be on fire   BURN **1**
fire: be playing with fire   RISK **5**
fire: catch fire   BURN **3**
fire: make/build a fire   FIRE **4**
fire: set fire to sth/set sth on fire   BURN **4**
fire: there's no smoke without fire   TRUE **5**
fire: under fire   SHOOT **5**
fire/fire up   ENTHUSIASTIC **4**
fire questions: ask questions/fire questions at sb   ASK A QUESTION **3**
fire risk: be a fire risk/health risk   DANGEROUS **2**

fire
which meaning?

fire, flames etc	● **FIRE**
make something burn	● **BURN**
make someone leave their job	● **LEAVE A JOB OR ORGANIZATION**

● FIRE

1 an uncontrolled fire that has started accidentally
2 a fire that someone has made in order to keep warm, cook on etc
3 the heat and light produced by something that is burning
4 to make a fire

Appendix 3
A one-page display of the main features of the *Oxford Learner's Wordfinder* Dictionary

- wanting sth to happen ⇨ HOPE
- thinking that sth is likely to happen ⇨ POSSIBLE¹

expensive ⇨ PRICE

experience
- things that you have done ⇨ ACTION
- a way of learning ⇨ LEARN
- work that you have done ⇨ WORK

experiment
- science and research ⇨ SCIENCE, STUDY
- trying sth ⇨ TRY

explain ⇨ UNDERSTAND

explore ⇨ TRAVEL

export ⇨ BUSINESS

extremely ⇨ FAIRLY/VERY

eye
> other parts of the head ⇨ HEAD
> see also SEE

- one of the two parts of the body that you use to see with: **eye** ○ *She opened/closed her eyes.* ○ *I've got brown eyes.*
▷ picture at FACE
- the whole of the eye, including the part which is hidden inside your head: **eyeball**
- the coloured part of the eye: **iris**
- the round black hole in the middle of the eye: **pupil**
- the piece of skin that can move to cover the eye: **eyelid**
- one of the hairs that grow on your eyelids: **eyelash**
- the part at the back of the eyeball that is sensitive to light: **retina**
- the colour of a person's eyes can be **blue**, **green**, **brown**, **grey**, **hazel** (= light brown) ○ *a girl with blue eyes* ○ *green-eyed*
- unable to see: **blind**; *noun* (U): **blindness** ○ *He is blind in one eye.*
- if your eyes do not move together properly, you have a **squint**
- the thing that people wear to help them see more clearly: **glasses** (*AmE* **eyeglasses**) (*noun plural*) ○ *to wear glasses* ○ *a new pair of glasses*
▷ other problems in seeing ⇨ SEE
▷ more on glasses ⇨ GLASSES

- to shut your eyes and open them again very quickly: **blink** ○ *She blinked as he took the photograph.*
- to close and open one eye quickly, usually as a signal to sb: **wink** (**at** sb); an act of winking: **wink** ○ *My friend winked at me across the room.* ○ *He gave her a big wink.*
- to look at sth with your eyes almost closed: **squint** (**at** sb/sth) ○ *to squint in bright sunlight*

- a drop of water that comes from your eyes when you are crying: **tear** ○ *She had tears in her eyes.*
- if your eyes fill with liquid, they **water** ○ *Peeling onions makes my eyes water.*
- if you feel a sudden sharp pain in your eyes, they **sting*** ○ *Soap makes your eyes sting.*

■ MORE . . .
- if sb hits you on the eye, you may get a **black eye** (= a dark mark around the eye)

- a piece of material that you wear over one eye: **patch** ○ *He had a patch over his eye.*
- to cover a person's eyes with a piece of cloth, etc, so that they cannot see: **blindfold** sb; the piece of cloth is called a **blindfold** ○ *The prisoner was blindfolded.*

face

1 parts of the face
2 the appearance of the face
3 facial expressions
other parts of the head ⇨ HEAD
see also BEAUTIFUL/ATTRACTIVE, COSMETICS

1 parts of the face

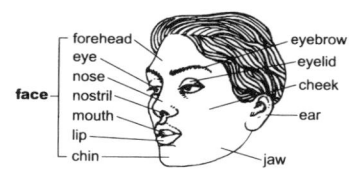

forehead — eyebrow
eye — eyelid
face — nose — cheek
nostril
mouth — ear
lip
chin — jaw

▷ more on eyes ⇨ EYE
▷ more on noses ⇨ NOSE
▷ more on mouths ⇨ MOUTH
▷ more on ears ⇨ EAR

- the front part of your head: **face**; *adjective*: **facial**
- a part of the face, for example the mouth or the nose: **feature** ○ *strong/handsome features*
- a small round hollow on your chin, cheek, etc that is often only seen when you smile: **dimple** ○ *She has a very attractive dimple on her left cheek.*

2 the appearance of the face

- a person's appearance in general: **looks** (*noun plural*) ○ *He has good looks and intelligence.*
- the natural colour and quality of the skin on your face: **complexion** ○ *a healthy complexion*
▷ the appearance of the skin ⇨ SKIN

- the hair which grows on a man's cheeks and chin: **beard**
- if a man does not have any hair on his face, he is **clean-shaven**
▷ beards and other hair on the face ⇨ HAIR

190

15

Culture-bound and trapped by technology: centuries of bias in the making of wordbooks

[A paper commissioned for and published in *Cultures, Ideologies, and the Dictionary: Studies in Honor of Ladislav Zgusta*, edited by Braj B. Kachru and Henry Kahane, in the Lexicographica Series Maior 65, Tübingen, Niemeyer, 1995.]

When biologists look at cells under a microscope they do not usually think about *cell*, a word that serves them as impartially as it serves monks, convicts and electricians. Most of the time, for most people, a cell is a cell is a cell, whether on a slide, or in a cloister, penitentiary or battery. The three nouns in the title of this book are similarly obvious in meaning yet variable in application. The phrase *Culture, ideology and the dictionary* clearly indicates that some scholars have written about the relationships between a particular kind of reference book and behaviour, politics, beliefs, bias, propaganda and so forth, but it achieves this brief clarity at a price: polysemy affects (or infects?) these words as much as it affects *cell*, but is not so easily resolved. Whereas the contexts of biology, religion, penal establishments, and electricity only occasionally overlap, the multivalences in *culture*, *ideology*, and *dictionary* occur within the very bounds of lexicographical scholarship itself. For that reason I will look at these terms one by one before using them to make some points about historical biases that have influenced several genres of lexical reference.

Culture

The word *culture* originates in Latin *cultura*, whose core sense is 'tilling the soil'. Most current uses have kept something of that ancient sense: in *agriculture* and *bee culture* the link is clear, in *tissue culture* it is still detectable, and in *physical culture* and *a cultured way of speaking* the metaphorical tie between kinds of training and preparing the ground for seed can still be found. To this last sense, however, a second metaphor has been added, in terms of which people assess such matters as training, activity and status as 'higher' or 'lower' on various social and aesthetic scales. Finally, close to this 'social-judgement' use but far from tilling the soil is the 'anthropological' sense in such phrases as *classical Greek culture* and *twentieth-century Western culture*. This last appears to be the sense intended in the title.

It is not easy, however, to separate this 'anthropological' sense, which addresses in a highly abstract way a major aspect of the human condition, from the 'social-judgement' sense, which (often emotively) identifies something one has or lacks, as one has or lacks charm, good looks or money. Typically of polysemic relations, the two senses are not walled off from each other, but are rather fuzzy points on the same continuum. Tension between them is commonplace, including in the making, selling and use of dictionaries.

Although, in recent years at least, dictionary compilers have tried to be neutral and objective when preparing entries, their publishers often exploit social insecurity to promote sales, using subtexts like 'Cultured people own dictionaries—the rest don't'. Lexicographers commonly agree that one should *describe* words and usages, not *prescribe* some and *proscribe* others, but many users of dictionaries see things differently: they want help and reassurance on the 'proper' uses of words. The tension between what lexicographers do and what many people think they do (or ought to do) can be considerable, as witness the furore over the philosophy, style and content of *Webster's Third International Dictionary* in the early 1960s (cf. Sledd and Ebbitt, 1962). In the remoter past, before the anthropological approach to culture and society emerged, there were few such problems. In Johnson's and Webster's day, for example, the degree of psychological fit between makers and users of dictionaries was close: they all knew they were concerned with maintaining the lexical proprieties of 'high' national cultures: one in the Old World, one in the New.

The anthropological sense covers ways of living, behaving and thinking that communities build up and pass on, including art, artefacts, rituals, customs, ideas, beliefs, and values. To study such matters calls for a certain 'distance' from what is studied (another spatial metaphor), but the concept of such a distance is itself culture-bound, and nurtured among people who, by virtue of their training, activity, and status, are already high on the social list (whether they like such an idea or not). The social-judgement sense relates to artistic, intellectual, and linguistic activity, aesthetic refinement, educational attainment, and attitudes about good and bad and right and wrong in such matters. Anthropological *culture* is supposed to describe and explain the workings of social-judgement *culture*, but not (nowadays at least) to aid and abet them. Academics are not supposed to be socially and culturally biased in their work, although we know that they have been and sometimes still are biased (often despite their best intentions). We may suspect that things will never be otherwise; experience—both commonsensical and scholarly—suggests that no one has ever existed outside a sociocultural matrix that shapes behaviour and thought, or ever could.

The shift that has taken most scholars away from the social-judgement approach towards the anthropological approach (in their professional lives at least) belongs to the nineteenth and particularly the twentieth centuries. It was slow and patchy in developing, has occurred at different speeds for different people and disciplines, has not occurred at all, or to any great extent, for many people (including some scholars), and has no guarantee of permanency. It is, by and large, an aspect of the powerful social bias inherent in the 'scientific method' itself, and could in due course give way to something else.

Ideology

The term *ideology* is an infant compared with *culture*, dating back no further than the French Revolution. In 1796, the philosopher-count A.-L.-C. Destutt de Tracy coined *idéologie* to name a 'science of ideas' in which knowledge is seen as deriving from the senses alone (making this study very different from metaphysics). In his view, the application of ideology to society at large could strengthen reason, education, democracy and the egalitarian aims of the Revolution. Napoleon at first approved of the policies of the *idéologistes*, but later blamed them for the Republic's defeats in battle. He applied the term contemptuously to the confused and confusing politics of the late 1890s, scorning de Tracy and his colleagues as impractical *idéologues*. The term has often been used pejoratively since then.

A split has also subsequently developed in the way the term is used, leading to what may be called its *modernist* and *universalist* senses. The modernist sense retains de Tracy's revolutionary credo, and refers to any 'system of ideas that aspires both to explain the world and to change it' (Cranston, 1986). Such an ideology, as the *Oxford English Dictionary* puts it, is 'regarded as justifying actions', is 'held implicitly or adopted as a whole', and is 'maintained regardless of the course of events' (1989). Such ideology dates from the Enlightenment, and cannot include any sociopolitical system from before that time (whether defunct or on-going) or any that comes from beyond Europe and its diaspora. The evolution of the modernist sense has been complex (as in the writings of Hegel, Marx, Weber, Camus, Popper, and Sartre), and it usually refers to consciously contrived totalitarian secular systems such as Fascism and Communism.

During this century, however, a universalist sense has emerged that covers any sociopolitical system whatever, modern or ancient, defunct or on-going, European or other. Islam and Hinduism may therefore have ideological aspects insofar as Muslims or Hindus engage in sociopolitical theory-building and in kinds of mental and social control. Their ideologies may derive as freely from and interact as freely with their worldviews, hierarchies and canons as any in Europe and its diasporas. In this sense, ideology need not be consciously contrived, totalitarian, secular, or even coherent. This *may* be the sense intended in the title of this book, but is not the only sense that could emerge in it. A writer might, for example, in a 'classically' modernist sense, discuss only the nature and use of dictionaries in, for example, Fascist Italy, Nazi Germany, or the Soviet Union.

My own preference is for the broader terms *belief system* and *idea system*. Although they overlap (both relating to worldviews, hierarchies, canons, doctrines, laws, propaganda, publications, media, and the like), they usefully cover conditions that develop organically in whole communities rather than as the intellectual exercises of a self-selected élite (who may well develop specific ideologies within them). Partly ordered and variably coherent, such systems are not by nature 'well-edited'. To say that someone is *Christian* is not usually enough; the complexity of Christian culture demands that we find out more, even if it is never quite enough. To talk about an *archetype* needs more than a knowledge of Carl Gustav Jung; the term has resonances beyond analytical psychology. Because many people feel the need to understand belief and idea systems more fully, describing them attracts the de Tracys of this world— ideologists who, for their own reasons or as servants of particular masters, seek to impose greater rigour and direction on them than they traditionally possess or even need.

The Japanese generally practice Shinto but are not usually comfortable describing it. The compiler of a dictionary of Shinto terms or an encyclopedia of Shintoism might therefore need to define the word or edit the subject into a sharper focus than it has usually needed. Achieving *new* clarity of this kind may well be a prime function of works of reference; if so, such an aim and undertaking are ideological in the sense that they are intended to influence how people perceive certain things (and perhaps also how they then behave in relation to them). Traditional belief and idea systems are closer to Shinto than to Communism; they are likely to influence reference materials only in implicit and indirect ways, and are probably too large and diffuse to be significantly shaped by them in return. In this, they are not like the regimes that Orwell had in mind when he described the 'Newspeak Dictionary'. In *Nineteen Eighty-Four* (1949), both the modernist view of ideology and the craft of lexicography are at their most bleak.

The dictionary

Although the term *dictionary* almost archetypally refers to books about words, books about words such as *Roget's Thesaurus* differ greatly from the dictionary 'properly so called'. In addition, some works of reference not concerned with words are called dictionaries, as for example the *Oxford Dictionary of Natural History*, which is an encyclopedia, and the *Oxford Dictionary of Quotations*, which is an anthology. There are also works that have all or many of the features of dictionaries, yet lack the name: for example, the *Longman Guide to English Usage*, which competes with Fowler's *Dictionary of Modern English Usage* (Oxford). However, the feature usually regarded as crucial to the term *dictionary* is A-to-Z ordering, and as a result the phrases *alphabetical order* and *dictionary order* are synonymous.

The source of the above disparities lies in the Middle Ages, when the Latin terms *dictionarium* and *dictionarius* came into vogue. There were, however, no firm conventions about how books about *dictiones* ('words', 'phrases', 'sayings') should be shaped and named. Indeed, a variety of names arose, in Latin and in its vernacular adaptations. They include: *abecedarium* (English *abecedary, absee*) 'ABC book'; *alvearium* (English *alveary*) 'beehive'; *glossarium* (English *glossary*) 'collection of glosses'; *hortus* 'garden'; *lexicon* 'wordbook' in Greek; *liber floridus* 'flowery book'; *manipulus* (English *maniple*) 'handful'; *medulla* 'kernel', 'marrow';

promptuarium, promptorium (English *promptuary*) 'storehouse'; *thesaurus* 'treasury', 'storehouse'; *vocabularium* (English *vocabulary*) 'wordbook' in Latin; *vulgaria* (English *vulgary*) 'book of common things'. Neither compilers nor publishers have ever systematized the use of these terms, and the terms that survive mark the age-old veneration of a 'golden age' of Latinate culture in terms of which later Europeans have tended to see themselves as dependent and derivative.

In English, the slowly decaying preference for high and ancient names survives in attitudes to *wordbook*, a humble Anglo-Saxon term that, some years ago, I pressed into service as a superordinate for *dictionary* and *thesaurus*. I have from time to time been asked—especially by German-speakers (thinking of *Wörterbuch*, which translates *dictionary*)—whether this is in fact a 'proper' word of English. It seems proper enough to me, and is indeed defined in 'the dictionary', but I recognise that for many people, including some lexicographers, it is problematical. In the eighteenth century, Lord Chesterfield disdained it, and he was widely held in high esteem—though latterly not by Johnson. Chesterfield wrote in a letter to *The World* (1754), the year before Johnson's Dictionary appeared: 'I cannot but think it a sort of disgrace to our nation, that hitherto we have had no such standard of our language (as the French); our dictionaries at present being more properly what our neighbours the Dutch and Germans call theirs, WORD-BOOKS, than dictionaries in the superior sense of that title'. That superiority has been considerable.

Alphabetic bias

I am assuming here that all alphabetically ordered wordbooks, whether called dictionaries or not, are covered by the title of this book. I am not so sure about alphabetically-ordered books that, though called dictionaries, function as encyclopedias, anthologies, and the like. And I am even less sure about wordbooks that are not organized alphabetically and not normally called dictionaries: especially those with thematic formats, such as *Roget's Thesaurus* (1852), the *Longman Lexicon of Contemporary English* (1981), *What's What: A Visual Glossary of the Physical World* (1981) and the *Random House Word Menu* (1992).

Such works inhabit a lexicographical closet, from which they are only occasionally let into the front room. Clearly not dictionaries 'as such', they get some recognition because they are more like dictionaries than they are like anything else. Jackson (1988:216) refers to the traditional *Roget* and similar works as 'non-alphabetical dictionaries', a usage that (though its intent is clear in his context) only points up the confusion:

Roget is widely cited as the polar opposite of a dictionary. One can only conclude from this that *dictionary* has two virtually antithetical senses: a narrow, 'proper' sense ('book that defines words in alphabetically ordered entries') and a broad, very 'loose' sense ('book that may or may not define words, may or may not be called a dictionary, or may or may not have alphabetically ordered entries containing definitions').

Such an odd state of affairs is unlikely to be accidental. For most of recorded history and in most literate cultures, thematic order (also called *topical* and *classified order*) has been the norm. It was dominant throughout the Middle Ages in Europe, when the term *dictionary* did not imply any specific genre or format. Alphabetic order at that time was largely confined to glossaries of hard words culled from Latin manuscripts, used in training young readers of Latin (Matoré, 1968; Mathews, 1933; McArthur, 1986; Read, 1976; Whitehall, 1971). Otherwise the format was little used and had no prestige. During this period, the compiler's aim was to fit the *omne scibile* ('everything that can be known') into one circle of topics; as a result, most literate medieval Christians appear to have considered the scattering of nuggets of knowledge from A to Z as irrelevant and perhaps even perverse (McArthur, 1986: 50–80).

After the development of movable type in fifteenth-century Europe, however, printers and writers grew used to lifting metal letters out of trays organized alphabetically, putting them in lines of type, then putting them back in the trays till needed again. This novel manipulation of metal, which soon became routine, appears to have made it easier for producers of printed books to think about using the ABC ordering developed centuries earlier for tutorial purposes. The alphabetic arrangement of concordances, indexes and dictionaries, now technically easy, became socially valuable as Latin grew less and less of a lingua franca for Europe and people began to need ever more help with it and other languages, such as Italian, French and English, whose social status was steadily rising. As more and more dictionaries were prepared for such new vehicles of knowledge, their prestige rose too.

During the sixteenth and seventeenth centuries, thematic and alphabetic formats were common in works of reference, but in the seventeenth century the alphabetic began to outnumber the thematic (despite even the great success of John Amos Comenius with the *Ianua linguarum reserata* in 1631 and the *Orbis sensualium pictus* in 1657). In the eighteenth century, A-to-Z dictionaries (now very much 'properly so called') served as models for novel non-lexical works to which the name 'encyclopaedia' was given (making them for the first time also 'properly so called'). Although thematic lexical and encyclopedic reference books have continued to be produced into this century, alphabetic order had by 1750 become the format of preference with publishers, printers, compilers and the public alike. What had been a minor feature of scribal culture became a major feature of print culture.

A further social factor seems likely to have helped in this development, beginning in the puritanical individualism of the Reformation and strengthened by the rationalism of the sixteenth century and the distrust of social and religious élites that emerged in the eighteenth century. The French exile Pierre Bayle, for example, compiled in the Netherlands a *Dictionnaire historique et critique* (1696), in which he avoided the use of any hierarchical structures, describing the result with satisfaction as 'a shapeless compilation of passages all stitched to each others' tails' (my translation: cf. Matoré 1968:97). In England, Ephraim Chambers set the standard for vast and 'shapeless' alphabetic egalitarianism in his *Cyclopedfia* (1728), Denis Diderot followed with his *Encyclopédie* (35 volumes: 1751–80), and a 'Society of Gentlemen' in Scotland reinforced it with the *Encyclopaedia Britannica* (3 volumes: 1768–71). With their stitched-up head-to-tail entries, all three celebrated the liberation of thought, setting the style for dozens of scholarly and popular works that would be published in the nineteenth century for the newly literate masses.

Thematic bias

In 1972, I undertook a year of lexicographical research for Longman, to see whether a new kind of reference book for foreign learners of English could be developed from recent descriptions of structural semantics (Lyons, 1968; Tyler, 1969). When I began this work, neither the Longman executives and their advisers nor I had any idea what would emerge from it. However, Longman had published the most famous thematic wordbook in English, *Roget's Thesaurus*, and made a great deal of money from it, and so the company may have been more open to unconventional lexical adventures than most other publishers at the time.

After two years of research I was asked to produce something often called for convenience 'a semantic dictionary'. The result, the *Longman Lexicon of Contemporary English* (1981), was far more like *Roget* than like the *Longman Dictionary of Contemporary English* (*LDOCE*) (1978), an A-to-Z work compiled at much the same time. The *Lexicon* has been a success (going through thirty impressions to 1993), but not on the scale of *LDOCE*, the flagship of Longman's EFL reference programme. Many EFL/ESL teachers, reviewers, students, and others have had difficulty assessing the *Lexicon*, whose words are defined and exemplified in hundreds of sets within fourteen semantic fields, with an additional network of cross-references. For them, a single A-to-Z list has had the advantages of both familiarity and a one-step process of consultation (factors that, for most purposes, are hard to beat). In addition, the idea of learning several words at a time in associated groups, especially if this means two or more steps to get started, has been rather novel and not universally attractive. It presupposes a concentrated effort rather than a quick in-and-out service.

The *Lexicon* received few detailed early reviews, taking seven years or so to attract the attention of scholars (cf. Jackson 1988:219–23; Lipka 1992:38–9, 157–9, 175–81), whereas learners' dictionaries have for several decades been subject to intense study by applied linguists and others. There may be two further reasons for this: first, that the *Lexicon* is an event and not a genre, and needed time to gain institutional status; second, that it was out of cultural phase. That it is now much more in phase is due to a development that could hardly have been predicted: the worldwide technological and social change that took place after 1977, when Apple introduced the desktop computer. By the time the *Lexicon* was six years old personal computers were ten years old and used by millions, in the process changing the habits and assumptions of those millions. Among other things, such people have learned that desktop computers do not need alphabetic order to access information quickly, and that the software offers quite different techniques for searching out and displaying information.

There is an unintentionally ironic reference to the topicality of the *Lexicon* in Landau's *Dictionaries: The Art and Craft of Lexicography*. In the section 'Current Computer Uses in Lexicography', he describes it as a 'work produced automatically from a database . . . important evidence that computers can be used to produce substantially new language reference books if the database has been carefully prepared' (1984:273–4). No computers or database, however, carefully prepared or otherwise, were used in compiling the *Lexicon*, which was produced with paper, pencil, pen and typewriter, although electronic equipment was used in-house at about the same time for *LDOCE*. To this day I do not have a copy of the *Lexicon* on disk, a situation that indefinitely delays a second edition and prevents fuller experimentation with the format.

Many computer techniques, highly innovative in the ways in which they are used, may yet be as old as the pyramids: PCs benefit from a layered inheritance of communicative styles. For example, while the keyboard is relatively recent and derives from the typewriter (a nineteenth-century miniaturization and personalization of printing), scrolling goes back through the medieval parchment to rolls of ancient Egyptian papyrus wrapped round spindles. The icon is linked less to the paintings of Orthodox Christianity than to the ideograms of Chinese and, more fundamentally, the cuneiform of ancient Mesopotamia and the hieroglyphs of Egypt. Menu-driven procedures for specifying and locating services and data, though they sound new and suggest restaurants rather than libraries, are grand-children of the hierarchies that Bayle and Diderot avoided but Francis Bacon and John Comenius greatly favoured. Hypertext in its turn is a maze-like cousin of all the devices deriving from hands and signposts that cross-refer from one text to another in one or many documents.

In the electronic culture of the late twentieth century people are acclimatizing quickly to thematic order and complex cross-referencing. In the process, these devices are losing their low peripheral status and in tandem with the PC are gaining high cultural value. In effect, the pendulum is swinging back again from an era in which alphabetic order, losing its low peripheral status in scribal culture, attained high central status in print culture. The changes are already considerable, even though electronic culture is only just beginning. It is already common for publishers to spin off works in diverse formats (printed or otherwise) from one database, to blend elements from two or more databases to produce a single hybrid product of whatever format makes more sense, to convert an existing work in one format into a companion work in the other, or even so to design a database that works of various kinds in various formats can be efficiently projected from it.

Consider, for example, the *Bloomsbury Dictionary of Quotations* (1987), a work modelled on long-established 'proper' dictionaries of quotations, which was followed a year later by the *Bloomsbury Thematic Dictionary of Quotations* (1988), whose name speaks for itself. Consider also the *Collins Dictionary and Thesaurus in One Volume* (1987), which combines elements of the *Collins Dictionary of the English Language* (2nd edition, 1986) and the *New Collins Thesaurus* (1984). In such developments, a balance appears to have been struck—for the first time ever—between the two great moulds for reference materials, initiating a considerable change in the culture and ideology of dictionaries, whether they are properly or improperly so called.

16

Guides to tomorrow's English: dictionaries for a universal language

[An elaboration of a paper given to the Dictionary Research Group of the Japanese Association of College Teachers of English (JACET), at Waseda University, Tokyo, 26 August 1997, published in *English Today* 55, July 1998.]

In order to talk about tomorrow's English, and the works of reference that could serve it, I would like first of all to say something about yesterday's English and today's English, and the works of reference associated with *them*. Having done that, I will try to project some lines forward into the early twenty-first century, despite the awful risks of futurology. Some things can, I believe, be usefully said towards the end of the 1990s.

Yesterday's English

My first point is that 'yesterday's English' is not really so long ago. Conventionally, the beginnings of the English language are dated from the arrival of the Angles and Saxons in the island of Britain 1,500 years ago. However, the dialect complex at that time (much later referred to as 'Old English' and 'Anglo-Saxon') was utterly remote from today's usage, and its life cycle ended in the twelfth century. It was in fact a predecessor language, as distinct from English as we now know it as Latin is from French.

The dialect complex that followed Anglo-Saxon—and continued till around 1500—was later called Middle English, and was hardly the same language as what preceded it or what followed. It also had its own detectable life cycle, and is most notably the outcome of hybridization between an indigenized French and a Scandinavianized Anglo-Saxon. The dividing line between *that* deeply diverse complex and the English I wish to discuss here was a cluster of developments that included the Great Vowel Shift, the development of a print culture, the stabilization of orthography under the influence of that culture, and the emergence in the sixteenth century of a high cultural variety based on the dialect(s) of London and influenced by the written usage of the Chancery (the Lord Chancellor's court). The term 'Standard English' is often used by present-day scholars to label the high London English which emerged at that time, but this term did not in fact come into use until the later eighteenth century, when it was applied to the 'good' or 'proper' usage of the educated and socially dominant people of that time. This is a variety that we still comfortably understand today, as for example when we read the unadapted novels of Jane Austen.

So, for my purposes here, 'yesterday's English' ran from Elizabethan to earlier Georgian times, and 'today's English' has been running from the early nineteenth century onward: varieties that philologists call 'Early Modern' and 'Modern' English. The lexicography of Early Modern differs from later dictionary-making in being primarily geared to other languages. Thus, in the late sixteenth century there were unidirectional bilingual dictionaries such as William Salesbury's Welsh-to-English compilation of 1547 and John Florio's Italian-to-English compilation of 1599, and in the earlier seventeenth century there were a number of so-called *hard-word dictionaries,* which I would like to call 'crypto-bilingual', because they served to explain the foreignisms that were pouring into English at the time—mainly from Latin—to people who did not want to fall behind the latest linguistic fashion. Such works included the first ever 'proper' English dictionary, Robert Cawdrey's *Table Alphabeticall* (1604), John Bullokar's *The English Expositour* (1623), and Edward Phillips's *The New World of English Words* (1658). The broad procedure with such books was to take an Anglicized foreignism—usually polysyllabic and from Latin—and gloss it in the everyday language (as for example where *acquisition* is defined by Cawdrey as 'getting, purchasing').

One can make a useful comparison between these Early Modern works and genres in Japanese lexicography today: with on the one hand the mainstream unidirectional bilingual English-into-Japanese dictionaries for students and on the other those works that list and define *gairaigo* terms (foreignisms) in Japanese. Such terms are nowadays overwhelmingly drawn from English, as with the abbreviations *sekuhara* (from 'sexual harassment') and *wapuro* (from 'word processor'). The inflow of

Latin into English in Renaissance times can also be compared to the inflow, centuries ago, of Chinese words into Japanese. It would appear therefore that the same kind of lexicographical needs can arise on islands off the shores of continents on opposite sides of the world, but at very different times and with very different realizations.

Today's English

Today's English came into being around 1800, when the stream of standardizing English had already divided between the United Kingdom on the one side and the United States on the other, the latter's usage being consolidated in relative isolation by c.1900. By the end of the nineteenth century, the English language complex had become extremely widespread and influential, the outcome of such forces as sea-borne mercantilism, the Industrial Revolution, the British Empire, and the enlargement of the US, which was in linguistic (and other) terms an extramural extension of that Empire. At about the same time Japan was opening its doors to the world, as a result of which it has from the start been conscious of two national approaches to Standard English and its dictionaries, whereas for example mainland Europe and Africa were in the main conscious of only one, the dominant British variety.

The lexicography of today's English arose equally in both of the Atlantic traditions, the beginnings of each being identified with a single mythologized man: Samuel Johnson in the UK and Noah Webster in the US. But where the Americans have kept the Webster name vigorously and competitively alive, the British have fossilized and virtually forgotten Johnson, except as a wordy and rather pompous eccentric. Most general dictionaries in the nineteenth century, following in the Johnsonian and Websterian traditions, were self-help books more than school books, but a tradition of dictionaries for schools as well as homes established itself at an early stage in the US. There was also a good deal of re-printing and cross-fertilization between the UK and US, but even so rather different kinds of dictionary had emerged by the end of the century in three distinct locations: in England (with the primary focus as time passed on Oxford); in Scotland (characterized in particular by Chambers in Edinburgh as 'publishers for the people'); and in the United States (with its centre of gravity in Springfield, Mass., the home of the G. & C. Merriam company, which promoted books in the main Webster tradition).

Tomorrow's English

Paradoxically, *tomorrow's* English and its dictionaries do not quite belong to the future: rather, they had their beginnings around the Second World War, when some observers were already making statements about English not simply as the language of an ageing worldwide empire and of a vast republic in its prime, but as a language that girdled the world. At least one such commentator, the best-selling educational writer Lancelot Hogben, referred to this linguistic juggernaut not as 'English' at all but as 'Anglo-American', acknowledging in this way a core duality within the international complex (1964:17). Although we talk freely in the 1990s about going 'global', the globalization of English in general and Standard English in particular began decades ago, passing almost unnoticed by lexicographers whose attention was focused on the doings of the UK or the US. And this supranational state of affairs will soon be altogether clear when the world's linguistic demography shows that more non-natives than natives use English with educated success.

Such things were not so easy to see between 1940 and 1970. In that period, the British and the Americans were first of all waging a hot war against a German-speaking European empire then for decades afterwards a cold war against a Russian-speaking Communist empire with a huge Chinese-speaking partner. The first competitor is long gone, the strength of the second is now dissipated, and the global impact of the third as a force in its own right is as yet uncertain. Many international bodies, however, currently use English as a key language (the UN, the EU) or as *the* key language (NATO, CARICOM, ASEAN) in running their affairs. Even speakers of such other world languages as Arabic, Chinese, French, German, Hindi-Urdu, Malay, Portuguese, Russian, Spanish, and Swahili use English extensively, and as a result the rapid growth of a stratum of linguistic universalization is clearer now than ever before—and is proceeding apace. [For details and comment see Crystal, 1997; Graddol, 1997; McArthur, 1998.]

A cardinal development for English lexicography at large was the emergence in the 1930s of dictionaries entirely in English for foreign learners of the standard language. The pioneers who compiled these books were British: pre-eminently Michael West (who did his seminal work in Bengal, in India), A.S. Hornby and his colleagues E.V. Gatenby and H. Wakefield (whose key work was done in Japan), and—importantly but often forgotten—C.K. Ogden (the creator of Basic English, in Cambridge in England).

Hornby was influenced by the lexicological work of Harold E. Palmer at IRET (the Institute for Research in English Teaching) in Tokyo. The dictionary that Hornby and his colleagues produced was published (after they left Japan) by Kaitakusha in 1942, as the *Idiomatic and Syntactic Dictionary of English*. After the war, it travelled to England, where it was re-published by Oxford University Press as *A Learner's Dictionary of Current English* (*LDCE*, 1948), then in a revised edition as the *Advanced Learner's Dictionary of Current English* (*ALDCE*, 1963), and in a further revision and development as the *Oxford Advanced Learner's Dictionary of Current English* (*OALDCE*, 1974), since when there has been a fourth edition in 1989 and a fifth in 1995. Here we see the institutionalization —indeed the Oxfordization—of a book that initially had no link whatever with Oxford University Press, which has not by and large perpetuated the memory of the Japanese connection. In its several incarnations, this work has sold over twenty million copies (a figure far beyond any of its rivals) and has had a vast impact not only on learners' dictionaries at large but also on perceptions of English as an international language. It is the Bible of the genre and the pre-eminent exemplar of the view that one should seek explanations for the words of a target foreign language in that language itself. This view derives from the language-teaching reforms in Europe in the 1880s, and is one with which I have never been entirely comfortable.

I just used the phrase 'English as an international language' (EIL), which is not the same as 'English as a foreign language' (EFL) or 'English as a second language' (ESL). It is wider in its scope than both and fits in with a development which has recently become widely recognized and is now probably irreversible: that everyone who uses English (native or foreign) has to negotiate its standard forms at an international level. Mikie Kiyoi, a Japanese working for an international organization in Paris, writing in the *International Herald Tribune* ('Dear English Speakers: Please Drop the Dialects': 3 November 1995), spoke up for the non-Anglophone world as follows, when she invited native speakers to leave their dialects behind when attending international gatherings:

> I have to live with this unfortunate fate: My native tongue is remote from European languages. Yet I believe I have the right to request that my Anglo-American friends who are involved in international activities not abuse their privilege, even though they do not do so intentionally. First of all I would like them to know that the English they speak at home is not always an internationally acceptable English. Nowadays, non-natives learn English through worldwide media such as CNN or BBC World Service. Whether CNN's

English is a good model is arguable. My point is that most nonnatives do not learn dialects such as Scottish or Australian. . . . I sincerely believe there exists a cosmopolitan English—a lingua franca, written or spoken—that is clearly different from what native English speakers use unconsciously in their daily life. There are also good manners that go along with a cosmopolitan English: not monopolizing the floor, giving equal opportunity to usually silent nonnatives and refraining from interrupting non-natives when they do speak. We non-natives are desperately trying to learn English; each word pronounced by us represents our blood, sweat and tears. Our English proficiency is tangible evidence of our achievement of will, not an accident of birth. Dear Anglo-Americans, please show us you are also taking pains to make yourselves understood in an international setting. [Paragraphs conflated.]

Here, native speakers are seen as needing to adjust linguistically, socially, and culturally in international situations just as much as anyone else: speaking with care, avoiding unnecessary idioms and slang, and toning down their regionalisms: that is, using—or aiming at—an International Standard English (ISE) rather than any of their own particular 'Englishes' (including what to them may already be standard). To a significant degree *no one* has ISE as a mother tongue. Indeed, it *cannot* be anyone's mother tongue—it is too artificial and artful for that, and (as yet) it is far from rigorously standardized. What it does have, however, is enormous and increasing prestige. Two markers of this in Japan are, firstly, its presence on signs, packets, and a host of other things and, secondly, its Japanization as *wasei eigo* ('Made-in-Japan English').

Tomorrow's dictionaries

An unusual but trend-setting development in British lexicography emerged in the 1990s out of a short-lived alliance in the later 1980s between the Scottish publisher W. & R. Chambers and the English publisher Cambridge University Press. At that time, Chambers wanted better worldwide distribution of its products and Cambridge wanted a dictionary list to compete with Oxford, Longman, and Collins, as a consequence of which a joint imprint, Chambers Cambridge, was created in 1986. As part of this shared endeavour, a fully international advanced learners' dictionary was to be compiled by Chambers, with the title the *Cambridge International Dictionary of English* (*CIDE*), and I was engaged as its editor-in-chief.

A great deal of work was done on the project despite difficulties in operating the joint imprint. The partnership failed in 1990 for reasons unconnected with *CIDE* itself, and as part of the settlement each company inherited its policy-and-planning documents and embryo database, to be used if each so chose as the foundation for dictionaries to be developed separately. For reasons that included difficulties relating to the collapse of the joint imprint, illness in my family, and my editorship of the *Oxford Companion to the English Language*, I did no further work with either company on the project. Paul Procter became editor-in-chief of a *CIDE* that was re-worked and completed in Cambridge and published in 1995. In the meantime, Chambers was taken over by the French company Larousse, which had earlier taken over the London reference publisher Harrap. A re-worked Chambers-Harrap version of the joint-imprint proto-dictionary came out not as a Chambers title, however, but as *Harrap's Essential English Dictionary* (also 1995), with Anne Seaton (an editor on the original *CIDE* project) as Senior Editor. This book was presented not as an advanced but an intermediate dictionary. Both titles have, however, emphasized their internationalism, in the spirit of the original project.

International dictionaries may however be localized. In 1997, Federal Publications of Singapore brought out the *Times-Chambers Essential English Dictionary* (*TCEED*), whose introductory remarks describe a three-way project among Chambers-Harrap, Federal, and the Department of English Language and Literature at the National University of Singapore. Chambers had co-operated on various titles with Federal long before becoming Chambers-Harrap, under the 'Times-Chambers' joint name. The introduction to the *TCEED* distinguishes between 'Core English' (Standard British and American), English words specific to Singapore and Malaysia (marked 'SME' in the text), and regional words adopted into SME (listed in an appendix). There is in addition a brief account of SME (including pronunciation and grammar) and a list of further reading. Such *localization* of a universal learner's dictionary has immense potential worldwide.

We see here two complementary processes at work: *globalization* (books for all people and places) and *localization* (the same books customized for one country or group of countries that have close linguistic associations). Linked to these is a third process, unidirectional *bilingualization* (now widespread and likely to increase), in which the entire explanatory content of a major work is translated, so that it is available to users in both English and their mother tongue: a process with which I *do* feel comfortable. This has been a marked success with Chinese learners, as in the cases of the *Longman Dictionary of*

Contemporary English (1976 onward) and the *Longman Lexicon of Contemporary English* (1981), and has also done well with various titles in Japanese, Arabic, and Spanish-language markets. The opportunities for profitable extensions here are considerable, alongside more traditionally bidirectional bilingual works of reference.

Related in turn to straightforward bilingualization is an as yet modest but noteworthy fourth process, *semibilingualization*, in which translation equivalents for dictionary headwords are dropped economically into white space already available on the pages or provided in slightly recast pages, offering the student quick fixes in terms of the key mother-tongue meanings of the English words. Pioneers in this field are Lionel Kernerman and his son Ilan in Israel, with the Kernerman Semi-Bilingual Dictionaries, which add other-language items to straightforward English-language dictionaries, as for example: (1) Ya'acov Levy and Raphael Gefen, editors, *Passport: English Hebrew Learner's Dictionary*, Kernerman & Kahn, Israel (1996), based on the *Passport English Learner's Dictionary*; (2) Catherine M. Schwarz, M. Anne Seaton, and Jadwiga Fisiak, editors, the *English Polish Learner's Dictionary*, Wydawnictwo Naukowe PWN, Warsaw (1996), based on the *Chambers Concise Usage Dictionary* (1985), with a Polish-English Index and a Phonetic Index; and (3) the *Password English Dictionary for Speakers of French*, also based on the *Chambers Concise Usage Dictionary*, and with a team of French-language editors under Michèle Morin in Quebec (1989).

So, there we have four pragmatic developments associated with tomorrow's English: *globalization, localization, bilingualization*, and *semibilingualization*. And with their emergence we may have entered the twilight stage of the long-standing pedagogical view that Standard English is best learned through direct use (immersion), unmediated by the student's own language(s).

There is also no shortage of developments in native-speaker lexicography, developments so closely associated with the autonomy of nation-states that I will call the process that especially interests me here *nationalization*, and will take as prime examples works created in Australia and Canada, although New Zealand and South Africa also bear watching. Until recently, we have generally conceived of International English in terms of two main varieties and their standards: British in traditional and American in contemporary terms. Now, however, Australian has broken free, with norm-related institutions of its own, including the Macquarie dictionaries (based at Macquarie University in Sydney) and government and other style guides (centred on Canberra). These include the *Cambridge Australian English Style Guide* (1995), edited by Pam Peters at Macquarie—who has now been engaged by Cambridge University Press to produce a *world* style guide, based among other things on computer corpora and the Langscape Survey questionnaires which began appearing in *English Today* in January 1998.

Canada is currently in the process of breaking free. Its first 'national' dictionaries were Canadian editions of American dictionaries (comparable to Australian 'national' editions of British dictionaries). Now, however, there are indigenous Canadian dictionaries, and Oxford University Press Canada has recently brought out the *Guide to Canadian English Usage* (1997), edited by Margery Fee (a research colleague of Pam Peters and the Canadian editor-contributor for the *Oxford Companion to the English Language*, 1992) and Janice McAlpine (of the School of English at Queen's University, Kingston, Ontario). In addition, last month Oxford University Press Canada published the *Canadian Oxford Dictionary* (Managing Director Susan Froud) with the promotional banner 'Defining Canadian English'. This work clearly sets out to do for Canada what the *Macquarie* has done for Australia. Once such nations establish their own dictionaries and style guides (whether the publisher is entirely indigenous or a transplant from the former 'mother country'), their English becomes endonormative and their standard home-based —or, to use a term popularized in Canada in the 1980s, when the constitution finally moved from London to Ottawa, they have 'patriated' their usage.

The next and last process I'd like to identify here can be called *regionalization*, where the region is much larger than a single state—and the only example I know for this development does not (yet) exist. However, the project in question is radical in various ways. First, it proposes to produce a native-speaker-style dictionary for a huge and varied area where there are few traditional native speakers: Asia or, more properly, South and East Asia, where there are few pan-regional lingua francas. Second, it too has been undertaken by Macquarie in Australia, perhaps as part of a policy of (as it were) Asianizing Australia and Australianizing Asia: fitting Australian English more firmly into the Asian context (and its markets). Certainly one sees here a process in which (massively, from India and Malaysia to Japan and Korea) the middle classes are welcoming English into work and home *as an Asian language*. The Macquarie approach to this novel situation has already led to related lexicographical conferences in Bangkok and Manila.

None of which exhausts the possibilities. Everything I have mentioned so far has been traditionally alphabetic. There is also, however, a surge in *thematization*: that is, of works with formats more or less like the

LEXICOGRAPHY

traditional *Roget's Thesaurus* and my own *Longman Lexicon*. I am aware of at least six new works more or less in this area, published by three publishers: (1) three bilingual works in the Cambridge Wordroutes series, General Editor Michael McCarthy, Chief Editor Elizabeth Walter: the *Cambridge Anglais-Français Word Routes: Lexique thématique de l'anglais courant* (1994), the *Cambridge Inglés-Español Word Selector: Diccionario temático del inglés contemporaneo* (1995), and the *Cambridge Angliká-Ellinika Word Routes* (1996); (2) the two *Activator* volumes by Longman, Director Della Summers, Managing Editor Michael Rundell, the *Longman Language Activator: The World's First Production Dictionary* (1993) and the *Longman Essential Activator: Put Your Ideas into Words* (1997); and (3) Hugh Trappes-Lomax's *Oxford Learner's Wordfinder Dictionary* (1997). These, it seems to me, are more than just straws in the wind.

The eight *-izations*

There is no shortage of *-izations*: *globalization, localization, bilingualization, semi-bilingualization, nationalization, regionalization,* and *thematization*. But the most awesome of them all has been under way for some time now everywhere, touching on all the others and on almost every aspect of our lives: *electronicization*. This has had at least three stages: (1) from the 1960s, with the use of computers to make dictionary-making less laborious and more consistent, primarily in keying in, storing, and printing; (2) from the 1980s, on the one hand, with the use of desktop computers by compilers and editors, and, on the other, with the development of corpus linguistics and concordancing, providing more extensive and reliable data on how words work, most particularly in print, than ever before; (3) increasingly, with works of on-line reference without any equivalents on paper—some hundreds of them already set free in cyberspace and (especially in the case of non-copyright technical lists and definitions) capable of rapid and cheap improvement and updating by means of feedback from their own users. (See Li Lan, 'Cyber-dictionaries', *English Today* 54, Apr 98.)

Because such electronic activities are still in their infancy, they often consist of standard A–Z lists that could just as easily have been made available on paper—and may indeed originally have been paper products whose virtue for Internet purposes is that they are safely out of copyright. But hypertextuality is increasingly available within and among such products, so that users can pass freely from one lexical region to the next, wherever they may be based, whether within a single work of e-reference or from one to another. This lusty cyberbaby will, I suspect, soon outgrow A–Z storage and retrieval, and we will see words defined in sets, in the company they naturally keep, and supported by a rich supply of citations drawn from concordanced corpora, every item reached by menu or by hotlink. Oh brave new world, that has such things in store for us.

Part 4: The knowledge revolution

17

What then *is* reference science?

[An integration, adaptation, and expansion of: (1) 'What is reference science?', a lecture given in September 1997 to the Iwasaki Linguistic Circle, Tokyo, a first printed version of which was published in their annual journal *Lexicon* in 1998; (2) 'Why reference science?—Extending the reach of lexicography', the opening paper of 'Reference Science', a conference held under the auspices of the Dictionary Research Centre, the University of Exeter, in May 1996.]

It was born in Exeter in the spring of 1996. The birth was on time, the baby was small but healthy, and made very little noise. As a result, few people knew it had arrived. At the same time, however, there has been a steadily increasing interest in the new arrival. I believe it is a subject whose time has come, but it will take a little more time before the precise nature and relevance of 'reference science' become clear.

Before I go on I would like to look at a rather basic issue—the matter of inventing a science. Can one just *invent* a science when one feels like it? And if you do, how does it *stay* invented? Does a new science occupy new semantic or conceptual space, does it 'steal' space from other sciences, or does it overlap, flowing in and out of them? Or are these the wrong metaphors? And if you do invent a science, when and how do you know if you've succeeded— ten, twenty, a hundred years later? I would argue that these questions are not just interesting in general terms: they are questions for which reference science could itself provide a framework for answers—and for further questions. Looking back over the year since we launched our fledgling science, four things particularly stand out for me:

- Reinhard Hartman creating the Dictionary Research Centre at the

University of Exeter, an institution that has played a pivotal role in getting practitioners of lexicography and other enthusiasts for the subject to talk to each other, take degrees relating to it, *create* degrees relating to it, write articles, dissertations, and books about it, and organize conferences and other activities relating to it.

- Specific study programmes developed at Exeter, from the doctoral level to Interlex, the one-week international course on aspects of lexicography, that encourage open-ended consideration of everything that relates to lexicography. Nothing referential has been arbitrarily excluded in such programmes, and as a result minds have been able to extend the subject and themselves.

- The formulation over time of first Euralex then Afrilex (both initiated at Exeter), then this year in Hong Kong, Asialex. These organizations, alongside the Dictionary Society of North America, provide a firm base for lexicographical debate worldwide, without which one could not even contemplate anything more fundamental or far-reaching, such as an eventual world federation of reference professionals.

- The publication by Cambridge University Press in 1986 of my own survey *Worlds of Reference: Language, Lexicography and Learning from the Clay Tablet to the Computer*. The book was widely and constructively reviewed, and—somewhat surprisingly—the most enthusiastic reviewers were not lexicographers at all but librarians and computer specialists who appear to have felt that the book gave them a history and even a charter, something that had been lacking without their ever previously noticing the lack. Lexicographers also responded well, but some considered that I did not give enough attention to 'proper' lexicography. However, the book wasn't about any single art, craft, or science. It was about how we refer and inform, how we communicate, and ultimately how we *know* and can pass on what we know to others.

One of the most powerful developments in recent years has been our expanding understanding of DNA—dioxyribonucleic acid, 'the building blocks of life'. In a few short years, humankind has uncovered and begun to map a referential software system (a *genome*) that is built into us and into all other life known to us, and one that is often compared with language, as for example when DNA elements are called 'letters' and

WHAT THEN *IS* REFERENCE SCIENCE?

'words' and the entire system is called 'the language of the genes'. It seems to me that we need a framework within which we can ask questions such as 'how similar *are* human language and DNA?' and 'how similar to and different from DNA are our systems of information storage and retrieval?' It is not enough to talk figuratively about genetic language and letters. We have to ask: are these expressions simply metaphors, or do language systems and gene systems share a pattern that might also underlie some third or fourth system that we have not yet encountered —or have encountered but have not yet recognised? This is just one of the possible areas that reference scientists might in due course look at.

We can consider next something not quite so cosmic, but nonetheless large: what I describe at the end of *Worlds of Reference* as an emerging 'global nervous system'. In the twelve years since the book came out, that nervous system has immensely, almost incalculably, increased—a vast multiplex of older copper cable and newer fibre optics, older terrestrial TV and newer satellite TV, and many other things. Technology is one thing, however, and content and use are another, and part of that content and use relates to asking for information, either from other humans by e-mail or from the system itself on, say, the World-Wide Web. Reference science has a place in observing and reporting on this largest and most integrated reference and communicative service humanity has ever known, into which many of the resources of the world's great libraries and others sources of stable information are currently being woven, to form the largest and most widely consultable work of reference that has ever existed. The word *Internet* is already not large enough to contain it.

When pushed, users and observers of works of reference will concede that both the dictionary and the telephone directory have much in common, as do indexes, concordances, atlases, manuals, and catalogues (whether the mail-order kind or in libraries). It is hard, however, to conceive of the circumstances in which the compilers of a telephone directory, an atlas, a computer manual, or a catalogue would be accepted as members of Euralex, Afrilex, Asialex, or the Dictionary Society of North America. Yet these varied products are all linked by both their reference function and a range of content, technique, and technology. The current electronicization of all such materials by much the same means only serves to emphasize this point.

Indeed, all such materials belong within something larger than, but closely associated with, traditional lexicography, have never had any cover-all name or names, and at the close of this century need such names. On offer since at least 1986 have been, for the practical business of producing artifacts, such terms as *reference art* and *reference technology*, and since 1995 the term for their description, discussion, and assessment has been *reference science*, the study of all aspects of organizing data, information, and knowledge in any format whatever, for any purpose whatever, using any materials whatever. The lack of such a level of study may be due at least in part to a historical current which, in the terminology of postmodernist literary theory, has 'privileged' the position of dictionaries and to some extent also of encyclopedias, gazetteers, chronologies, concordances, and indexes (all of them generally arranged in archetypal A–Z order), and along with them has to some degree privileged the position of lexicography and its practitioners—certainly in relation to, say, the makers of such markedly practical things as phonebooks.

Lexicographers might, in Johnson's term, be 'harmless drudges', but *their* drudgery has for centuries been held in higher esteem than that of makers of catalogues, directories, time-tables, ready-reckoners, travel guides, and the like. It might, however, be wise in McLuhan's age of information to seek greater egalitarianiam in the worlds of reference, by focusing on reference itself rather than on language and alphabeticism (significant as these are), and to examine and exploit *all* techniques and insights associated with *all* works of reference from any time, place, language, and encoding system.

Of course, it is only relatively recently that lexicography has been systematically critiqued, a development that has however proved both successful and useful. Nowadays, by and large, lexicographers no longer compile dictionaries according to hand-me-down formulas that seldom change, but are instead more liable to develop opinions about—and even theories of—what they are doing along with novel practices tied to those theories. Given this advance, is it asking too much to say now: look beyond this recently raised consciousness and recognise a greater link with other information professionals and products?

It is not surprising that the academic world has paid little or no attention to the making of directories and catalogues: it has paid little enough attention to dictionaries and encyclopedias, which have grown up as part of its own concern—an adequate definition of terms and the description of reality. So crucial, however, is the business of organizing data, information, and knowledge in our time, and on a global basis, that it may soon be difficult—impossible—to *avoid* bringing all the tools and vehicles of reference together within one labelled area. This will happen, I suspect, if for no other reason than that anything informational and referential, when stored in a computer, becomes quite simply a *database*, regardless of whatever name or function or prestige or lack of prestige it might traditionally have had. The electronic revolution is nothing if not a leveller.

At the moment, however, we can identify three areas of immediate concern to reference science, the first with a traditional name, the second with a new name, and the third with no name at all:

- The first is *lexicography*, that aspect of reference art and technology which deals wholly or mainly with language and pre-eminently with words, regardless of the format used (in the main alphabetic, thematic, or a hybrid of the two).

- The second is *encyclopedics*, that aspect of reference art and technology which deals with information about the world, and for me includes atlases, gazetteers, almanacs, manuals, and quite possibly also textbooks.

- The third covers tabulations (such as time-tables), directories (as for telephone subscribers), and catalogues (in libraries, of goods for sale, etc.). This may prove to be several areas, requiring us to conclude that certain divisions of reference science necessarily overlap with other disciplines (such as library science) and activities (such as social and business life), because they have common concerns.

Fairly obviously, the bulk of research and commentary in reference science in the immediate future will focus on dictionaries and perhaps encyclopedias. I anticipate, however, that increased interest in databases, hypertext, multimedia, and information structures at large—from satellite linkups, Internet structures, and libraries to supermarket layouts, transport systems, theme parks, star maps, and descriptions of DNA—will ensure that more attention is paid to my third, unnamed element, which to date has been the part of the iceberg below the referential waterline.

There are all sorts of fertile possibilities within the framework that the concept *reference science* makes possible. I will close by looking at only one of these, a contrast that has become important in lexicography in recent years: *macrostructure* and *microstructure*. This dichotomy is usually interpreted as covering on the one hand the overall ('macro') organization of a dictionary and on the other hand any single entry within such a work (the 'micro' organization). I would argue here, however, that the contrast is valuable not only in terms of dictionaries and their entries (and by extension library catalogues and whatever their constituent units may be) but also in other levels of organization among information structures, knowledge structures, and communication structures.

Thus, just as an entry is microstructural within the macrostructure of a dictionary, so such a dictionary is microstructural within a publisher's list of dictionaries. Such a reference list is in its turn microstructural within the macrostructure of all publishers' reference lists everywhere. The same is true with each microstructural bibliographical entry within the macrostructure of a catalogue, which is in turn microstructural in the macrostructure of a library, which is in turn microstructural within the macrostructure of all bibliographical collections within all libraries and similar institutions in a city, state, or the world—especially if such resources are linked electronically. Similarly, within such a system as the World-Wide Web, each website is microstructural within the WWW as a whole.

Such matters become discussable if we have such a framework, whose findings and postulations can feed back into the practical business of making books and other artifacts. Reference science can be a liberating and integrating discipline, in which lexicography would not be eclipsed but strengthened, in intriguing theoretical and practical ways. The term proposed is neither a cute neologism nor a novelty for its own sake, but at the end of this century a necessity.

Notes

1. *Coining the term.* The term *reference science* was informally coined in 1995 by Reinhard Hartmann, on the analogy of *library science* and *information science*. It seems to me an excellent choice, despite the fact that the term *reference* has two distinct technical meanings, as in *work of reference* on the one side and *reference and sense* on the other. In the former case, a dictionary, thesaurus, or encyclopedia is a work of reference; in the latter, words have in semantic terms a *referential function,* as for example when the word *horse* refers to (or labels) a particular class of animal, in contrast with the *sense relations* that exist within various lexical systems, as for example between *horse* and *mare* (gender), *horse* and *donkey* (species), *horse* and *racing* (activity, sport), and *horse* and *saddle* (physical association). This multiple meaning does not however interfere with the value of the term *reference* in naming a scientific discipline; indeed, it might well make it more useful in that role. The phrase *reference science* also fits in comfortably with the long-established set *reference book,*

reference shelf, reference materials, reference technology, and of course *work of reference.*

2. *Other 'reference' terms.* Even if many people find the term *reference science* acceptable and useful, and start propagating it, it could take at least a decade to see whether the majority of *reference professionals* and *reference critics*—and in due course thorough-going *reference scientists*—are likely to use it as a matter of course. Whatever happens, university departments of reference science are hardly imminent.

3. *Meanings of 'dictionary' and 'lexicography'.* The *Reader's Digest Great Illustrated Dictionary* (1984) provides the following definitions of *reference* and *lexicography*:

> **dictionary** 1 A reference book containing an explanatory alphabetical list of words, as: **a** A book listing a comprehensive or restricted selection of the words of a language, identifying usually the pronunciation, grammatical function, and meanings of each word, often with other information on its origin and use. **b** Such a book listing the words or other units of a particular category within a language: *a slang dictionary.* 2 A book listing the words of a language with translations into another language. 3 A book listing words or other linguistic items from particular fields, with specialized information about them: *a medical dictionary.* 4 A reference book dealing with a particular subject: *a dictionary of modern history.*
>
> **lexicography** The writing or compiling of a dictionary or dictionaries.

These definitions express rather well both the commonsensicality of lexicography and the chaos of words in the real world. By and large, users of dictionaries expect compilers to reduce the disorderliness of life and language to clear-cut statements, but the better the lexicography the more likely it is that the inherent fuzziness of words and meanings will emerge. Here, the first sense of *dictionary* emphasizes the alphabet and focuses on language. But where the second and third senses reinforce this emphasis, the fourth demolishes everything that precedes it, because it allows *any* kind of reference book, alphabetic or not, linguistic or not, to be a dictionary. And it offers lexicographers a blank cheque, because they are, in terms of the entry *lexicography,* the people who write dictionaries senses 1 to 4 and not just senses 1 to 3. Intentionally or not, lexicographers appear here to be people who produce reference books of any kind.

The *Reader's Digest* dictionary has reported accurately here on how things are, but imagine if we were discussing the word *horse* rather than *dictionary*. Senses 1 and 2 would be fine: horses would be large equine animals, whether they are racing thoroughbreds or Clydesdales. But Sense 3 would stretch the point, allowing a donkey to be a horse, or at best 'a small, horse-like animal', and Sense 4 is wild, because it would allow a cow to be a horse, on something like the relaxed semantic grounds that it has a head and four legs, and is about the same size. What is needed here is a suitable superordinate term covering both horses and cows, such as *quadruped*—even if this brings in all sorts of other animals as well, such as dogs, sheep, armadillos, and wombats. It is much the same with a superordinate term like *reference science*. It helps out with our professional horses, donkeys, and even cows, but only if we allow all the dogs, sheep, armadillos, and wombats in as well, because all such animals share important features, as do works of reference from the *Oxford English Dictionary* to the Yellow Pages.

18

The scholarly guild

[An invited article published under the title 'The fifth estate' in *Verbatim: The Language Monthly*, 15.2, 1988 Old Sarum, Connecticut, and Aylesbury, Buckinghamshire.]

It began in medieval Europe, and in the late twentieth century it is everywhere in the world. Its overall influence is profound but undiscussed, although aspects of that influence are discussed constantly, under such headings as language, education, standards, literacy, literature, science, and medicine. There is little that it does not touch, being physically present in the architecture of schools, psychologically present when we talk and think about what makes us civilized, and linguistically present in much of modern communication and especially in what we call educated (or standard) usage. Yet it has no name.

Let me therefore give it a name: *the scholarly guild*. The phrase is a reminder of its medieval provenance, its academic focus, and its corporate style. This guild of scholars is one of the most successful enterprises in the history of our species. Indeed, some of its eighteenth-century members even gave our species the elevated Latin title *Homo sapiens sapiens* ('wise wise human') as if thinking of themselves while also labelling all the birds, beasts, and bugs in creation. The guild takes many forms now, but it retains much of the Middle Ages and the ecclesiastical Schoolmen who gathered in their quasi-monastic colleges, behind walls that marked them off from the rest of the world—a separation that in England is still marked by the contrast, especially in Oxford and Cambridge, of 'town and gown'.

The men (and increasingly the women) who have inherited the mantle of the Schoolmen have no trouble recognising each other. They live similar lives, conduct similar courses, and with similar subventions go to similar conferences and give similar papers on every continent—much as one of their members, the English novelist David Lodge, describes them in his novel *Small World*. They are not as tightly knit as other fraternities, past and present, such as the Knights Templar, the Freemasons, the Jesuits, the Mafia, the Ancient and Mystical Order of the Rosy Cross, the corporate executives of Coca Cola or Chrysler, or the managers of labour unions. The guild's gentler cohesion and lack of obvious international hierarchies have contributed to its marked success and curious anonymity. Its institutions take many forms and survive under many different political regimes. They possess neither a Vatican nor a Vicar-General to report back to, and, although the guild can at times be arcane (with its Latin charters and medieval capping ceremonies), by and large its doings are overt and to all intents and purposes benign.

Historically, the bulk of the human race has never known a classroom, leave alone a cloister or an ivory tower, or encountered teachers who have been empowered by letters placed after their names. Nowadays, however, there are few people who have not come across colleges and college graduates or (at the periphery of things) at least gone to primary school and learned the elements of reading and writing under the guidance of such graduates, or people trained by them. That is the physical and social measure of the guild's success. Its continuance seems assured, and working in its favour is a social contract with a three-part system that has been established in every country in the world:

- *Bottom-up progression.* The young are inducted into school at an early age and proceed, level by level, to institutions of ever 'higher' learning, stopping for various reasons at various levels, which are usually validated by tests and the distribution of certificates that provide a kind of social grade. These processes are often reinforced with such comments from parents and others as, 'You'll never get anywhere nowadays without a college education' and 'I wish I'd had your opportunities when I was your age'. There are even league tables among nations, showing the percentages of those who stay in the system longer, a state of affairs generally considered to be a measure of national success, as well as league tables of how different countries do in such matters as linguistic and mathematical instruction. The guild and its influence are marked by many things, not the least of which are:

- *Top-down rank.* There is an apex of professors and doctors buttressed by holders of first-level bachelor's and second-level master's degrees, many of whom become lower-level administrators, teachers, researchers, and other workers within the system. These in turn are surrounded and supported by holders of school certificates and other qualifications. Spreading out from the base of the pyramid are those who have less prestigiously certified educations or no formal education at all, people who may have mixed feelings about such matters as book learning, big words, and fancy degrees, and about such people as eggheads, highbrows, and absent-minded professors —as well indeed as the inherent perils of scholarship, science, and technology: 'Filling your head with nonsense. I had no time for all that. I went to the University of Hard Knocks.' And within the system itself are people with similarly mixed feelings, but by and large it remains intact; we all send our children to school.

- *Language appropriate to level.* Things start with a basic ability to read and write, followed by the capacity to handle abstractions, and, at a higher level, to be at ease with what Philip Gove in Webster's *Third International Dictionary* (1963) has called ISV (International Scientific Vocabulary). For English, this means a capacity to add the Latinate to the vernacular, then the Greek to the Latinate, so that you can eat a *hearty* breakfast and be *cordial* afterwards without suffering from *cardiac* arrest. For users of other languages, entry into the guild may mean acquiring an entire language as a medium of education (such as French in Senegal and English in Kenya), because many of the world's tongues are not (yet, and may not ever be) part of the circle of standardized print languages in which the work of the guild can be suitably conducted.

You and I, gentle reader, are accredited members of the guild, something that is demonstrated in various ways, such as: a shared literacy and the assumptions and biases that go with it; an awareness of what books are for, and a willingness to use them; a knowledge and use of innumerable cultural allusions and educated idioms; and a relative ease in reading a periodical called *Verbatim*, with for example sections entitled *Epistolae* (letters) and *Obiter dicta* (expressions of opinion). We are also, by and large, capable of conducting ourselves suitably in the company of others who have been group-educated to college level, so that we do not let the side down.

In school, college and university, people have for some six centuries been receiving diplomas and titles to prove that, to varying degrees (a loaded word), they are educated. Oftener than not, use of language establishes membership and social-cum-educational rank as clearly as any parchment. One of the less pleasant ways in which such rank can be pulled is labelling the linguistically less secure 'illiterate'. They too can read and write, but for many collegiate folk in Western societies over the last two hundred years the 'solecisms', 'barbarisms', and 'vulgarisms' perpetrated by 'substandard' language users have called for rebuke, and what better rebuke than to treat them as if they did not belong at all—to assign them to the outer darkness of analphabetism? Subtler still is the label 'self-educated' applied to people who have had little formal learning and seek knowledge by any means open to them; Thomas Hardy described an extreme case of such treatment in *Jude the Obscure*.

The scholarly guild has always interested itself in language, its standards and usage, its literature and classics, its mediums (?media) of manuscript and print, its academic apparatus, and its Latin tags. It places a high value on success with such things, and a lower value on such matters as rural and urban dialect, popular culture, and folklore (along with 'folk etymologies' and 'folk beliefs'). These are only accepted into the canon of good usage and literature after a long and vigorous rearguard action. Only now, for example, is the soap opera (with its enormous social impact) beginning to be seen as a fit topic for academic study. Such things as movies and soaps begin to attain a special kind of social respectability when there are enough papers in learned journals and theses in bound volumes to elevate them beyond the 'merely' popular. It is similar with guild members who are low on the ladder of rank. Once upon a time there was a playwright who knew 'little Latin and less Greek'. Much of his skill was acquired in the hurly-burly of life, but his works had—an occasionally disputed—merit. But with the passage of time he was canonized by the guild, and his *Complete Works* have since been annotated and organized by men and women with doctorates in Shakespearian Studies. He made it to the highest heights, so it *can* be done, but it is rare.

The guild's institutions have, in their unobtrusively ubiquitous way, become more powerful than both the Catholic Christianity which gave them birth (having first been inseminated by Islamic influence) and the imperial and expansionist European regimes that have scattered them round the world. Their diaspora has been so successful that most of us unreflectingly see school (a Greek word that once meant 'leisure') as the natural dispenser, controller, instrument, and structure of education— and therefore of educated discourse—*everywhere* on earth, and for more and more purposes. It is another measure of the guild's success that we are hard put to imagine an alternative to it. The communes of anarchists, socialists and hippies, for example, have not even dented it, although they have sometimes seemed close to taking it over. The degree mills still turn, and more busily than ever, so that the once-cherished bachelor level is hardly enough, masters programmes proliferate, and even the doctorate risks over-subscription, making post-doctoral fellowships a further height to scale.

After centuries of social and cultural direction from the guild's leaders (the professorial élite, the academic, scientific, and medical establishment), it is hardly possible for anyone in the Western or Westernizing world today to be reckoned or to feel educated *without* having been to school, and the more school the better—especially in American English, in which *school* stretches all the way from kindergarten to doctoral research. It may only be possible to imagine alternatives (or significant adaptations, if we wish them) after we have found the right label for what has been going on. Societies seldom see what is central to—and perhaps problematic in—their own cultures, having much less trouble identifying it in the cultures of others.

Historians have often discussed the 'three estates' of the Western world—nobility, church, and commons. A 'fourth estate'—the media—is also widely acknowledged. The ancient idea of social estates can be taken one stage further, however, to the global agglomeration of educational and scientific communities, which in effect constitute a 'fifth estate', an entity as worthy of anthropological investigation as the Yanomama of the Amazon or the Dinka of the Sudan. Unfortunately, just as we find it hard to imagine the scholarly guild as a whole, and to envisage alternatives to it, so no organization exists outside this fifth estate that could investigate it. Who will assess the assessors?

There is probably only one solution. A traditional role of the guild has been searching for the truth, and if that aim is sincere (and, by and large, it seems to be), the fifth estate may yet turn the bright searchlights of scholarship and science on itself, and consider with care what it finds.

19

Knowledge, knowledge everywhere: the global library

[The opening plenary address at the conference 'Serials 86', held at the University of Exeter in March 1986, and subsequently published in *SERIALS '86: Proceedings of the UK Serials Group Conference*, 1986. The presentation was undertaken at short notice, hence the opening remarks. The text in the proceedings was an edited transcript of the tape recording of the talk, from which the following has been developed.]

A couple of weeks ago, my wife Feri and I came off a plane from Los Angeles, and after we had more or less settled back into our normal routine, one of our daughters said something to me that I heard as 'Dennis Forbes phoned and asked if you would give a talk to some cereals people'.

What with jet-lag and ignorance, I didn't interpret this the way *you* might. Dennis Forbes of Cambridge University Press publishes the magazine I edit, and is with us here today. I know him to be a man of initiative, snap, crackle, and pop, but I didn't know what connection he might have had with the wheat industry. The next day, I looked at the note my daughter had written and discovered that in fact you are *serials* people with an S and an I, which was enough for me to misinterpret the whole thing again. I can't tell how many of you here, like me, belong to the generation who were boys and girls in the late 1940s in the UK and at 6.45 every week-day evening on the BBC heard the signature tune for 'Dick Barton Special Agent', the serial before the one before 'The Archers'. You can see I was still in a bit of a quagmire but at least I was getting nearer to the area that interests you.

Seriality

The next stage in the evolution of my thoughts related to the word *serial* itself. My main professional concerns are triangular: first, language, and in particular the English language, then language teaching, then lexicography. In the process of trying to discover for myself exactly what I have been doing over the last twenty-five years or so, I wrote the book *Worlds of Reference*, something I would have welcomed myself when I first became involved in lexicography and reference materials. I wanted a history of the development of externalized knowledge, and that's more or less what the book is, with the subtitle 'Language, lexicography, and learning from the clay tablet to the computer'. I began my research with dictionaries, found myself deep in encyclopedias shortly afterwards, then went on to the technology and uses of writing and print, much more fundamental matters.

In the process of doing this, I became interested in the *universals* and the *contingencies* of the subject. The contingencies are easy. To begin with there were bits of soft wet clay in ancient Mesopotamia. You took a quantity of it, slapped it into your hand, flattened it out, and with a bit of reed cut some wedges on the surface, and this eventually became a fully fledged form of communication. The universals of the subject are abstract, and one of them is the idea of *seriality*—the need for one quantum of discourse to follow another, just as the episodes of 'Dick Barton' had to be in one specified sequence. At the moment, I am imposing a line or flow of sound on your ears and your brains are doing something with it as I go along. I can stop that line of sound at any moment. [PAUSE.] And if instead I offer you a book to read and you open it, like this, I impose on your eyes a line of print. The universal here is the abstract line; the contingent is either the sound or the ink marks.

This idea of seriality or linearity invests everything that people like you and me do in our business much of the time. One example is alphabetic order, which came into existence about 3,000 years ago, but did not come into serious practical *referential* use until the beginning of the Renaissance. It then took another 150 years or so before indexes and dictionaries arranged in the alphabetic mode became established, after which they became the dominant form, classified or thematic arrangements ceasing to be the immediately interesting form for many people in the business of recording, storing, accessing, and otherwise handling information.

So that was my next stage along the line of thinking what you, the UK

Serials Group, could conceivably be and do. And of course I was still slightly wrong. In addition, as a lexicographer, I was interested in the fact that you call yourselves *serials people*, in the plural, dealing with things which the rest of the world does not think of as serials in the way you do. That fascinates me.

Three waves

Having wondered what I could say that would be valuable to you, I decided that I would go over the entire history of the human race in the next twenty minutes or so. I would start by mentioning Alvin Toffler, and check how many of you have heard of him. Mm. About half. Well, Toffler is an interesting writer, although his books could have been half as long as they are, and academics might have hoped he would be less sensational in his approach to the future. His form of apocalyptic enthusiasm divides the human race into three parts. In his first book, *Future Shock*, with which he leapt into prominence in 1970, he talks about 'yesterday's people, today's people, and tomorrow's people'. In his second book, in 1980, he refers to 'the first wave, the second wave, and the third wave' of humanity in such a strict and clearly categorized form that people are forced to ask themselves into which of Toffler's containers they might go.

For Toffler, yesterday's people, the first wave, are the part of the human race that is still bonded to the Neolithic agricultural revolution. There was a stage, some 10,000 years ago, when some of the human race settled down and became farmers, a move that in the course of time made possible the development of cities. I suppose when mentioning such people now he is talking about a large part of the Third World, as well as a number of people in the Second World (the Soviet Union and its satellites?), and the First World, which is presumably us. I suspect that most reasonably educated people nowadays wouldn't like to be considered yesterday's people, bonded to the Neolothic agricultural revolution. Toffler's today's people may sound better, as though we are properly up to date, but instead of farming *today's* people are bonded to the Industrial Revolution, starting about 200 years ago. So today's people are in fact relics of the dark satanic mills and other horrors of the nineteenth century. That leaves us with tomorrow's people, the precursors of what he calls the new 'post-industrial super-society'. Since the micro-chip crossed Toffler's horizon—between his first and second book, and not predicted in the first—it will come as no surprise to you that one of the primary elements in being one of tomorrow's people is a capacity to move on to the new high-tech plateau, a clean and beautiful place where apparently the sun always shines.

Four communicative shifts

Toffler's division of humankind greatly interested me, and I began to wonder whether it was possible to draw a professional parallel to what he offers us. In my field—and yours—I think one *can* do this, but instead of having three stages we appear to need four. Instead of worrying about whether we belong to yesterday's, today's, or tomorrow's people, or a first, second, or third wave, I will describe the moves from one stage to the next as *communicative shifts*. The first shift, which has usually been ignored by students of communication, is that point—many thousands of years ago and probably lasting thousands of years—when our ancestors moved from a primary use of certain physical apparatus to a new secondary use: that is, from the primary use of breathing, eating, and drinking to the secondary use, what I am doing now. In other words, linear (or serial) speech. What was previously only possible in a limited way through gesturing and a restricted range of vocal sound became 'language'—what the tongue does.

About 5,000 years ago the second great communicative shift took place. This one cannot be called more radical than the first, but it made all the difference for people like you and me. The process of linear speech was transferred to a medium that no one could possibly have imagined till it happened: a series of sounds (the work of mouth and ear) was converted to a line of marks on a surface (the work of hand and eye). The line might go from left to right and start again at the left, or go first one way then the other, reversing the letters every other line, or go up and down, or in any other way one might wish as long as it had a degree of consistency and others could therefore 'follow' it (like a path). So the clay-and-cuneiform technology of Mesopotamia was created, and then the reed-and-hieroglyph technology of Egypt, as well as in due course the bamboo-and-ideogram technology of China and the parchment-and-alphabet technology of ancient Greece. Elizabeth Eisenstein (1979) has described what followed as the period of *scribal culture*, half-way between the total orality of all the preceding millennia and what we have now. In a scribal culture, people still depend a great deal on rote memorization, because only a small number of them possess tablets or scrolls or books. They read aloud and their listeners have mnemonic systems to help them remember what was in the 'magic' texts. That's the second shift.

The third shift is a neglected area, hardly looked at seriously by scholars before Elizabeth Eisenstein. It arose from the development in the fifteenth century of that most radical machine, the printing press. Nowadays, as Walter Ong (1982) has pointed out, we who live in a print culture find it hard to imagine what it was like to live in a wholly scribal culture, without access to printed matter of any kind—and virtually impossible to imagine what it was like to live in an entirely oral, pre-literate culture where nothing could be written down at all. In the processes through which our society has gone, and which we recapitulate in our education, we are marked irrevocably by certain attitudes towards the periods before the latest shift has taken place. First of all, our society has tended to be disdainful of the 'deaf and dumb'—who can nonetheless have rich gestural language. Then, if we move beyond the first shift, we can see how disdainful literate people are of societies which, or of individuals in a society who, can't read or write. We call them all sorts of things: 'subliterate', 'semi-literate', or plain '*il*literate'; but now and again, if we want to be a little kinder, we call them 'unlettered'. Illiteracy, as many of the educated people in our society see it, is a kindergarten condition. We watch over our children to see how quickly they can flee from this illiteracy and become civilized, because we often use the word 'literate' to mean *civilized* as opposed to, say, *heathen* or *barbaric*.

The fourth shift is what is happening now, with computers as the centrepiece. Toffler has noted that things are accelerating. Think of the tremendously long time it took humanity to learn to speak, then of the 5,000 years or so from the development of writing to the development of printing. After several hundred years of print culture we cannot even begin to consider what society might be like after this new shift has fully established itself, not having yet stabilized the technology of the culture we are moving into. Looking at things from my professional point of view, from the point of view of studying communication, we *can* think in terms of a yesterday's culture of speech and script alone, a today's culture of these plus print, and a tomorrow's culture of whatever emerges from our current revolution—not a bad approximation to Toffler's tripartite concept.

The question of literacy arises again. There is a new kind of literacy developing, and you serials people with your journals and other periodicals are intimately involved in the process of becoming what I will call, if you do not mind too much, 'computerate'. There is, alas, every indication that people who are now computerate from childhood will be just as disdainful of predecessors bonded to the culture of the printing press as they in their turn have disdained *their* predecessors back down the line.

'Lost in information'

I have tried from time to time to investigate the antecedents of the things that *you* deal with—serial publications. I suspect such ancestors are the tally-bones found in caves, made from the antlers or other bones of animals, with various things marked on them, perhaps to indicate the number of rituals performed at a certain time or the phases of the moon. These bones are tangible objects, but we do not know exactly how they were used. One can imagine someone in Cave A sending his tally-bone to someone in Cave B as a regular monthly message, but we do not know anything for sure. Yet this is where serials people first came into the communicative picture. You also come into this picture—in Tofflerian terms—in that *if* there are people who can (broadly and emotively) be called yesterday's people, today's people, and tomorrow's people, then maybe there are also yesterday's librarians, today's librarians, and tomorrow's librarians.

What does it mean to be yesterday's librarian? What does it mean to be an insecure today's librarian? Are there such creatures as insecure librarians anyway? I suspect there are and I would like to address myself briefly to the question of why we tend to be insecure in our professional lives. You are not alone: teachers are insecure, academics at universities are insecure, because of the bombardment of potentiality that we suffer from towards the end of the twentieth century. Let me quote T.S. Eliot. In 1934, in a poem called 'Choruses from *The Rock*', Eliot uttered these precisely three lines:

> Where is the life we have lost in living?
> Where is the wisdom we have lost in knowledge?
> Where is the knowledge we have lost in information?

This was written before the computer was even a gleam in a cryptologist's eye and well after Charles Babbage's Analytical Engine had been prematurely consigned to the scrap heap of history. Eliot in his pessimism reckoned he knew where the human race has been and is going. We once had real humanity, knowledge, and wisdom, he says, before the word 'information' became fashionable.

Always something new

To go back to Dennis Forbes. After I had done my thinking about what a serials group could be, Dennis came round to tell me, and explain exactly what he hoped to commit me to—and we began to swap possibilities. I told him a bit about what I had been doing in California and I asked if he had heard about it and he had not. I tried something else and he had not heard about that either. Then he tried a couple of interesting developments on me and I knew nothing about *them*. The extent of our mutual ignorance about things that were legitimately within our professional range was startling and chastening. But this is the position we are all in. Although we live in a situation where there is knowledge, knowledge everywhere, at our very fingertips, there is far more than we can comfortably handle. We are millionaires of information and we have still to work out how to use it properly. But perhaps we are beginning—slowly—to be literate in the technology of organizing information so that it does not just flood our systems, either in institutional terms or inside our heads.

Dennis told me something you all know about already. He said that the traditional method of distributing material from libraries is reaching crisis point, and he mentioned the division of the British Library at Boston Spa, which has been producing 1.8 million photocopies of journal articles a year, and the authors and publishers received no kind of royalty payment whatever. Even so, the cost of each copy to the British Library's end-user is about £2.00, which is not cheap when you think about it. Then he asked if I knew about the Elsevier jukebox, and I didn't. This is a system that uses optical disks about the size of an LP. Each disk will hold several tens of thousands of pages in digital form. A number of disks in such a 'jukebox' can store a million pages or more. The millennium has come, and it is electronic. He also asked me if I had heard of the CD-ROM. I hadn't, and so he told me about that too.

Then it was *my* turn. I asked Dennis if he had heard of what was happening to Dr Frank Stockdale at Stanford University, and (as I knew very well) he hadn't. Frank is an oncologist whose primary work is in breast cancer but who has other interests relating to DNA and muscle development. When I visited his lab during our trip to California he was using an Apple Macintosh to store his research material and could call up all sorts of things by means of a drop-down menu system, which particularly intrigued me because I could apply it to my own lexicographical activities. After I had watched him using the Mac, a young man of prodigious intelligence arrived whose doctoral research was concerned with how to put Frank's expertise into a computer. So I was watching Frank put his stuff into a computer at the same time as this man wanted to put a version of Frank into another computer, to create an 'expert system'. He will evidently keep talking to Frank till he knows what kind of clinical and cognitive process makes Frank the good specialist and researcher he is. He will then try to model this in a computer and make the result available to other people who do not have access to Frank Stockdale the human being.

There are a number of other things I could mention. For example, at the University of Pisa in May there is going to be a symposium funded by the European Economic Community, for people to talk about the computerization of dictionaries. For those of you involved with reference materials the time may soon come when you can start from a menu of themes or semantic fields and work your way through the system to get to the word you want, like a thesaurus, all done without a keyboard, and scroll up and down like an ancient Egyptian with a papyrus, to find a word and the company that it keeps. Dennis did not know about that. We are all in different states of relative knowledge and relative ignorance —all the time. This tends to frighten us, but it should in fact make life more rather than less interesting, as long as we concede ignorance when we *are* ignorant.

Tomorrow's library

I owe an enormous personal debt to librarians. When I was growing up in Glasgow, the public libraries made my future possible. I had no access to books except through second-hand bookshops and the various public libraries in the city, the first step on my professional ladder. So I'm well disposed to librarians and those libraries where you can smell the polish, and people behind vast smooth desks slide a book across to you, or if you want to read the translation of the Epic of Gilgamesh that they don't make available to the general public you are taken into a room where they can check on you now and again. You feel special when this happens to you. This is yesterday's library, peopled no doubt by yesterday's librarians, but it was yesterday's librarians who helped me.

Today's librarians are hybrids, caught between the technologies of yesterday and tomorrow. Will tomorrow's librarians escape from this hybridity and become clean-cut technicians of knowledge? I think not. Toffler's concepts don't quite fit in this particular sphere. Consider the four shifts I put to you. When we learned to speak we didn't stop breathing, eating, or drinking. When we learned to write we didn't stop speaking or breathing or eating and drinking. When the printing press came along we didn't stop writing by hand, or speaking and so forth. So once the new electronic revolution is stabilized we'll continue to print and handwrite and speak, breathe, eat, and drink.

You have an interesting prospect ahead of you, one which I think leaves room for more optimism than pessimism. You can have all your different technologies, just as I have described the human race as having all its communicative levels. Of course, there are Luddites of various kinds who fear the changes, but within a library system in the next century there could be something of everything. We can't throw the past away completely. Manuscripts will continue to be stored as manuscripts. Books will continue to be consulted as books, because they have a certain kind of efficiency about them. They are one of the great—and abiding —achievements of the human race.

But built on these earlier strata will be that most magnificent new stratum of my title, the global library. Each of your institutions will be a node, an element in the global integrated circuit of communications. Whether you're in New Zealand and someone else is in Oregon, or you're in Yorkshire and the information is in India, it won't matter; what will matter is that you can get the information from the system. At the same time, within the library itself you'll continue the various activities which have characterized libraries down the years. I don't expect the word 'library' to vanish from the lexicon; it will simply extend its meaning. There is one note of caution to be sounded, however. I hope it won't be forgotten that we have a choice about how humane we shall be when we engage in this kind of multi-level librarianship. I hope we'll always remember that human contact is the whole point of the thing, that no mechanical device—printout or diskette—is as important as a real living human being with whom one can talk.

20

Themes and dreams: the romance of the database

[The keynote address at the Third Annual Conference of the University of Waterloo Centre for the New Oxford English Dictionary, Waterloo, Ontario, Canada, November 1987.]

Μῆνιν ἄειδε, θεά, Πηληϊάδεω Ἀχιλῆος
οὐλομένην, ἣ μυρί' Ἀχαιοῖς ἄλγε' ἔθηκε,
πολλὰς δ' ἰφθίμους ψυχὰς Ἄϊδι προΐαψεν
ἡρώων, αὐτοὺς δὲ ἑλώρια τεῦχε κύνεσσιν
οἰωνοῖσί τε πᾶσι, Διὸς δ' ἐτελείετο βουλή,
ἐξ οὗ δὴ τὰ πρῶτα διαστήτην ἐρίσαντε
Ἀτρεΐδης τε ἄναξ ἀνδρῶν καὶ δῖος Ἀχιλλεύς.

The words you have just heard are the opening lines of Homer's *Iliad*. The poet has asked the Muse to sing of Achilles' deadly anger, a rage that condemned many heroes to become food for dogs and birds, and sent their pale shades to the underworld. These words were stored in the hardware used at the time the epic was created (a human brain) and were transmitted to you by means of the original delivery system (a human mouth). Unfortunately, I could not sing them to the accompaniment of a harp, but I have done my best with the dactylic hexameters, the favoured mode of delivery among ancient Greek epic singers.

There is a considerable gulf fixed between the bards who sang wingèd words in ancient Greece and the people—their brains and their mouths—in this room tonight. I want to talk about that gulf, about what it is and how it has arisen, but, at the same time as I say something about what separates us from the singers of Homeric times, I would like to say something about the line of cultural and technological evolution that links us with them—indeed, with all the communicative styles of the ancient world.

There is, however, a second gulf to be considered, that between different contemporary scholars when they talk to each other about the technologies of communication, past and present. In this area there is a lack of shared terminology, indeed a lack of shared perspective. When, for example, classicists with an interest in Homer meet computer specialists with an interest in large-text databases, they may have difficulty finding common theoretical ground to stand on. Such common ground *should* be available to them—they do, after all, operate in the same broad area of communication, linguistics, and education—but it is not easy to locate. This distance between different present-day specialists interests me just as much as the distance between ourselves and Homer, and I would like to start my discussion of both gulfs by considering the meaning of the word *database*.

When preparing this talk I looked at a number of dictionaries and other works of reference, to see how they define *database*. The *Oxford Reference Dictionary* (1986) proved to be representative, calling a database 'an organized store of data for computer processing'. The glossary in Joost Kist's *Electronic Publishing* (1987) calls it 'an organised collection of machine-readable records containing bibliographic descriptions, subject-oriented information, dictionary content and/or actual texts or data (numerical or textual)'. You probably can't say fairer than that, in strictly contemporary terms, but neither Oxford nor Kist was quite what I wanted for my purposes. I found a more co-operative definition in the *Collins English Dictionary* (1986), which says: 'A systematized collection of data that can be accessed immediately and manipulated by a data-processing system for a specific purpose'. This description, by omitting words like 'electronic', 'computer', and 'machine-readable', offers me the freedom I need. The Collins definition does not exclude the idea of a non-mechanical database. Probably quite inadvertently, it allows for the possibility that Homer was also in the database business.

Over the last few years, I have been working on a theory of communicative shifts. This theory seeks to bring together and extend the observations and conclusions of a number of scholars in various fields. In terms of the humanities, its antecedents date at least from the American classicist Milman Parry in the 1920s and 1930s, working on the structure of Homeric epic verse. On the technological side, it ranges back to Johannes Gutenberg and beyond, and includes the contributions of such inventors and theorists as Charles Babbage and Alan Turing. In recent years, Elizabeth Eisenstein, Jack Goody, Eric Havelock, Walter Ong, and Anthony Smith, among others, have discussed major 'shifts' or 'revolutions' in the history of human communication, and the theory owes a great deal to them. In 1986, in *Worlds of Reference*, I briefly outlined a model of four great communicative shifts: speech, script, print, and what we currently think of as the electronic revolution. Let me take them in order here, in somewhat greater detail.

Speech is ancient and fundamental, but by no means unitary. There is, for example, a considerable difference between our general capacity for spoken language (which appears to be genetically primed and environmentally stimulated), and the skills once needed for the oral preservation of information (which were acquired through more or less strict and formalized training). This, it seems to me, is the point at which the database enters history—not with the invention of computers and the coining of the word itself, nor with the advent of the printing press, and not even with the creation of the first written texts.

To discuss the primordial mental-and-oral database, I need to propose a communicative 'subshift'. In it, everyday talk was augmented by a novel and highly formal register. This may have occurred around 10,000 years ago, perhaps earlier. The everyday business of chatting, gossiping, and reporting shaded— in various ways in various times and places—into a range of ritually elevated language. This high style served to signal certain intentions on the part of a speaker and to organize certain kinds of information. Its 'data' related to two main areas: great people and events (in the genealogies of chiefs and in accounts of heroic exploits) and approaches to the powers of nature (through prayers, hymns, incantations, and the cycles of myth which structured various worldviews).

I would like to call this development *storage speech*, which could be accompanied by such mnemonic aids as tally sticks, notched bones, and strung beads, rhythmic tapping, and kinds of music. Its rhythms, structures, themes, and formulas made the longer-term retention of knowledge more efficient, less vulnerable to mental lapses, and more easily transmitted, in the first place to audiences, and in the vital second place to apprentices who could carry its themes and dreams into the next generation. Through the conventions of storage speech, the lore of a community was gathered, shaped, elevated, and edited across the generations. In the specific form of *orature*, with its powerful poetic conventions, storage speech served as precursor to *literature*.

With the second shift (the creation of writing systems and their accompanying containers and layouts), we pass from a single oral-cum-auditory medium to a dual system: the older oral-cum-auditory medium used for one range of purposes, and the newer tactile-and-visual medium for others—often with a degree of overlap and rivalry. As regards the storage of quantities of information, the new medium proved seductive; it was more efficient, permanent, and directly consultable than stylized sound (however beautifully that sound might be rendered). As a result, more and more matter from the older oral tradition was transferred to new visual 'databases', using the hardware of clay-and-cuneiform technology, of reed-and-hieroglyph technology, of bamboo-and-ideogram technology, and so forth, up to the print-on-paper technologies of our own time.

In the transition from the entirely oral to the oral-scribal we can see emerging the basic sequential patterns—I will call them *frames*—that still dominate the production, storage, retrieval, and presentation of information. These are three-fold: first, the *list frame*, equally useful in speech or writing for handling genealogies and formulaic sequences generally; second, the *narrative frame*, for the presentation of events and descriptions; and third, for many of the purposes of orature, literature, reference, and administration, a *hybrid frame*, making use of both listing and narrating. The essential difference between list and narrative is that lists are more or less item-bound, and have little or no grammar and discourse, whereas narrative uses grammar and discourse to the full.

The *Iliad* and the Bible are large, complex works within hybrid frames. In them, catalogues of various kinds co-occur—and often blend—with various kinds of narrative. They are also examples of primary works that have generated a range of secondary genres. Scribes and scholars, while studying and editing such works, have created such aids as chapter and verse, numbered lines and pages, indexes and concordances, cross-references, annotations and commentaries, thematic companions, anthologies, textbooks, readers, and versions for special markets, such as children. One outcome of all that effort is the modern reference book in all its subgenres, an excellent example of the hybrid frame at work.

Progress has, however, exacted its toll. Although script was slow in supplanting storage speech, it has progressively displaced and downgraded it. Later, just as the use of script downgraded storage speech, so movable type downgraded the manuscript (no matter how beautifully indited), and marginalized scribes and copyists. Throughout those communities touched by literacy the traditional oral-auditory database declined. Although rote memorization was still a crucial feature of education in scribal and early print societies, it was text-based, and owed little directly to the unlettered skills of the bards. In turn, scribal rolls and codices, the first hardware for the visual database, declined in

THEMES AND DREAMS: THE ROMANCE OF THE DATABASE

importance when the print medium proved to be more stable, economical, labour-saving, and abundant.

The fourth shift is centrally a matter of electronic innovation, but there is more to it than that. It is a cluster of some ten linked subshifts that constitute the media mix of the later twentieth century, its constituents falling into three types: (1) *auditory* (the telephone, telecommunications, radio, and audio-recording); (2) *visual* (photography, and primary cinematography, television, video-recording, and computing); (3) *hybrid* (secondary cinematography, television, video-recording, computing, and some applications of laser technology).

Earlier on, I talked about gulfs. What I have tried to do here is bridge the gulf between ourselves and the ancient world by creating a model of communicative shifts, then manage the gulf among specialists by offering the shift model as a paradigm for where we have been, where we are now, and where we may be going. The different specialists may be able to locate themselves and their fields of interest within the paradigm, and make use of the attendant terminology. One of the model's virtues is the analogies it throws up. For example, it suggests that, although the achievements and prospects of the electronic age seem unique, potent, and *sui generis*, they are not. In an important sense, we have been this way before, at least three times—and more than three, if we count such subshifts as the creation of the alphabet, the switch from the papyrus roll with its spindles to the bindable parchment sheet, and the development of printing blocks. Analogies drawn across the shifts are creatively useful, a point that I would like to illustrate with only one from among many possible examples, taken from electronic publishing.

The Knowledge Warehouse is described in the second issue of the *International Publishers Bulletin* of 1987 as one of the world's first 'active electronic archives'. Developed in the UK by Publishers Databases Limited in London, its aim is 'to build a store of electronically held works from which data can be extracted and manipulated to provide a base for new knowledge works aimed at new markets'. It uses a system whereby machine-readable versions of currently published works can be stored, indexed, edited, excerpted, blended, and re-combined in a virtual infinity of forms, none of which requires the involvement of conventional third-shift publishing.

It all seems so up-to-the-minute, yet what intrigues me about the Knowledge Warehouse is its antiquity. A memory trace of an earlier incarnation lurks in the word 'text' (from the Latin *texere*, 'to weave'). Prior to the Latin, however, came the singers of Greek epic verse. They were *rhapsodes*, or 'stitchers of songs'. Theirs was not the heavy, slow warp and woof of scribal text on costly surfaces, but a fast, light, spontaneous blending of verse formulas and prefabricated episodes —right there in front of a live audience. The bards were not just inspired dreamers who invoked the Muse; they were thematic editors. Or, in computational terms, their poesy was menu-driven. In the heat of creation, a bard like Demodokos in the *Odyssey* could choose this theme rather than that, this episode rather than that, this version of the episode rather than that, this length rather than that, blending the whole in this way rather than that, weaving it all together as he went along.

His was a flexible craft, rendered less flexible when it passed into the care of scribes, and less flexible still when handed to the printers. Now, however, we find ourselves in a curious situation, in the Knowledge Warehouse or any other large electronic project. We are the new stitchers and weavers, but this time we can handle fixed text as if it were fluid voice, without necessarily suffering from the transience of speech. Available to us, through the new media, are both the creative fluidity of the bards' oral database and the efficient fixity of the visual database built by the scribes and printers. That, it seems to me, is both the romance and the utility of modern databases as defined by Oxford and by Kist.

The idea of authorship and copyright was largely implicit in scribal cultures, and only became explicit in print cultures. In purely oral times, no one owned the wingèd words of Homer, and no one now knows who Homer was. His name is no more personal than Oxford or IBM. In the world of knowledge warehouses, we will no doubt seek to protect authorship, ownership, and copyright, but we are intriguingly close to storage speech again, in our return to infinite blendability, adaptability, and copiability. There is a primitive communalism in the new fluency that the fourth shift offers us, copying discs on to cassettes, photocopying this document so that it can go into that customized collection, transferring software programs, and combining by electronic means chunks from many different textual sources. We will no doubt learn to handle it all, blending freedom with licences, but there will be some interesting moments in store, as we go back to the future.

21

Representing knowledge for human consumption

[An adaptation and updating of the keynote paper at the conference 'Informatics 9', held at King's College, Cambridge, March 1987, and organized by ASLIB (the Association of Librarians), the ASLIB Informatics Group, and the Information Retrieval Specialist Group of the British Computer Society, and published in the proceedings *Informatics 9: Meaning, the Frontier of Informatics*, ASLIB, 1987.]

This paper takes a panoramic historical look at the representation and presentation of knowledge, within a linguistic and cultural frame of reference. The first half discusses the four great communicative shifts: firstly, the adaptation of our physical apparatus for speech; secondly, the creation of an analogue to speech by means of organized marks on surfaces (including the invention of the alphabet as such); thirdly, the nature and impact of the printing press; and fourthly, in our own time, the coming of the computer and other high-tech communicative devices. This has been a cumulative process the recognition of which may enable us to step back and look more objectively at the interests, aims, and activities of knowledge engineers and information technologists. The second half relates the four shifts to three perennial interacting factors in the representation of knowledge: technology, technique, and content. The shared evolution of these three factors is concisely reviewed, so as to relate them to such areas of interest as: (1) past and current presentational technologies (from clay-reed-and-cuneiform in Sumer to silicon-screen-and-text today; (2) Popper's three-worlds model of knowledge; (3) the universal of knowledge management; (4) Walter Ong's concept of 'secondary orality'; (5) neurology and artificial intelligence; and (6) the problem of meaning.

The four shifts

Computation and artificial intelligence, expert systems and knowledge engineering have a *sui generis* quality about them. It is as if, for their practitioners and the general public alike, they came out of a virginal electronic womb, unassisted by any historical or cultural midwives, and without anything in the nature of a pedigree.

Certainly the electricity-based and electronically-contrived marvels of the late twentieth century are new and unprecedented by any measure, but this latter-day novelty serves at the same time to obscure two things: first, the fact that our species has in a serious sense been here before, several times, and second, the likelihood that we can learn from studying what happened on those previous occasions and afterwards. Following on from a variety of recent research and commentary (such as Eisenstein, 1979; Smith, 1980; Ong, 1982; McArthur, 1986), I would argue that the technocultural events and artifacts of interest to such people as those attending this conference are fourth in an on-going series. In addition, that series is not simply linear but cumulative, encouraging a mutually valuable interplay among technologies and techniques developed over thousands of years within the social and intellectual dimension of human evolution. One result of this interplay is that, after each breakthrough, the options that become available to *Homo sapiens* for the representation and presentation of knowledge are extended and enriched—and certainly not diminished or corrupted, whatever some traditionalists and purists may say.

Drawing on the model that I have used in *Worlds of Reference* (1986), I would like to outline here the four major communicative shifts (or jumps: a number of metaphors are possible) as follows:

(1) *The shift from a primary use of the physical apparatus of breathing, eating, and drinking to a secondary set of skills that we now call in English 'spoken language'.*
This shift belongs within a biological and geological time frame rather than to historical and social time as we normally conceive it. In bio-geological time, however, although it was itself no doubt a process spanning thousands of years, it was rapid and radical in terms of the species *Homo*. It was in all probability part of a cluster of developments, including the hemispheric lateralization of the neocortex of the brain, which indeed produced the variant to which we belong: so-called *Homo sapiens*, the Wise Human. Provisionally, we can suggest a broad date

such as between 100,000 and 50,000 years ago for this paradoxically sudden yet gradual shift.

(2) *The shift from the primary form of language as speech to a secondary analogue of the spoken language that we now call in English 'writing': signs scratched or inked on to surfaces of various kinds.*
This radical development not only belongs in historical time but in effect makes the concept of historical time possible, beginning some 6,000–5,000 years ago with what would now be called 'ideograms'. It was also greatly enhanced—at least as far as the Western and Westernizing world has been concerned—by a subshift around 1000 BC, when the alphabet was invented and disseminated. The second shift took centuries to establish itself, adding to our neurophysical repertoire the linguistic power of hand and eye where previously we had only the power of mouth and ear. The result was, as it were, a doubling in the strength of the 'grip' (a rather appropriate metaphor) that we have on communication. In the process, as Ong points out (1982), we added to our perception of language-as-action that of language-as-object. Communication was no longer simply audible and transient; it was also visible and more permanent, with all that this has meant for cultures with literate élites. The social experience of a socially restricted literacy was imposed on the wider, prior, and on-going experience of universal orality.

(3) *The shift of the primary form of the written language as scribal (Ong's chirography) towards a secondary and labour-saving process of print (typography).*
Towards, in other words, the first kind of mechanized multiple copying using a standardized range of formats and surfaces. The invention and adoption of the printing press contributed greatly to the vigour of European civilization from the fifteenth century onward (cf. Eisenstein, 1979). This contribution was not only in the area of text dissemination and an increase in the number of readers for such texts, but also in assumptions about what terms like 'literacy' and 'illiteracy' entail in societies that propelled themselves in post-scribal times towards the remarkable goal of 'universal literacy' within schemes of 'universal education'. In such societies, everyone would belong to the vastly expanded guild of scribes and copyists (but not—yet—of printers). This third shift began just over 500 years ago, affecting some varieties of speech more than others and as a result affecting people's attitudes towards them. Some, like French, became centralized and standardized relatively swiftly, while others, like Occitan (the language of the

troubadours in southern France), could not do so and as a result became peripheral, with such labels as 'patois' and 'dialect'. Indeed, within a 'language', 'dialect' often became the term for a subvariety opposed to a more elevated 'good', 'refined', 'cultivated', 'literary', 'correct', 'proper', or 'standard' supervariety with a name like English, French, German, Spanish, and Swedish. In the process, the orthographies of the standard languages tended to freeze at the point when printing truly came into its own for them, giving in the process a tremendous boost to scholarship and 'book learning'. Concepts like *book*, *text*, and *page* have reigned supreme since Gutenberg went to press.

(4) *The shift from the primary form of print on paper to a secondary form of (mainly) electronic composition and display, embodied in a variety of new devices that are by no means yet stabilized.*
From mainframe computers through 'smart' typewriters to PCs. This radical shift is so recent that, although we are greatly involved in its development and exercised about its potential, we can no more be sure of where it can take us than Alexander Graham Bell, working on a device to help the deaf, could see where his telephone would be a century later: part of a network that encircles the planet like an embryonic nervous system.

Perhaps the most cogent point about these shifts is their cumulative nature: everything which developed earlier is capable of interaction with everything that has developed more recently. All four shifts have powerful implications as regards how we think: that is, how our consciousness is structured and how it operates. Using the terminology of the fourth shift, we can say that each stage in turn has required an educational 're-programming' of the brain, both with regard to handling the new technologies as crafts and in relation to the ways in which these crafts have influenced our worldviews. If, for example, pre-literate people are viewed as 'savage', 'primitive', or 'pre-logical' (all terms used by men of science until quite recently), both the judgemental terms and the 'savage' state of affairs are tied to the systems available to savages and men of science alike for the representation of knowledge and the shaping of thought (cf. Lévi-Strauss, 1966). It appears to have been like this on every rung of the technocultural ladder, as the unreflecting recipients of the products and the *mentality* of a particular rung have chosen to down-value the *illitterati* below 'below', while those caught below have looked 'up' with alarm, envy, resentment, and indeed awe at the *illuminati* above.

However, in spite of the manifest and often Luddite tendencies that arise when a new shift or subshift begins to take effect, the layering of stage upon stage in this progression (if not progress) seems to be largely benign. No later arrival has yet erased any of its predecessors, although competition does occur among variant technologies and practices within shifts: we can speak, write, print, and compute, but vary greatly in the languages, scripts, typographies, and operating systems we may use. Each new shift does, however, over time alter both our perceptions and our use of prior technologies and techniques. Each shift produces a 'hindsight effect', in that it is hard for the beneficiaries of a later shift to get at prior states of mind and action except through the filter of their own experience; as a result they may misassume that predecessors or contemporaries in oral, scribal, and print cultures have been either (favourably) 'really just like us' or (unfavourably) 'naive and unsophisticated' and therefore lacking in the full truth.

Whereas our remoter ancestors needed to be articulate in only one area (speech and gestures, for example), many people today have to be multiply articulate—or suffer the consequences—in speech, reading and writing, handling print in all its forms and formats, and now, increasingly, in the new literacy [by 1998 of word-processing, electronic mail, and the Internet], all of which further affects our perceptions and our attitudes to others. Large residues of people are 'left behind' when such things happen. Nowadays, no one is left untouched by computers and the information-cum-knowledge revolution, however remote or intransigent that person may be. But millions are varyingly and in varying degrees (in)articulate in computational terms. This inarticulateness could also be true, not just for the less educated, but also for people who are marvellously articulate in other, 'earlier' modes: bards, genealogists, and praise-singers; calligraphers, hot-metal typographers, traditional artists, conventional typists, and off-line journalists, all of whom have found niches in the on-going crafts of earlier shifts. This appears to be inevitable in a cumulative civilization like ours, whose strata have built up since the days of the Sumerian clay tablet. It is part of human experience and it is entirely human to strike attitudes about it all.

One might bend Linnaean biological classification and talk about a *Homo electronicus* emerging out of *Homo typographicus*, who came in turn from *Homo scribalis*, who was preceded by *Homo oralis*. I use these evolutionary labels only partly in fun; they do serve to point up the psychological and cultural gap between people who have experienced the layers of literacy in full, those with less experience, and those with no experience beyond the oral. Alan Turing's people are as different from Gutenberg's people as the first printers were from the makers of

Mosaic tablets. Or to use an analogy taken from Richard Dawkins (1976), whereas between the chimpanzee, *Australopithecus*, and *Homo* differentation is built into 'genes' ('words' in the 'book' of life), the more recent and less primeval differences created by the various technocultural shifts belong in the 'memes' (communicable ideas, a sort of mental viruses) that are passed on, generation by generation, through socialization, education, and communication (whether casual or profound).

All of this may at first seem rather far removed from informatics and its ramifications, but that is not really the case. A general theory of information and knowledge that covers us and all our informatic activities requires the kind of historical backdrop that I have been outlining. Set against such a backdrop, the subject matter of this conference looks different. It is not an isolated modern event and a novel law unto itself; it belongs in the latest of four shifts. One day, in all probability, there will be a fifth shift. It is characteristic of such shifts that people cannot imagine them in advance, because they require a cluster of developments to trigger them, after which they take on their own distinctive shapes. Both Marshall McLuhan in 1964 and Alvin Toffler in 1970 were insightful about various present and future trends, but neither foresaw the microchip and miniaturized computers. And yet the relevant people were well into electronic research and experimentation when McLuhan and Toffler were writing about mediums, messages, and future shock.

Technology, technique, and content

I would like now to move from a general discussion of the shifts to the question of what exactly shifted with them. In this, I need to talk about three fundamental interlocking components in any representation and presentation of knowledge for any purpose. These are:

(1) *Technology*, covering the design, construction, maintenance, and use of delivery systems. This is by and large the hardware side of things.

(2) *Technique*, which refines and operates on technology, and is to a great extent conditioned by it while governing the quality of its use. It is therefore linked to the software side of things, but is not co-terminous with the concept of software.

(3) *Content*, which has such a high degree of autonomy that it is often considered to have an objective reality independent of the technologies and techniques that deliver and shape it. This apparent autonomy may,

however, be more apparent than real, and is routinely affected by technology and technique.

Natural language is an instructive example of how the three components work. A message in a particular language is as it were 'poured' into one of two mediums: on the one hand, the oral or phonic medium whose primary delivery system is 'human-body technology' (using vocal tract and bodily movements and positions), and on the other the graphic medium, which ranges through three shifts and across many technologies (for example, from clay-reed-and-cuneiform through paper-pen-and-alphabet to silicon-keyboard-and-screen). The linguistic message in each medium (and in each subform of the graphic medium) is structured and delivered in a distinctive way. A simple example of this is the part that intonation plays in speech: the closest correlate to this on paper or screen is punctuation and layout, and that is far from close. There is in fact no content without some kind of vehicle, and each vehicle affects content in its own way. A message 'incarnated' in speech is not the same as one incarnated on clay tablet, paper, or screen; the medium may not *be* the message, but it certainly affects it.

In terms of models and metaphors, one can represent these three interlocking components as boxes set side by side, as layers one above the other, or in any other kind of containerizing diagram. I prefer a mixture of triangle and circle to handle them, so as to allow for their continuum qualities and to indicate the bidirectionality of their relationships (see Figure 1).

Figure 1

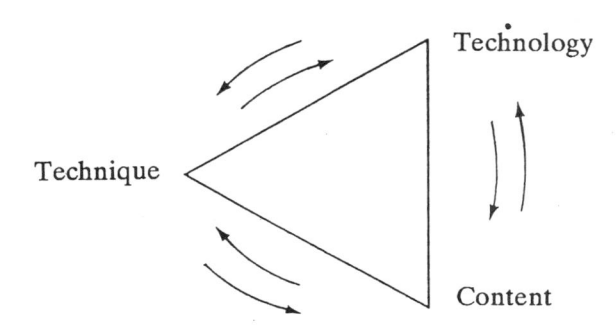

This model reminds us of the degree to which technology, technique, and content serve to shape and constrain one another, offering within the frames created by the different shifts (separately or together) a package for any particular purpose that has certain inevitable strengths and weaknesses. In terms of high theory, one can relate this triangular relationship to Karl Popper's three-worlds model of life and consciousness. As presented in Popper and Eccles (1981), this model is a rigid construct consisting of three containers set side by side (see Figure 2).

Figure 2

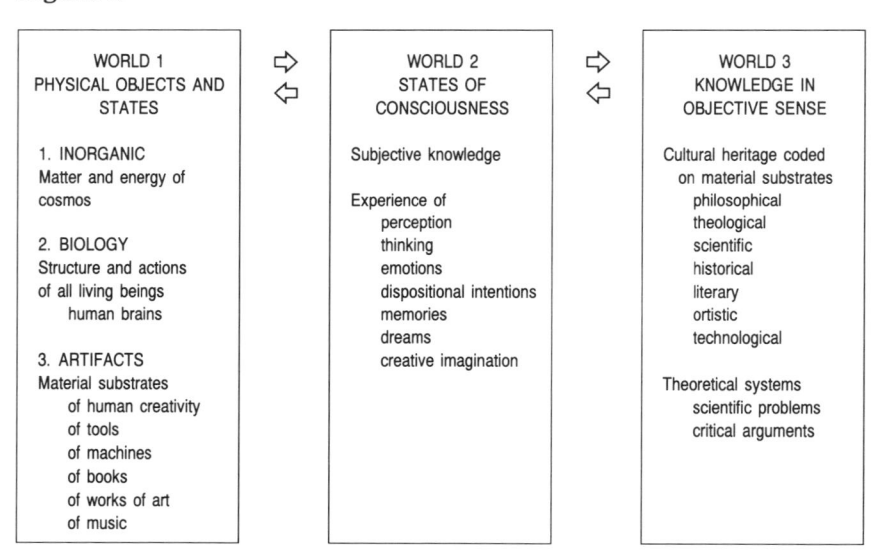

WORLD 1 PHYSICAL OBJECTS AND STATES	WORLD 2 STATES OF CONSCIOUSNESS	WORLD 3 KNOWLEDGE IN OBJECTIVE SENSE
1. INORGANIC Matter and energy of cosmos 2. BIOLOGY Structure and actions of all living beings 　human brains 3. ARTIFACTS Material substrates 　of human creativity 　of tools 　of machines 　of books 　of works of art 　of music	Subjective knowledge Experience of 　perception 　thinking 　emotions 　dispositional intentions 　memories 　dreams 　creative imagination	Cultural heritage coded on material substrates 　philosophical 　theological 　scientific 　historical 　literary 　artistic 　technological Theoretical systems 　scientific problems 　critical arguments

Popper's World 1 of physical objects and states is the bedrock of everything, providing the matter and energy, living beings, artifacts, and products that we are concerned with. This is the world of technology *par excellence*. World 2 lacks the objective hardness of World 1. It is the soft subjective world of our consciousness, both individual and collective, including our perceptions and conceptions, our emotions and dispositions, our memories, dreams, and creative imaginings. World 2 plays upon and plays with World 1, observing and experimenting, drawing analogies, creating logical relationships, extending what *does* exist towards what *could* exist. Technique depends centrally on this world, although its consequences are obvious everywhere in World 1. In the intimacy of the perceived images of World 1 and the conceived images of World 2, ideas shape and develop the felt everyday world.

Popper's World 3 is the most controversial of these constructs. It represents or consists of knowledge in the objective sense; it is all of our cultural heritage as it is tangibly and visibly coded in the materials and formats of World 1. It is our honey store, all of the religions, philosophies, sciences, arts, histories, and other taxonomically neat 'subjects' that we have created and boxed for ourselves in order to handle the flux of existence. Content as such is a chameleon among the various worlds proposed by Popper; it is conceived (in both senses of that word) in World 2, systematized for general consumption in World 3, drawn in various ways from the quarry of World 1 and then poured back into that world in the form of books, periodicals, notices, printouts, displays, tapes, and every other artifact ever constructed for the representation and presentation of knowledge and news.

As Popper might put it, we need a good falsifiable theory of all this, a unifying theory that draws together whatever conception and observation we have about orality and primary oral cultures, about scribes and chirographic cultures, about printers and others concerned with typographic materials, and now the information scientists and knowledge engineers in the brave new world of the fourth shift. My assumption, of course, is that a comprehensive theory would be good for us. An appreciation of its universals and of all the contingent circumstances from clay to silicon would help us now, in the onrush of the fourth shift, and would apply in broad terms to any fifth or sixth shift that our species may experience in days to come. If we do not have such an integrated theory of all knowledge systems throughout recorded history and across all relevant cultures, we impoverish the basis on which we seek to understand any one shift with its attendant interplay of technology, technique, and content.

One area of impoverishment is that people interested in exploiting the new tools of the fourth shift—computer hardware and software, database organization, electronic networking, telecommunications, still photography, motion photography, video technology, sound recording and replay, and others—may fail to appreciate relevant past analogues to what they are doing, condemning themselves as a result to reinventing the wheel in their new media. They may also carry over unexamined into the fourth shift many techniques that have worked well enough for the third-shift world but that may act as a brake on their efforts in the new medium. Disdain for 'electronic page-turners' has been one way in which many people show an awareness of this danger, but there may be subtler influences at work than the power of the fixed-frame page. Another area is the growing awareness that although alphabetic order has worked quite well for dictionaries as third-shift 'books', it may be a primitive and inhibiting technique in the new world of menu-driven programs and mice (or mouses). Lastly, there is the matter of backflow: uncertainty about the aims and achievements of an infant fourth shift should not prevent third-shift publishers from deriving ideas from the world of computer software that can enliven the pages of traditional publications.

The subject is of course enormous and its ramifications lead in every direction across the Western and Westernizing world. Let me, however, try to highlight some of the more significant features of the trio of technology, technique, and content.

In terms of technology, we have a tendency to under-appreciate and misperceive what I have called 'human-body technology', especially as it relates to the first-shift culture of knowledge and news processed orally. One reason for this is of course that it is the oldest shift and is therefore taken for granted as not being a 'shift' as such at all. Another is that we tend, reasonably enough, to discern and define technology as extra-anatomical—existing out there in apparatus separate from our own physique, which is not usually thought of as apparatus at all. This may be a mistake, and the interest that many artificial intelligence enthusiasts are taking in human intelligence and so-called 'natural language' indicates that the whole area is being re-appraised in challenging ways. First-shift orality is of course ephemeral and dependent on memory—and memory is not a straightforward commonsense thing. Because of the flightiness of memory it has always entailed strict mental and physical training, whether on the part of a Homeric rhapsode performing in ancient Greece or a Shakespearian actor portraying Hamlet in Stratford-upon-Avon. Teachers, actors, dancers, singers, oral poets, priests, orators, and lawyers have all had access—crudely or in highly sophisticated ways—to apprenticeships in techniques for controlling brain, breath, lips, tongue, teeth, throat, tone, voice quality, accent, expressions, gestures, stance, movement, and relation to situational context all of which contribute to the whole professional package. We all know when the apparatus—the human technology—is defective and the technique is deficient in such areas.

We also all know that through radio and television, audio- and video-tape recordings, and the like (as part of the intensely complex fourth shift), all this ephemeral first-shift use of body and brain has in an instant of geological time been rendered repeatable, copiable, and therefore much more permanent than ever before, and we can see and hear the actors and poets and lawyers, etc., again and again on tape (and perhaps some day in holograph), where our ancestors could only see one performance at a time from one angle at a time and only hear anything once. This new state of affairs is what Walter Ong calls 'secondary orality', a novel extension and adaptation of the ancient, primary process.

In addition, if we are to fulfil the hope of robotics and artificial intelligence and to have machines that can do more than mimic the rawest forms of human communication, then a new and full appreciation of first-shift linguistic craftsmanship on the part of fourth-shift information specialists will be essential.

Technology is more obvious when we move away from the human body and its cruder analogues and turn to the various kinds of surfaces that our species has made use of. The range of such surfaces is wide and runs the gamut of animal, vegetable, and mineral. The animal is skins for parchment and goose quills for pens, entailing the slaughter of herds of young animals for the codices of scribal times and the maintenance of huge flocks of geese before pens with metal nibs were invented. The vegetable is papyrus reeds, wood pulp, clay tablets, bamboo strips, palm leaves, and the like, while the mineral is stone (and especially marble), clay, and now silicon chips set in metal and plastic, animated by current running along wires. All of this is the contingent world, the messy stuff we have to manipulate, whether we are plucking geese and sharpening quills, or etching microchips and downloading data. We may yet get back to animal matter, if one day someone steps aside from silicon and lasers, and in proper Frankenstein style begins to use quasi-neurons in assemblages of pseudo-tissue. Neurologists and computer scientists already write books like Ernest Kent's *The Brains of Men and Machines* (1981).

It would not surprise me if one day we worked with organic computers. If and when that time comes, the mass of humankind will feel the same awe for organic 'cybrains' as the peasants of ancient Egypt must have felt for a papyrus of *The Book of the Dead* (as we call it), in the hands of a literate priest. That awe is one of the universals.

I have already mentioned a range of techniques used by oral performers because of the nature of the human-body technology at their disposal. Most such oral/visual techniques have their analogues in the mediums that use surface and script, thus: voice quality is matched by handwriting, typeface, and layout; voice projection is matched by size of lettering; voice and breath control are matched by punctuation and white space, as well as the sizing of phrases, sentences, and paragraphs; stance and delivery are matched by format and accessibility; and body language and physical movement are matched by design and illustration.

Just as writing was the first great analogue of speech, so within the second, third, and fourth shifts we can detect, in their various uses of surfaces, minutiae which match quite closely the minutiae of first-shift orality. As I have already suggested, the fourth shift will incorporate the technologies of 'secondary reality' (audio- and video-recording, etc.) into the general technology of the computer in ways that will attempt to capture or imitate the spontaneity and even the transience of speech in the world. We already see in disk technology certain procedures for the incorporation of sound and animation into databases for encyclopedias and reference-related services, and movements towards integrated systems that combine hi-fi, televisual, and computer facilities in one high-tech complex. Here, the interplay of technology and technique will do interesting things to linearity and sequence, as users find themselves able to enter and exit at all sorts of points for all sorts of purposes, and may provide interactive facilities allowing not just for the manipulation of data in standard packages but also for privately editing and adapting that data.

This will of course cause headaches for people interested in copyright and intellectual property. Such matters belong in the main to third-shift print culture, where fixity and the incorrupt text have been highly valued. Creative editing does however occur all the time in the dissemination of information through print media, while the margin annotation of second-shift and the plagiarism of third-shift culture are only writ larger in the new freedom and licence of electronic adaptation. Curiosly enough, as things loosen up in the fourth-shift world of interactive facilities, hitherto sacrosanct texts may well in many situations attain a fluidity comparable to the flux and ease of general conversation. Textual transformation may well begin to resemble the inpressionism and low attributability of everyday speech. The more the output of smart machinery begins to resemble natural language, the truer this picture will become.

This could then bring into the discussion of text a secondary version of an ancient oral requirement: that while most speech may be casual and ephemeral, some speech must be kept inviolate. That kind of speech consisted of tribal genealogies, heroic exploits, and religious poetry, all structured to facilitate a greater fixity than ordinary speech. In the high fluidity of computer-based texts, certain 'touchstone texts' may become mandatory. They may even be kept in traditional third-shift book format, for checking against, much as the perfect metre is kept in certain shrines of standard measurement.

In talking about texts, we have overlapped out of technique into content, which is intimately involved with the idea of 'meaning'—a quagmire in which philosophers of language have wallowed for centuries.

REPRESENTING KNOWLEDGE FOR HUMAN CONSUMPTION

Part of the problem of meaning is the assumption that it exists apart from its vehicles and circumstances, in some high Platonic place where it is free from human corruption. This is a classic concept, but a hard one to work with. Much easier to suppose that we do not draw on meaning and content as if from some celestial bank account, but select our data from the flux of life in accordance with our needs, our ideologies, our current technological capacities, and our repertoire of techniques for presentation and representation. In practical terms, there is no refuge from this view of meaning and content, because we cannot find such entities in a pure and unalloyed condition. The best way of achieving decent objectivity appears to be by cross-checking. You get a fix on a word by consulting one dictionary, a better fix by looking at two, and a decent triangulation by bringing in a third. It is likely that one service which the fourth shift will offer us in abundance is the freedom to compare and contrast, and then to synthesize. And that of course applies not just to artifacts such as dictionaries and encyclopedias (which are a particular concern of mine), but to all the artifacts of all the shifts, from oral genealogies in poetic form to an international stock market printout.

This brings us back to the cumulative and enveloping quality of the four shifts that our species has experienced. Speech goes on in all its rich allusiveness and elusiveness, but has been enveloped and augmented by and reinterpreted in terms of writing. Speech and writing go on, expanded and enriched by the vigour and fixity of the printed page. Speech, writing, and print go on, further augmented first by photography, the telephone, radio, and television, then by the developments in computation, from early valves, tapes, and mainframes to the transistor, the silicon chip, and the 'personal' computer, as available to everyone as a watch or a pocket calculator. The result is a remarkable media soup, where high technology will not mean simply more 'high' artifacts, but better access—if we play our cards right—to all the products of the older 'low' technologies.

Graphics on high-resolution screens and top-quality scanners and printers will do things for hieroglyphs and calligraphy that the old scribes would have marvelled at, while the options for kinds of print and presentation will make a Gutenberg out of anyone with access to a desk-top publishing package. The fascination and promise of the fourth shift is not so much that it now deals in ROM, RAM, megabytes and terabytes, mice-cum-mouses, the Internet, AI, and virtual reality, but that it uses these to let us have all the old tricks back again in novel—almost magical—settings. That is a properly encyclopedic service, in the ancient sense of the *enkyklios paideía*, the circle of learning.

Appendix: The Unabridged *Devil's Dictionary of Language Teaching*

[An unofficial glossary of terms in applied linguistics and language teaching, published in serial form (in a less complete version) in the monthly newspaper the *EFL Gazette*, January to September 1988.]

Dedication To the unhallowed memory of Ambrose Bierce (1842–?1914), journalist and compiler of *The Devil's Dictionary*. Three definitions from the master's work (posthumous unabridged edition, 1967): *Aberration* Any deviation in another from one's own habit of thought, not sufficient in itself to constitute insanity. *Dictionary* A malevolent literary device for cramping the growth of a language. *Disabuse* To present your neighbor with another and better error than the one which he has deemed it advantageous to embrace.

Accent. What other people speak with.

Acrolect. A basilect that made it to the top.

Advanced learner. Someone who owns a copy of Hornby's dictionary of current English.

Alphabet. A set of symbols so organized as to persuade us that, although spoken language came first, written language comes first.

Applied Linguist. An English-language teacher who applies, has applied, or intends to apply for a job at a university.

Applied Linguistics. An academic discipline consisting of two sub-disciplines that operate sequentially: *applied Applied Linguistics*, the province of masters and doctoral students, who still have one foot in the classroom; and *theoretical Applied Linguistics*, for after their graduation.

APPENDIX

Approach. A method with a conscience.

Appropriacy. What your students should have said in any given situation.

Attention span. What you remember when you're sitting in the audience but forget when you're standing beside the water jug.

Audiolingualism. A revolution in language teaching that encourages students to be audio and teachers to be lingual.

Audiovisual aids. Those materials and gadgets in a classroom designed by somebody called Murphy.

Authentic materials. Genuinely true-to-life materials used in genuinely artificial conditions.

Basilect. An acrolect with no ambition.

Behavio(u)rism. The psychological theory that expects learners to salivate whenever a bell rings, whether the goods have been delivered or not.

Bilingualism. The condition in which one person learns to confuse two languages with equal skill.

Body language. Your body talking when you wish it would leave the job to your mouth.

Child language. The kind of language a child produces when wired for sound by parents working for a doctorate in psycholinguistics.

Child language acquisition. A natural phenomenon so beautifully designed as to make language teachers permanently open to attack.

Cloze test. A test in which the students have to guess certain words that have been systematically removed from a text that they can't understand because certain words have been systematically removed from it.

Cognitive code. A revolution in language teaching and learning for people who know what 'induction' really means.

Code-switching. What the CIA, MI5, and any other right-thinking group does when they don't want outsiders to know what's going on.

Colloquial language. Words that are so bad they have to be labelled 'informal' in trendy dictionaries.

Communication. What you and I do well but everybody else lets us down on.

Communicative approach. What they used to do on Friday afternoons when everybody felt like relaxing after a hard week of grammar, drills, compositions, and translation exercises.

Communicative competence. A skill worth cultivating if you want to perform a deletion transformation on a major theory of syntax.

APPENDIX

Community language learning. A philanthropic procedure in which the student community agrees to take on the teachers' work as well as their own.

Competence and performance. Two things that matter to all of us; unfortunately, only ideal people have the first and everybody else is stuck with the second.

Comprehensible input. What methodologists provide in their books.

Computer assisted language learning. A procedure by means of which students can use teachers as backup systems in the event of a power failure.

Correction. A game played by two people, only one of whom knows the rules.

Creole. A variety of language spoken near cruise ships.

Culture shock. An entirely tolerable experience if you have a return ticket.

Deep structure. The linguistic communion we would all share if surface structure didn't get in the way.

Definition. A use of one or more words as if to explain the meaning of one or two other words; particularly useful in EFL dictionaries for words like 'the', 'my', 'get', and 'must'.

Diagnostic test. A test that tells you the students are every bit as bad as you knew they were before you administered the test.

Dialect. A language variety that has everything going for it, except the government, the schools, the middle class, the law, the armed forces, and employers.

Dialog(ue). Something that happens between two students at the front of the class while the rest go to sleep.

Dictionary. A book which uses the alphabet to put words in their proper place, but which has so far failed to keep them there.

Direct Method. The late nineteenth-century revolution in language teaching that enabled students to converse fluently in languages they didn't know.

Discourse analysis. The study of long stretches of language undertaken by linguists after they found they couldn't get the hang of short stretches of language.

Drill. What dentists, army sergeants, and language teachers have in common.

Eclecticism. What you believe in when you've got a class to teach in five minutes and haven't prepared anything according to this year's panacea.

EFL. English for Fellow Linguists.

APPENDIX

EFL lexicography. The art of marshalling the words of the English language in various useful ways for people whose only problem is that they don't know the English language.

Elicitation. Something you would be arrested for if you did it in a public place.

ELT. English Language Tension, a debilitating syndrome to which publishers and conference organizers are particularly prone before sales conferences and annual conventions, and which also afflicts teachers who aren't sure which book *not* to photocopy out of.

English. The language ordained by Divine Providence for the employment of EFL teachers, ENL teachers, ESL teachers, ESD teachers, EAP teachers, ESP teachers, teacher trainers, teacher-trainer trainers, language school program(me) directors, language school administrators, government overseers, ELT publishers, ELT publishers' editors, ELT publishers' printers and binders, ELT publishers' accountants, ELT booksellers, ELT booksellers' accountants, ELT writers, ELT writers' bank managers, ELT writers' accountants, applied linguists, applied applied linguists, theoretical applied linguists, translators, interpreters, librarians, British Council English Language Officers, English Speaking Union organizers, ARELS organizers, IATEFL organizers, TESOL organizers, TESOL-Scotland-SATEFL-SATESL organizers, MEXTESOL organizers, TEXTESOL organizers, SEXTESOL organizers, ABC broadcasters, BBC broadcasters, CBC broadcasters, plenary speakers, keynote speakers, featured speakers, conference centre managers, hotel complaints staffs, language laboratory makers, CALL creators . . .

Error analysis. A mistake.

ESL. English for the Slow Lane.

ESP. Extra-Sensory Perception (and don't let anybody persuade you otherwise).

Exercise. Something that is mechanical, boring, sadistic, and useless for learning a language, but mechanical, boring, sadistic, and useful for keeping fit.

Feedback. The return to the input of part of the output of a machine, system, or language teacher, so as to produce electrical changes that improve performance.

Gender. A grammatical category, regardless of sex; a sexual category, regardless of grammar.

Gesture. The cognitive strategy employed by students when they respond to situations not covered in the course.

APPENDIX

Gradation. The careful staging of language teaching material from the difficult to the difficult.

Grammar. The residue of language left after you covered all the stuff that should have led to fluency but didn't.

Grammar-Translation Method. The undiscussable mess the human race made of language teaching and learning before we got to the discussable mess.

Holistic approach. That spirit of enthusiasm and good will in which you remember the global personal needs and aspirations of every single one of the students in your care but still put the cassette in backwards.

Humanistic approach. The scientific theory of language teaching which proves that nobody was nice to the students before 1978.

Idiolect. My personal guarantee that nobody else speaks the language properly.

Interaction. The same thing as intercourse before intercourse became something else.

Interactive approach. That view of language teaching and learning which says everything will be fine when teachers and students get their acts together.

Intermediate. The stage in language learning that covers everything between birth and death.

Jargon. What the other academics and presenters use.

L1 and L2. First and second language respectively, especially where English is the second language of the students until they have learned it, after which it becomes their second first language.

Language. 'Any interactive communicationally-oriented phonic-graphic-gestural patterning system for the purpose of manipulating situational, semantic, structural, discoursal, and pragmatic variables so as to facilitate or disfacilitate comprehension' (Quatsch and Kauderwelsch, 1985:1).

Language course. Any series of structured or non-structured, humanistic or non-humanistic, interactive or non-interactive, communicative or non-communicative, effective or non-effective institutionalized experience involving two or more people, one or more language, and every hang-up under the sun.

Language laboratory. A room full of audiolingual equipment so designed that there is always one functioning booth *less* than the number of students waiting to come in.

Language learner. A category that includes language students but may or may not include language teachers.

APPENDIX

Language learning. The social process by which a student, on joining a course or opening a book, progressively discovers the gulf fixed between promises and fulfilment.

Language students. People who may or may not want to be in the classroom, may or may not be capable of the work, may or may not learn, and may or may not care.

Language teachers. People who may or may not want to be in the classroom, may or may not be capable of the work, may or may not learn, and may or may not care.

Language teaching. The educational process in which one teaches today's students with yesterday's methods, and prepares tomorrow's teachers to use today's methods.

Langue and parole. Forerunners of competence and performance that made the mistake of being in French.

Lexicography. The art of marshalling words in various useful ways in order to convince us that words can be marshalled in various useful ways.

Linguist. Formerly someone fluent in two or more languages; now someone fluent in writing about one or more language.

Linguistics. The science that hopes one day to understand language but in the meantime helps everybody else to understand language.

Listening comprehension. A skill that is necessary for the student but optional for the teacher.

Method. Any way of teaching languages that is based on the collaboration of Divine Providence and at least one language teacher.

Methodology. The scientific study of how language teachers guess their way from course to course; any preferred set of such guesses.

Monitor Model. A Christian Science approach to language learning, which demonstrates that language learning doesn't exist.

Motivation. That which enables students to learn a language in spite of teachers, organizers, institutions, classrooms, methodologists, or any other obstacle that we have so far found to put in their way.

Multiple-choice test. None of the above.

Natural Approach. A revolution in language teaching and learning in which students are steadily filled with input until they feel the need to output.

Nature versus nurture. The controversy about whether our inability to communicate and live decently together should be blamed on our remoter ancestors or on our immediate ancestors.

Notional-functionalism. The theory of language teaching and learning that stresses the importance of the notional and the functional

APPENDIX

interpreted in terms of functions and notions, insofar as one can assert anything positively about either notions or functions, particularly in communicative terms.

Objective test. Any test that is easy for teachers to mark and preferably one that can be given to a machine instead.

Oral drills. What dentists and language teachers have in common.

Oral interpersonal exchange. 'The acquired capacity to initiate, sustain, encode, and decode direct non-graphic communicative interactivity on a strict person-to-person basis through the mediation of the mouth and ears' (Quatsch and Kauderwelsch, 1985:2).

Overhead projector. A piece of classroom equipment so designed as to project your first transparency upside-down no matter how you position it.

Pair work. The oldest approach of them all.

Part of speech. A category of language description that should be strictly avoided until it cannot be avoided any more, recursively.

Philology. What linguists did before the word 'synchronic' was coined.

Phonetic notation. A pronunciation system in earlier and simpler EFL dictionaries intended to help students manage the everyday alphabet by respelling every word in a different alphabet and between square brackets.

Phonemic notation. A pronunciation system in later and more complex EFL dictionaries based on the classic 1975 study by Quatsch and Kauderwelsch, which demonstrated that placing transcribed words between slanted lines makes RP diphthongs 3.1415 times easier to assimilate than placing them between square brackets.

Pidgin. A variety of language highly favoured by people who don't have to use it.

Prescription. Something we accept with gratitude from a physician but would never tolerate in a linguistics course.

Proficiency. The point at which a student's knowledge and ability begin to embarrass the teacher.

Proficiency test. A test that provides proof that the students are at least as good as they are.

Pronunciation. That part of a student which is exactly the same at the end of a language course as at the beginning.

Psycholinguistics. The scientific study of the gap between psychologists and natural language.

Reading comprehension. The capacity to understand a writer's meaning, useful for many purposes but not essential for the output of social scientists and linguists.

APPENDIX

Reception and production. What methodologists talked about before they began to talk about input and output.

Remedial teaching. What you do all the time, only more so.

Repetition. It cannot be said often enough that this is a bad habit.

Role-playing. What we do some of the time in the classroom and all of the time elsewhere.

RP. Real Pronunciation, a form of spoken English commoner among foreigners than natives, and endemic in EFL dictionaries.

Silent Way. The first ever language-teaching method that shuts teachers up and lets students do the talking.

Simulated situation. This occurs when a truly sincere language teacher turns a classroom into a cafe or a cafe into a classroom.

Small-group teachng. Large-group teaching on a small scale.

Social distance. The amount of space you need in order to escape from an importunate foreigner.

Sociolinguistics. The study of substandard dialects as if they were as good as the language they are described in.

Speech act. Something you wish you hadn't said but it's too late to do anything about.

Standard English. The variety of English that is least misunderstood around the world.

Stimulus-response. A way of getting pigeons to play ping-pong and to put human beings into comas.

Stress. What a language teacher feels when the student emphasizes the wrong syllable for the fortieth time.

Structuralism. The scientific revolution in language teaching and learning which so organized things that students couldn't make any mistakes while teachers and course-writers could make as many as they wanted.

Syllabus. Something you keep handy to prove that you know what you should have been doing that day.

Syllabus design. A programme designed to provide methodologists with steady employment.

TESOL. Teaching English to Speakers of Obsolescent Languages, a hierarchically structured, democratic, nationally based international organization that arranges for enormous numbers of people connected with teaching English to become over-excited once a year in a North American city.

Testing. What you do in order to measure the extent of your failure.

Textbook. A book whose production, distribution, purchase, and presence in a classroom is proof that somebody somewhere runs a paper mill.

Total immersion. A modern approach to language teaching that dates back to John the Baptist and presumes a similar faith.

Total physical response. What we would all like to get more of, but wonder why we don't.

Total recall. What you achieve with everything and everybody that you don't want or need to remember.

Transaction. Anything that allows me to be OK whether you're OK or not.

Transformational-generative grammar. A system of language description which demonstrates that English syntax underlies all the world's languages; so called because it transformed a whole generation of linguists into terminal strings of well-formed grammarians.

Usage. What people firmly deny doing till somebody plays the tape back.

References

Abercrombie, David. 1963. 'Conversation and spoken prose', *English Language Teaching*, 18:1. Reprinted in Abercrombie, *Studies in Phonetics and Linguistics*: Oxford: Oxford University Press, 1965.
———. 1967. *Elements of General Phonetics*. Edinburgh: Edinburgh University Press.
Bacon, Francis. 1620. *Novum Organon*. Book I, Aphorism 129.
Bailey, Richard W. and Manfred Görlach, eds. 1982. *English as a World Language*. Ann Arbor: University of Michigan Press. UK edition, 1984, Cambridge University Press.
Bailey, Richard W. 1985. 'The idea of World English', *English Today* 1.1.
Barber, Charles. 1964. Revised 1972. *The Story of Language*. London: Pan.
———. 1993. *The English Language: A Historical Introduction*. Cambridge: Cambridge University Press.
Bickerton, Derek. 1975. *Dynamics of a Creole System*. Cambridge: Cambridge University Press.
Bolinger, Dwight. 1968. *Aspects of Language*. New York: Harcourt, Brace, & World.
Bongers, Herman. 1947. *The History and Principles of Vocabulary Control*. Holland: Woopi-Woerden.
Bright, J.A. and McGregor, G.P. 1970. *Teaching English as a Second Language*. London: Longman.
Clark, Arthur Melville Clark and Harold Whitehall. 1974. 'Rhyme', in Alex Preminger, ed., *Princeton Encyclopedia of Poetry and Poetics*. New York: Macmillan.
Corson, David. 1985. *The Lexical Bar*. Oxford: Pergamon.
Couper-Kuhlen, Elizabeth. 1993. *English Speech Rhythm: Form and Function in Everyday Verbal Interaction*. Amsterdam and Philadelphia: John Benjamins.
Cranston, Maurice. 1986. 'Ideology', in *The Encyclopaedia Britannica*, 15th Edition (Macropaedia Vol. 20). Chicago: Encyclopaedia Britannica Inc.
Crystal, David. 1984. *Who Cares about English Usage?* London: Penguin.

REFERENCES

——. 1997. *English as a Global Language*. Cambridge: Cambridge University Press.

Dakin, Julian. 1969. 'The Teaching of Reading', in Hugh Fraser and W.R. O'Donnell, eds, *Applied Linguistics and the Teaching of English*. London: Longman.

Daniel, Samuel. 1599. *Musophilus: containing a generall defense of learning*.

Dawkins, Richard. 1976. *The Selfish Gene*. Oxford: Oxford University Press. New Edition, 1989.

Donaldson, Margaret. 1978. *Children's Minds*. London: Fontana/Collins.

Eisenstein, Elizabeth. 1979. *The Printing Press as an Agent of Change: Communications and Cultural Transformations in Early-Modern Europe*. 2 vols. Cambridge: Cambridge University Press. Single-volume paperback, 1980.

Eldridge, R.C. 1911. *Six Thousand Common English Words*. Niagara Falls.

Ferguson, Charles. 1959. 'Diglossia', in *Word* 15. Reprinted in Hymes (1964) and Fishman (1968).

Fishman, Joshua, ed. 1968. *Readings in the Sociology of Language*. The Hague: Mouton.

Fries, Charles C. and A. Aileen Traver. 1950. *English Word Lists: A Study of Their Adaptability for Instruction*. Michigan: Ann Arbor.

Fromm, Erich. 1950. *Psychoanalysis and Religion*. New Haven: Yale University Press.

Gibson, Kathleen R. and Tim Ingold, eds. 1993. *Tools, Language and Cognition in Human Evolution*. Cambridge: Cambridge University Press.

Goody, Jack. 1977. *The Domestication of the Savage Mind*. Cambridge: Cambridge University Press.

Graddol, David. 1997. *The Future of English?* London: The British Council.

Gromm, Bernard. 1934. *A Short History of English Words*.

Grove, Victor. 1950. *The Language Bar*. London: Routledge and Kegan Paul.

Handscombe, R. J(ean). 'The Sunrunners: ESL by TV for grade 3 in Ontario', *TESOL Quarterly*, 9:3.

Havelock, Eric A. 1963. *Preface to Plato*. Cambridtge, Mass.: Harvard University Press.

Hogben, Lancelot. 1964. *The Mother Tongue*. London: Secker & Warburg.

Howard, Godfrey. 1985. *A Guide to Good English in the 1980s*.

Howatt, A.P.R. 1984. *A History of English Language Teaching*. Oxford: Oxford University Press.

Hulbert, James R. 1955. *Dictionaries: British and American*. London: André Deutsch.

Hunter, Karen. 1987. 'New technologies, publishing and copyright: an introduction to database publishing', *Rights*, 1:2.

Hymes, Dell, ed. 1964. *Language, Culture and Society*, New York: Harper & Row.

——, ed. 1971. *Pidginization and Creolization of Languages*. Cambridge: Cambridge University Press.

REFERENCES

Jackson, Howard. 1988. *Words and Their Meaning*. Harlow: Longman.
Kent, Ernest. 1981. *The Brains of Machines and Men*. New York: McGraw-Hill.
Kist, Joost. 1987. *Electronic Publishing: Looking for a Blueprint*. London: Croom Helm.
Labov, William. 1972. *Sociolinguistic Patterns*. Philadelphia: Philadelphia University Press.
Landau, Sidney. 1984. *Dictionaries: The Art and Craft of Lexicography*. Cambridge and New York: Cambridge University Press.
Leakey, Richard and Roger Lewin. 1992. *Origins Reconsidered: In Search of what Makes us Human*. New York: Little, Brown & Company.
Le Page, Robert B. and Andrée Tabouret-Keller. 1985. *Acts of Identity: Creole-Based Approaches to Language and Ethnicity*. Cambridge: Cambridge University Press.
Lieberman, Philip. 1991. *Uniquely Human: The Evolution of Speech, Thought, and Selfless Behavior*. Cambridge, Mass.: Harvard University Press.
Lévi-Strauss, Claude. 1966. *The Savage Mind*. London: Weidenfeld and Nicolson.
Lipka, Leonhard. 1989 (1st edn), 1992 (2nd edn). *An Outline of English Lexicology*. Tübingen: Niemeyer.
Lord, Albert A. 1960. *The Singer of Tales*. Cambridge, Mass.: Harvard University Press.
Lyons, John. 1968. *Introduction to Theoretical Linguistics*. Cambridge and New York: Cambridge University Press.
Mathews, M.M. 1933. *A Survey of English Dictionaries*. New York: Russell & Russell.
Matoré, Georges. 1968. *Histoire des dictionnaires français*. Paris: Larousse.
McArthur, Tom. 1978. 'The vocabulary-control movement in the English language', in the *Indian Journal of Applied Linguistics*, 4. (Chapter 5 in the present volume.)
——. 1979. 'The Status of English in and furth of Scotland', in A.J. Aitken and Tom McArthur, eds, *Languages of Scotland*. Edinburgh: Chambers.
——. 1983. *A Foundation Course for Language Teachers*. Cambridge: Cambridge University Press.
——. 1986. *Worlds of Reference: Lexicography, Learning, and Language from the Clay Tablet to the Computer*. Cambridge: Cambridge University Press.
——, ed. 1992. *The Oxford Companion to the English Language*. Oxford: Oxford University Press. Notably, the entries *communicative shift, rhythm, stress, syllable*.
——. 1998. *The English Languages*. Cambridge: Cambridge University Press.
McCrum, Robert, William Cran and Robert MacNeil. 1986. *The Story of English*. London: Faber & BBC Publications. 2nd edition, 1992.
McLuhan, Marshall. 1964. *Understanding Media: The Extension of Man*. New York: McGraw-Hill.

REFERENCES

Morton, Herbert C. 1994. *The Story of Webster's Third: Philip Gove's Controversial Dictionary and its Critics*. Cambridge: Cambridge University Press.

Murray, James A.H. 1900. *The Evolution of English Lexicography*. Oxford: Clarenden Press (The Romanes Lecture).

Ogden, C.K. 1930. *The Basic Dictionary*. London: Psyche Miniatures.

———. 1933. *The Basic Words: A Detailed Account of their Uses*. London: Psyche Miniatures.

———. 1935. *Counter-Offensive: An Exposure of Certain Misrepresentations of Basic English*. Cambridge: The Orthological Institute.

———. 1940. *The General Basic English Dictionary*. London: Evans.

Ong, Walter J. 1982. *Orality and Literacy: The Technologizing of the Word*. London: Methuen.

Orwell, George. 1949. *Nineteen Eighty-Four*. London: Secker & Warburg.

Palmer, Harold E. 1917. *The Scientific Study and Teaching of Languages*. London: Harrap (reprinted Oxford University Press, 1968, ed. D. Harper).

———. 1930. *Interim Report on Vocabulary Selection*. Tokyo: Institute for Research in English Teaching.

———. 1931. *Second Interim Report on Vocabulary Selection*. Tokyo: Institute for Research in English Teaching.

———, Michael West and Lawrence Faucett. 1936. *Interim Report on Vocabulary Selection*—the Carnegie Conference Report. London: King & Son.

———, and A. S. Hornby. 1937. *Thousand-Word English: What It Is and What Can Be Done With It*. London: Harrap.

Parry, Milman. 1971. *The Making of Homeric Verse: The Collected Papers of Milman Parry*, ed. Adam Parry. Oxford: Oxford University Press.

Peñalosa, Fernando. 1981. *Introduction to the Sociology of Language*. Rowley, Mass: Newbury House.

Piaget, Jean. 1972. *Problèmes de psychologie génétique*. Paris: Denöel. Translated by Arnold Rosin as *The Child and Reality: Problems of Genetic Psychology*. London and New York: Penguin, 1976.

Popper, Karl R. and John C. Eccles. 1981. *The Self and its Brain: An Argument for Interactionism*. Heidelberg: Springer International.

Preminger, Alex. 1974. *Princeton Encyclopedia of Poetry and Poetics*. New York: Macmillan.

Quirk, Randolph, Sidney Greenbaum, Geoffrey Leech and Jan Svartvik. 1972. *A Grammar of Contemporary English*. Harlow: Longman.

Quirk, Randolph. 1983. 'The English language in a global context', in Randolph Quirk and Henry Widdowson, eds, *English in the World: Teaching and Learning the Language and Literatures*. Cambridge: Cambridge University Press.

Read, Allen W. 1976. 'Dictionary', in *The Encyclopaedia Britannica*, 15th Edition (Macropaedia Vol. 5). Chicago: Encyclopaedia Britannica Inc.

Rushton, Dorgan, 1985. *The Queen's English: High Taw Tawk Prawpah-Leah*. London: Michael Joseph.

REFERENCES

Seuss, Dr (Theodore Seuss Geisel). 1960. *Fox in Socks: A Tongue Twister for Super Children*. New York: Random House.

Sinclair, J.M., ed. 1987. *Looking Up: An Account of the COBUILD Project in Lexical Computing*, London and Glasgow: Collins.

Sledd, James and Wilma Ebbitt. 1962. *Dictionaries & THAT Dictionary: A casebook of the Aims of Lexicographers and the Targets of Reviewers*. Glenview, Ill: Scott, Foresman.

Smith, Anthony. 1980. *Goodbye Gutenberg: The Newspaper Revolution of the 1980s*. Oxford: Oxford University Press.

Starnes, DeWitt T. and Gertrude E. Noyes. 1946. *The English Dictionary from Cawdrey to Johnson, 1604–1755*. Chapel Hill: University of North Carolina Press.

Strang, Barbara M.H. 1970. *A History of English*. London: Methuen.

Thorndike, Edward L. 1921a. *The Teacher's Word Book*. Columbia University: Teachers College.

——. 1921b. 'Word Knowledge in the Elementary School', in *Teachers College Record* XXII. New York: Columbia University.

——. 1932. *A Teacher's Wordbook of the 20,000 Words Found Most Frequently and Widely in General Reading for Children and Young People*. Columbia University: Teachers College.

——, and Irving Lorge. 1944. *The Teacher's Wordbook of 30,000 Words*. Columbia University: Teachers College.

Toffler, Alvin. 1970. *Future Shock*. London: Bodley Head.

——. 1980. *The Third Wave*. London: Collins.

Travers, J.F. 1977. *The Growing Child: Introduction to Child Development*. New York and London: John Wiley.

Tyler, Stephen A., ed. 1969. *Cognitive Anthropology*. New York: Holt, Rinehart & Winston.

Valdman, A., ed. 1977. *Pidgin and Creole Languages*. Bloomington: Indiana University Press.

West, Michael. 1927. *The New Method Readers*. London: Longman.

——. 1935. *New Method Dictionary*. London: Longman.

——. 1953. *A General Service List of English Words*. London: Longman.

——. 1965. *An International Reader's Dictionary*. London: Longman.

——, et al. 1934. *A Critical Examination of Basic English*. Toronto: Toronto University Press.

Whitehall, Harold. 1971. 'The development of the English dictionary', in Leonard F. Dean, Walker Gibson and Kenneth G. Wilson, eds, *The Play of Language*. Oxford and New York: Oxford University Press.

Widdowson, H.G. 1968. 'The teaching of English through science', in Julian Dakin, Brian Tiffen and H.G. Widdowson, eds, *Language in Education*. London: Oxford University Press.

Wilks, Yorick. 1972. *Grammar, Meaning, and the Machine Analysis of Language*. London: Routledge and Kegan Paul.

REFERENCES

For etymological statements on the words *rhyme, rhythm,* and *rime,* see for detail the *Oxford English Dictionary,* Second Edition, 1989, and/or for a more compact presentation of the same information the *New Shorter Oxford English Dictionary,* 1993.

Index

abbreviations, 48, 59, 202
Abercrombie, David, 126, 143, 178
academic world, 28–32, 223–7:
    bias and elitism, 27, 28–32, 33,
    94–5, 192–3, 225, 226; language
    use, 225, 226; public deference
    towards, 32, 37, 38; spoken
    prose, 126, 127
academies, language, 101
acoustics, 13
adjectives, 46
administrative standard, 111, 118, 128,
    204
advertising, 20
Aelfric, Abbot of Eynsham, 155–6, 157
affect, 27, 33–5
affixation, 35, 46
Africa, 123, 203, 216
Afrilex, 216
Alexander, L.G., 68–9
All India Radio, Delhi, 129
alliteration, 18, 19–20, 21, 26
almanacs, 219
alphabet, 231, 241, 245
alphabetic order, 149–53, 163–4, 195,
    196–8, 219: electronic presentation,
    210–11, 252; encyclopedias, 151,
    167, 176, 197–8; history, 90, 197–8,
    229; privileged position, 196–8, 200,
    218; print culture promotes, 197–8,
    200; thematic order interlaced,
    164–7, 219
American Council on Education, 69
American English, 123, 203:
    dictionaries, 39–40, 43, 96, 135,
    139, 143, 145–6, 203; Dictionary
    Society of North America, 216; in
    ELT, 142–3, 145–6; General
    American, 128, 139, 143, 145–6;
    and international standard, 128;
    Network English, 139; orthography,
    45, 108, 128; print standard, 127;
    school, 22
Amerindian languages, 18, 19
anarchy, 123, 227
Anglo, 34, 41
Anglocentricity, 28, 30, 32
Anglo-Saxon, 201, 202
animation in databases, 254
Anne, Princess, 109
anthologies, 195, 196
anthropology, 192–3: cognitive, 144,
    179
antonymy, 4, 6, 48, 144–5, 179
apes, 5, 11
apostrophe, 15, 108
apparatus, textual, 226, 240, 254
aptronyms, 48
Aquinas, Thomas, 156, 157
Arabic, 14, 19, 204
arbitrary sign, 4, 34
archetype, 194
Aristotle, 150
article, 28–9, 32, 33
ASEAN, 204
Asia, 123, 204, 209, 216 *see also*
    individual countries
Asialex, 216
assonance, 16, 18, 19, 26
Atkins, Beryl T., 143–4, 178

271

INDEX

atlases, 217, 219
Austen, Jane, 202
Australia, 115, 119, 123, 127, 208–9
Australopithecus, 11
authority: of books and print, 91, 122, 125–6, 129; in education, 77–80, 84
authorship, 242
awareness, language, 29

Babbage, Charles, 233, 238
Bacon, Sir Francis, 119, 122, 157, 158, 200
Bahamian English, 40
Bailey, Nathaniel, 134, 158
Bailey, Richard W., 120
Barber, Charles L., 28–32, 33
Barnes, William, 113–14
base words, 47
Basic English, 61–5, 66, 70, 72, 73, 114–15, 140: Ogden's dictionary of, 141, 204
Bathe, William, 157
Bayle, Pierre, 198, 200
BBC, 129, 139, 228
BBC English, 31, 129, 139
beat, rhythmical, 13, 14
Bell, Alexander Graham, 246
Berlitz, Maximilian, 137
Berlitz method of language teaching, 57, 154
'between you and I', 100
bias, social and cultural: academic, 27, 28–32, 33, 94–5, 192–3, 226; in classroom, 77–88; in lexicography, 191–200; of ordering schemata, 153; in vocabulary control, 53–4, 56; unintentional, 32, 38, 193; *see also* gender
Bible, 52, 53, 54, 110: Authorized Version, 89, 91, 93, 127
Biden, James, 52
Bierce, Ambrose, 256
bilingualism, *see under* dictionaries
blindness, 52
Bloomsbury Dictionary of Quotations, 200
Blount, Thomas, 134
Blue-eyed English, 114
Bolinger, Dwight, 7
bones, tally-, 233, 239
Bongers, Hermann, 58, 69, 71–3
books: authority, 91, 129; future for, 235–6, 254; reverence for, 91, 112, 125–6, 253; and standards, 90–1; *see also individual types*
brain, 12, 237, 244, 246
Brazil, David, 147
breaks in words, placement of, 108
Bright, J.A., 57, 66
British Broadcasting Corporation, *see* BBC
British English: American English parts from, 203; bias towards, 28, 30, 32
British Library, 234
broadcasting, 106, 128 *see also* BBC; radio; television
Buchanan, James, 134, 135
Bullokar, John, 134, 202
Burchfield, Robert, 101
burgessisms, 47
business language, 115, 116, 124, 128–9
buzz words, 47, 48

Calgary, Alberta, 102
Cambridge University, 92, 139, 223
Cambridge University Press, 133, 146, 167, 206–7, 209: Wordroutes series, 184, 187–8, 210; *Worlds of Reference*, 216, 229, 239, 244
Cameron, John, 143
camp languages, 82
Canada, 102, 115, 123, 127, 208, 209
Cannell, Mrs M.F., 107–8
Caribbean, 121, 127, 204
CARICOM, 204
Carnegie Report, 61, 63, 65–7, 69, 72, 140
Carroll, Lewis: *Jabberwocky*, 8
Carver, David J., 143
catalogues, 99, 217, 219, 220, 240
Catholic Church, 111, 112, 226
Cawdrey, Robert, 63, 64–5, 89, 109–10, 134, 202
CD-ROM, 234
Celtic languages, 19
Chambers, Ephraim, 151–2, 198
Chambers, W. and R., 43, 96, 135, 203, 206–7: ELT dictionaries, 133, 143, 146
chanting, 12, 37

272

INDEX

characternyms, 48
Chaucer, Geoffrey, 110–11
Chesterfield, 4th Earl of, 196
children, 3–9, 14, 15, 77 *see also* education
China, 204, 207–8, 231, 240
Chinese language, 19, 200, 203
Chomsky, Noam, 38
Christian, 194
chronologies, 218
Churchill, Winston, 20, 63, 115
cinema, 128
'circle of English', 166, 173
Clark, A.M., 18–19
class, social, 97, 106, 116–17 *see also* bias, social and cultural
classicism, 91, 103, 116, 136 *see also* Greece, ancient; Latin
COBUILD (COLLINS Birmingham University International Language Database), 146, 147, 185
Cockeram, Henry, 134
codex, invention of, 241
cognate vocabularies, 66
Cold War, 204
Coleridge, Samuel Taylor, 17, 24, 157, 158
Collins, 154, 200: *English Dictionary*, 43, 162, 200, 238; ELT dictionaries, 133, 135, 143–4, 146–7, 178; *see also* COBUILD *and under* McArthur, Tom
collocations, 20
colloquial English, 70, 74, 121, 129
colonies, 123, 226
Comenius, John Amos, 157–8, 197, 200
commercial standard, 118, 124, 128–9
Commonwealth, 123, 124 *see also individual countries*
communicative approach, 84, 85
compound words, 46, 47, 48; and vocabulary control, 62–3, 66, 71, 74
computer technology, 233–5: auditory and visual modes, 241; communications, 236 *see also* Internet; communicative shift, 232, 241–2, 246, 247, 251, 254–5; expert systems, 234–5; fluid/fixed texts, 242, 254, 255; graphics, 167, 241, 255; and lexicography, 144, 146, 147, 209, 210–11, 235; organic computers, 253; printing by, 121, 122–3; and scribal traditions, 199–200; thematic and alphabetical order, 158–9, 164, 167, 182, 199–200, 210–11, 235, 252; *see also* databases; Internet
conceptual wordbooks, 144, 158, 163, 178–9
concordances, 217, 218
confusibles, 48
conjunctions, 46, 70
Conklin, Harold, 158
connotations of words, 27, 33–5
consonance, 16, 17, 18, 19, 26
consonants, 12; syllabic, 15
constellations of words, 60, 74
containerization of life, 82, 83
content, 249–50, 254–5
content words, 46
context, 4, 36, 45
contingency, 229, 253
conventionality of words, 33–5, 47
copyright, 242, 254
Core English, 207
corporations, international, 124, 128
Corson, David, 116
counting of words, 47 *see also* vocabulary control
court dialects, 90
Courtney, Rosemary, 144
Cowie, Anthony P., 141, 144, 146
Cran, William, 120, 121
creoles, 82, 129
cross-checking and objectivity, 255
Crowther, Jeremy, 146
Crystal, David, 97, 105, 144, 158, 167, 179
Crystal Mark scheme, 116
culture, 191, 192–3 *see also* bias
cuneiform writing, 200, 231, 240

Daniel, Samuel, 120
databases, 218–19, 237–42, 254: pre-computer, 237, 238, 239, 240
datedness, 51, 57, 68
Dawkins, Richard, 248
Dayananda, James, 111
deafness, 12, 232

INDEX

definitions dictionary, 36:
whole-sentence, 146–7, 185; rolling, 182–3, 185
descriptivism, 37–8, 93–4, 97, 192
determiners, 46
Devil's Dictionary of Language Teaching, 256–64
Dewey, George, 52
Dhi Fonètik Titcer, 137
dialects, 129, 205–6: attitudes to, 77–80, 86, 92, 226, 246; teaching of English as a second, 79
dictionaries, 39–41, 133–6, 201–11: alphabetic, thematic and hybrid, 90, 150, 151, 154, 163–4, 195, 196–200, 219, 235; American English, 37–8, 39–40, 135, 203; authority, 37–8, 91, 125, 135, 218; Basic English, 64; bilingual, 134, 177, 184, 188, 202, 207–8; citation forms, 47; Commonwealth countries, 40, 207, 208–9; and computer technology, 144, 146, 147, 209, 210–11, 235; descriptive/prescriptive, 37–8, 92–4, 192; ELT/EFL, 39, 40, 133–48: advanced and specialized, 142–4; development, 141–8, 204–5; educational background, 136–7; lexicographical background, 133–6; and phonetics, 137–8, 147; pronunciation models, 142–3, 145–6, 147; vocabulary control, 60–1, 64, 140–1, 146; whole-sentence definitions, 146–7, 185;
hard-word, 134, 137, 142, 202; historical development, 37, 92–3, 133–6, 151–2, 195, 197, 202–3; hypothetical international, 40–1; international standard English, 206–10; Japanese, 202–3; Latin, 134, 197; macro- and micro-structure, 219–20; other than word-books, 191, 195–6, 221–2; and other reference works, 160–1, 195, 218
Dictionary Society of North America, 216
Diderot, Denis, 152, 157, 198, 200
diglossia, 79

Direct Method, 84, 85, 137
directories, 217, 219
division of words, 108
DNA, 216–17, 219
Donne, John, 89
Doublespeak Awards, 116
doublets, Latin and Latin via French, 15–16
drama, 24–5, 126
Dryden, John, 112
Dublin, 135
Duden pictorial wordbooks, 144, 151, 154, 164
Dyche, Thomas, 134

ear, middle, 11
Early Modern English, 202–3
Eastman, George, 6
Eaton, Helen, 72
Edinburgh, 135, 143, 152, 178
editors, 104–8, 122
education: authority, 77–80, 84; ideologies, 80–1, 83–5; international standard English, 124, 129; language attitudes, 77–80, 102–3; Latin, 110, 112, 113, 116–17, 136, 156, 197; marketplace and monastery models, 81–3, 85, 87; non-native-language medium, 110, 112, 113, 129, 225; school as prime institution, 224, 226–7; social bias, 77–88, 94–5, 116–17; and standard language, 92, 98, 202, 226; students/teacher/materials relationships, 83–5, 86–7; vocabulary control, 51, 52–3, 55, 57, 60, 68–9, 69–71, 73, 115; vocational courses, 85, 86; women's, 110; and written language, 85–6, 121–2, 136; *see also* academic world; ELT; literacy
EFL (English as a Foreign Language), 14, 123–4, 129 *see also* ELT
EFL Gazette, 256–64
Egypt, ancient, 200, 231, 240
Eisenstein, Elizabeth, 37, 122, 231, 239, 245
Eldridge, R.C., 53, 57
Eliot, T.S., 233
elocution, 134
Elsevier jukebox, 234

INDEX

ELT (English Language Teaching): methods, 84, 85–7, 136–7, 205; models, 31, 40, 129, 139, 142–3, 145–6, 147; and phonetics, 137–8; vocabulary control, 53, 60–1, 64, 69, 70, 71, 115, 140–1, 146; *see also* dictionaries (ELT/EFL)

Encyclopaedia Britannica, 151, 152, 198

encyclopedias, 197–8, 218, 219: relationship to other reference works, 151–2, 160–1, 164, 195, 196

Endicott, J.G., 141

English as a Foreign Language, *see* EFL

English Language Teaching, *see* ELT

English as a Native Language, *see* ENL

English as a Second Language, *see* ESL

English Today, 30, 39, 95–6, 98–108, 209

Englishes, English languages, 33–4

engineering, social, 77–9

ENL (English as a Native Language), 34, 123–4, 129

Enlightenment, 194

epic poetry, 237–8, 240, 241–2, 252, 254

eponyms, 48

ESL (English as a Second Language), 34–5, 115, 123–4, 129 *see also* ELT

Esperanto, 137

estates, social, 227

ethnocentricity, 28, 30, 32, 34, 39–41

Euralex, 216

European Economic Community, 235

European Union, 128, 204

evolution, human, 11–12

exclusion, social and linguistic, 110, 245

Exeter, University of, 215–16

expectations, social, 129

expert systems, 234–5

Faucett and Maki's wordlist, 55, 65, 72

Fee, Margery, 209

feminism, 34, 39

Ferguson, Charles, 79

Fisher & Bregonier: *What's What*, 154, 164, 196

fixity and fluidity of text, 126, 242, 254

Florio, John, 202

flow of sound, 13, 17

folk taxonomy, 179

folklore, 226

Forbes, Dennis, 228, 233–4

'foreword', 113

form, 27–8, 35–8, 71

form words, 46, 48

formulas, stock, 13

Fowler, Frank, 95

Fowler, Henry, 93–5

fractured English, 128–9

Freeman, John, 52

French language: in former colonies, 225; influence on English, 15–16, 111, 201–2; reference books, 151, 152, 154, 197; and Spanish, 45; standard, 101, 245; syllable-timing, 14

French Revolution, 193

frequency, *see* vocabulary control

Fries, Charles C., 51, 63, 65, 69–71, 72, 73

Fromm, Erich, 77

function and form, 71

function words, 46

gairaigo (Japanese, foreignisms), 202–3

Gatenby, E.V., 60–1, 141, 204–5

gazetteers, 218, 219

gender bias, 29–30, 32, 33, 34, 39, 66–7, 81

genealogies, oral, 239, 254

General American, 128, 139, 143, 145–6

General Service List of English Words (Michael West), 67–9, 140–1, 143, 182

genetics, 216–17

German language, 52, 152, 204

Germanic words in English, 63, 113–14

gestural language, 12, 46, 232

Gibraltar, 124

Gimson, A.C., 138, 139

glamour, 37

Glasgow dialect, 77–80

Glazier, S., *see Random House Word Menu*

global English, 39, 118, 123–4, 129–30, 204–6, 209 *see also* international standard English

glossaries, 154, 195, 197

glottal stops, 79–80

INDEX

Goldsmith, Oliver, 90
Goody, Jack, 239
Görlach, Manfred, 120
governmental standard, 111, 118, 128, 204
Gowers, Sir Ernest, 94
Grainger, Percy, 114
grammar, 37, 100: explicit vs implicit, 85–6
grammar-translation method, 85, 136
grammatical words, 46, 52, 55, 63–4
graphic presentation, 249, 255: reference works, 151, 164, 172, 189, 190
graphological words, 51
Gray, Arley, 145
Greece, ancient, 43, 126, 156, 231: influence on English, 113–14, 136, 225; see also epic poetry
Greenbaum, Sidney, 101, 123–4, 143
Grove, Victor, 116
Gutenberg, Johannes, 238

Haeckel, Ernst, 5
Hamilton, W.A.R., 99
hand dominance, 12
'handbook', 113
hard words, 48, 137, 142, 197, 202
Hardy, Thomas, 226
harmony, 16
Harrap publications, 146, 154, 207
Harris, Dolores, 145
Hartman, James, 139
Hartmann, Reinhard, 215–16, 220
Havelock, Eric, 239
Haycraft, John, 99
headwords, 58, 59, 60, 134
hierarchies, levelling of, 198, 218–19
hieroglyphs, 200, 231, 240
Higgleton, Elaine, 146
Hindi, 14, 204
Hogben, Lancelot, 204
Holland, 69, 71
homeoteleuton, 16, 18, 19
Homer, 237–8, 240, 242, 252
Homo, genus, 11, 223, 244
homogenization of languages, 90
homographs, 51, 54, 55–6
homonyms, 59, 66, 179
'hopefully', 100
Hornby, A.S., 60–1, 72, 141, 142, 145, 204–5
Howard, Godfrey, 96, 98
hypertext, 200, 210–11, 219
hyponyms, 48, 179

icons, computer, 200
ideograms, 200, 231, 240, 245
ideology, 191, 193–5, 200; educational, 80–1, 83–5
idiom, 20, 62–3, 66, 143–4
illiteracy, 92, 226, 232, 246
illustrations *see* graphic presentation
Ilson, Robert, 99, 102
immersion, 84, 86, 136–7, 205, 208
imperialism, 226
imply and *infer*, 99
indexes, 217, 218 *see also under* thematic order
India, 8, 111, 123, 127, 129, 178
Indo-European roots, 44
Industrial Revolution, 125, 203, 230
insecurity, linguistic, 32, 80, 91, 226: and books on usage, 89, 95, 97; and dictionaries, 37, 135, 192
Institute of Research in English Teaching, *see* IRET
integrated systems, 254
interjections, 46
interlanguages, 81–2
Interlex course, 216
international languages, *see* global English; international standard English; Latin
International Monetary Fund, 128
International Phonetic Association (IPA), 137, 138, 165, 170
International Scientific Vocabulary, 225
international standard English, 124–9, 204–6: dictionaries, 206–10; print base, 127, 130; standards within, 127–9; varieties not attuned to, 124, 205–6; vigour, 118, 129–30
Internet, 210–11, 217, 219, 220, 246: styles and usage, 121, 123, 129
intonation, 249
inviolate texts, 254
IPA, *see* International Phonetic Association
IRET (Institute of Research in English Teaching), Japan, 58, 59–60, 71, 72, 141, 205

INDEX

Irish English, 128, 135
ISE, *see* international standard English
Islam, 35, 226
island vocabulary, 66
-ism suffix, 47–8
isolation cry, mammalian, 11
ISV (International Scientific Vocabulary), 225
Italian, 197, 202

Jackson, Howard, 183–4, 196, 199
Jamaican Patwa, 121
James VI of Scots and I of England, 89
Japan: dictionaries, 202–3; Palmer and colleagues in, 57, 58, 60–1, 140, 141 *see also* IRET; Shinto, 195; UK and US English influences, 203; *wasei eigo* ('Made-in-Japan English'), 206
Japan Times, Tokyo, 129
Japanese language, 14, 202–3
jargons, 82, 154
Jeffrey, G.B., 67
Jespersen, Otto, 137
Johnson, Samuel, 134, 153, 158, 196, 203: prescriptivism, 92, 192
Jones, Daniel, 31, 40, 138–9

Kaeding, F.W., 52
Kaitakusha publishing house, 141, 205
Kasner, Edward, 6
Kenrick, William, 134, 135
Kent, Ernest, 253
Kenya, 225
Kernerman semi-bilingual dictionaries, 208
Kirkpatrick, Elizabeth M., 143
Kiyoi, Mikie, 205–6
knowledge, 233–4 *see also*, academic world; databases; libraries; reference science
Knowledge Warehouse, 241
Knowles, Revd J., 52

[l], syllabic, 15
laboratories, language, 85
Landau, Sidney, 181, 199–200
Langscape Survey, 209
Larousse publications, 146, 207
larynx, 5, 11–12
Latin: break-up, 119, 120, 133–4, 197; and European vernaculars, 15–16, 44–5, 119, 120, 133–4, 197; influence on English language: 15–16, 90, 100, 111, 202, 203, 226; attempts to control, 63, 66, 99, 113–14, 117; social effects, 110, 116–17, 225; as international language, 119, 130, 134; linguistic scholarship, 43; plain language, concept of, 112; *see also under* dictionaries; education
law, *see* legal language
Leech, Geoffrey, 101, 123–4, 143
legal language, 111, 118, 126, 128
Lewis, J. Windsor, 141
lexical words, lexemes, 46
lexicographical words, 47
lexicography, *see* alphabetic order; dictionaries; reference works; thematic order
lexicon, 195
libraries, 217, 219, 228–36
linearity, 229–30, 254
Lipka, Leonhard, 184, 199
Lippmann, Bertram, 100–1, 103
lists, *see* catalogues
literacy, 43–4, 135, 245: computer-, 247; and illiteracy, 92, 226, 232, 246
literature, 19–25, 85–6, 239
loan-translation, 90
loanwords, 48, 90, 99
locality, 77, 153, 207–8
Lodge, David, 224
London, 92, 138, 202
Long, Thomas H., 144
Longman publications: ELT dictionaries, 133, 139, 141, 142–3, 144, 145; *Activator* volumes, 184–5, 189, 210; *Dictionary of Contemporary English*, 40, 142–3, 144, 146, 147, 207–8 and *Longman Lexicon*, 145, 181–2, 198; *Lexicon of Contemporary English*, *see under* McArthur, Tom; *New Method* volumes, 60, 140, 141; *see also* Roget, Peter Mark
Lorge, Irving, 55–7, 67, 68
Lyons, John, 158, 179

McAlpine, Janice, 209
McArthur, Roshan, 3–9

INDEX

McArthur, Tom, 178–9, 235: and *Cambridge International Dictionary of English*, 146, 206–7; *Collins Dictionary of English Phrasal Verbs and Their Idioms*, 143–4, 178; *Devil's Dictionary of Language Teaching*, 256–64; *Longman Lexicon of Contemporary English*, 40, 144–5, 177–90: bilingual versions, 177, 208 concept and origins, 144, 152, 158, 161, 163, 178–9; cross-referencing, 165, 171, 199; format options, 164–6, 167, 168–72; illustrations, 166, 172; index, 165, 170, 180, 181; and *LDOCE*, 145, 181–2, 198; meaning as other words, 179, 180; offspring, 183–6; and pronunciation, 145, 165, 170; Roget tradition, 144, 180, 198; rolling definitions, 182–3; semantic fields, 144, 155–6, 165, 168–9, 180, 185, 199, 235; sets, 166, 171, 179, 180, 199; snowflake principle, 182; thematic arrangement, 151, 154, 177, 196, 198–9, 210; theoretical and other influences, 179–80;
Oxford Companion to the English Language, 164–5, 166–7, 173–6; *Worlds of Reference*, 216, 229, 239, 244

McCaig, I.R., 144
McCarthy, Michael, 184, 210
McCrum, Robert, 120, 121
McGregor, Charles, 142, 181
McGregor, G.P., 57, 66
McLuhan, Marshall, 248
Mackin, Ronald, 144
MacNeil, Robert, 120, 121
Macquarie dictionaries, 208–9
macro- and microstructure, 161, 219–20
magic power of words, 36–7
manipulative use of language, 38, 77–9
manuals, 113, 217, 219
Maori language, 40
marketplace tradition in ELT, 80–3
masculine, generic, 29–30, 32, 33
MBA English, 128

meaning: and context, 4, 36, 45; doublets, 15–16; figurative extension, 62, 71, 74, 221; as other words, 179, 180; technology, technique, content and, 254–5; and vocabulary control, 62, 70, 71, 74, 182; words as packets of, 27–8, 35–8; words relating to, 48
media, 122, 126, 128: international standard English, 118, 124, 127, 128; *see also* radio; television
memes, 248
memory, 231, 240: oral, 12–13, 237, 238, 239, 252
meronymy, 179
Merriam-Webster Co., 37–8, 40, 152, 203
Mesopotamian cuneiform script, 200, 231, 240
metaphor and rhyme, 26
metonymy, 26
metre, accentual and quantitative, 13
microstructure, *see* macrostructure
Middle Ages: break-up of Latin, 119, 120, 133–4, 197; dictionaries, 195; form of documents, 200, 241; rhyme and rhythm, 16–17, 19; scholarly guild, 223; thematic order, 150, 154, 197; trilingualism, Latin/French/English, 111; *see also* Schoolmen
middle class, 91
Middle English, 19, 111, 201–2
middle style, 112–13
Miller, Don Ethan, 154
miologs, 57–8, 59
mnemonic systems, 231, 239
Modern English, 202
monastery tradition, 80–3, 84, 223
monologs, 57–8
morphemes, 46
morphological words, 46
Morris, William, 22
Morris, William and Mary: *Harper Dictionary of Contemporary Usage*, 96
multimedia systems, 219, 254
music, 13, 17, 237, 239

[n], syllabic, 15
names, 44, 47, 56–7, 62
Napoleon, 193

INDEX

narrative, 13, 19–20, 237, 239, 240, 254
National Consumer Council, 116
nationalism, 90
native speaker; connotations of term, 34
native users of English, 34, 123–4, 129
nativized Englishes, 129
NATO, 204
natural language, 249, 252
Natural Method, 137
Neolithic agricultural revolution, 230
nervous system, 12, 244, 245, 253
Network English, 139
neurology, 12, 244, 245, 253
New Zealand, 40, 123, 127, 208
Newfoundland English, 40
newspaper headlines, 20
Newspeak, Orwellian, 195
nicknames, 20
Nigeria, 111
non-native users: and non-standard varieties, 124, 205–6; outnumber native, 121, 204; typology, 123–4; *see also* EFL; ELT; ESL
non-standard varieties, 92–3, 124, 129, 205–6 *see also* dialects
nonce words, 3, 48
Norse language, 19
nouns, 46, 47, 70
numeric organization, 151, 164

objectivity, 93, 255 *see also* descriptivism
Occitan language, 245–6
official status of languages, 123, 128, 204
official use of language, 115, 116
offshore English, 129
Ogden, C.K.: Basic English, 61–5, 66, 70, 72, 73, 114–15, 140, dictionary of, 141, 204; and West, 63–5, 115, 140
Old English, 19, 201
Ong, Walter, 36–7, 232, 239, 245, 253
onomasiological/semasiological distinction, 161–3
onomastic words, 47
onomatopoeia, 26
ontogeny and phylogeny, 5
-onym, words in, 48

operators, 70, 114
oral cultures, 10, 13, 92, 231, 237–8: flexibility of words and texts, 44, 242; information storage, 237, 238, 239; power of words in primary, 36–7, 38; *see also* storage speech
orality, 10, 249: secondary (Ong), 252–3, 254; *see also* oral cultures; speech
orthoepy, 134, 135, 137
orthographic words, 45, 51
orthography: American English, 45, 108, 128; 18th-century concern, 134, 135; prescriptivism, 137; reform movement, 137 'sic', 104–5, 108; standardization, 45, 90, 202, 246; varieties, 45, 128; and word formation, 6; and vocabulary control, 73
Orwell, George, 35, 195
Oxford English, 31, 92
Oxford University, 319, 223
Oxford University Press, 40, 96, 154, 161, 203, 209: *Concise Oxford Dictionary*, 151, 152; *Companion to the English Language*, 164–5, 166–7, 173–6; ELT dictionaries, 133, 141, 142–3, 144, 145; *Oxford Advanced Learner's Dictionary of Current English*, 60–1, 141, 142–3, 146, 181, 205; *Oxford English Dictionary*, 56, 68, 93–4, 136, 151; definitions cited, 42–3, 162, 194; *see also* Trappes-Lomax, Hugh

page organization, 90
Palmer, Harold E., 57–60, 63–4, 73, 115, 140, 204–5: on constellations of words, 60, 74; and IRET, 58, 59, 71, 72
papyrus rolls, 200, 241
parallelism and rhyme, 26
pararhyme, 22–3
Parnwell, E.C., 142
Parrott, Fred, 107
Parry, Milman, 238
particles, 46
Passy, Paul, 137
Patwa, Jamaican, 121
peristalsis, 8
Perry, William, 134, 135

279

INDEX

persecution, social, 79–80
Peters, Pam, 209
Petit Robert dictionaries, 151, 152, 154
Phillips, Edward, 134, 202
Philological Society, 93
philosophy, language for, 103
Phonetic Teachers' Association, 137
phonetics, 13, 137–8, 143: notation, 44, 147, 170
phonological words, 45, 51
phonology, see pronunciation
Phonotypic Journal, 50–2
photography, 255
phrase books, travellers', 154
physiology, human, 11–12, 244–5
Piaget, Jean, 77, 78, 86
pictorial wordbooks, 154, 164
pidgins, 82
Pisa, University of, 235
Pitman, Isaac, 51, 51, 54
plagiarism, 254
plain English, 109–17: institutionalization, 115–16; lexical bar, Latinate/vernacular, 116–17; and rhetorical styles, 111, 112–13; and Saxon English movement, 113–14
Plato, 150
playground and classroom language, 79
Pliny, 150
pliologs, 58, 59
plurality of Englishes, 33–4
poetics, 13, 17, 21
'polite society', 91, 134
politics of words, 34–5
polysemy, 179, 191–6: and vocabulary control, 51, 54, 55–6, 62–3, 66, 74
Popper, Karl, 194, 250–1
portmanteau words, 48
prayers, 239
pre-literate societies, see oral cultures
prepositions, 52
prescription, 37, 92–3, 97, 137, 192
prestige languages, 119
prestige varieties of language, 30–2: as EFL models, 31, 40; as standards, 90, 92, 122, 202, 246; see also Received Pronunciation
printing, 118–30, 202: and alphabetic order, 150, 197–8, 200; authority, 37–8, 122, 125–6, 137;
communicative shift to, 37, 231–2, 240–1, 245–6, 255; and computer technology, 121, 122–3, 255; and dissemination of text, 245; fixing of material, 242, 254; and international standard English, 127, 130; and notions of good usage, 37, 103; and orthography, 45, 90, 202; and punctuation, 90; standard, 45, 90, 104–5, 118, 125–6, 127, 202, 225
Procter, Paul, 142, 143, 146, 181, 207
pronouns, 46, 52
pronunciation: American English models, 142–3; ELT dictionaries, 142–3, 145–6, 147; Irish and Scots, in dictionaries, 135; prescriptivism, 137; variability, 5, 8; syllable boundaries, 45; see also dialects; Received Pronunciation
prose, spoken, 20, 126–7, 128
Protestantism, 112
Provençal language: rhyme, 19
Public School Pronunciation, 139
Publishers Databases Ltd, 241
publishing, 91, 122, 127, 128, 255
Puerto Rico, 124
pulses, chest, breath and syllable, 14
punctuation, 90, 249, 253
puns, 7
Puritan plain style, 112

quantity, metrical, 13
Queen's English, 31
Quirk, Randolph, 129–30, 179: *A Grammar of Contemporary English* (with Greenbaum, Leech and Svartvik), 101, 123–4, 143
quotation marks, placement of, 108

racial attitudes, 81, 114
radio, 126, 228, 255
Random House Word Menu (Glazier), 163, 185, 196
rationalism, 156, 198
Reader's Digest books, 38, 96, 151, 163
reading aloud, 37, 231
reasoning, inductive and deductive, 85–6
Received Pronunciation (RP), 31, 138–9: as ELT; model, 31, 40, 139, 142, 143, 147

280

INDEX

recitation, 37, 126
recording technology, 252–3, 254
reduplication, 4, 20
reference rectangle, 150–1, 164
reference science, 215–22: and DNA, 216–17, 219; macro- and microstructure, 219–20; scope, 217–19
reference works, formats for, 160–76: alphabetical/thematic/graphic/numeric, 163–4 *see also individual entries*; and computer technology, 167, 210, 217; dictionary/thesaurus/encyclopedia, 160–1 *see also individual entries*; format options, application of, 164–76; onomasiological/semasiological, 161–3
referential function of words, 4, 6, 220
Reformation, 99, 112, 156, 198
regional varieties of English, 128, 207, 209 *see also* dialects *and individual varieties*
religion, 35, 91, 111, 112, 226
Renaissance, 112, 156, 229: Latin and vernaculars, 133–4, 197, 203
repetition and rhyme, 26
rhapsodes, Homeric, 241–2, 252
rhetoric, 13, 126; tripartite typology of styles, 112–13; and rhyme, 24–5, 26
rhyme, 10–26: imperfect, 22–3, 25; initial (alliteration), 19–20; internal or interior, 21; medieval concept, 16–17, 18–19; rhetorical devices, 24–5, 26; rhyme schemes, 23–4; rhyme-1 (sound-play), 18–19; rhyme-2 (partial identity in sound), 18–19, 20–3, 24–5; and rhythm, 15–17, 25–6
rhythm, 13–15, 239: and rhyme, 15–17, 25–6
Richards, I.A., 59, 61, 114
ritual language, 13, 239, 254
Rix, Tim, 142
Roach, Peter, 139
Roget, Peter Mark: *Thesaurus*, 68, 152, 153, 158; and *Longman Lexicon*, 144, 180, 198; thematic order, 151, 152–3, 180, 195, 196–7, 210

Romance languages, 45
root words, 47
rote learning, 13, 85–6, 231, 240
Royal Society of London, 112, 157, 158
RP, *see* Received Pronunciation
rules, language teaching and, 85–6
Rundell, Michael, 184, 185
Rushton, Dorgan, 97
Russell, Bertrand, 103
Russian, 14, 204

Safire, William, 100
Salesbury, William, 202
Sanskrit, 19
Sapir, Edward, 158
Saussure, Ferdinand de, 158
Saxon English, 113–14
Scandinavian influence on Middle English, 202
scholarly guild, 223–7; *see also* academic world
Schoolmen, 29, 150, 154, 156, 223
schwa, 14–15
scientific words, 62
Scots language, 8–9, 37, 77–80, 121, 128, 135
scribal culture, 37, 199–200, 231, 240, 245: power of words, 37, 38, 253
scripts, variety of, 247
scrolls and scrolling, 200, 235
Seaton, Anne, 146, 207
'self-educated' label, 226
semantics: and Basic English, 61; change, in child word formation, 5; and thematic lexicography, 144, 155–6, 165, 168–9, 180, 185, 199, 235; structural, 4, 144, 158, 179, 198
semasiological/onomasiological distinction, 161–3
Senegal, 225
sense relations, 4, 6, 220
seriality, 229–30, 254
serials, 228–36: antecedents, 233; and communicative shifts, 231–2; future prospects, 233–6; and linearity, 229–30; and Toffler's three waves, 230–1
Seuss, Dr., 10, 26

281

INDEX

Shakespeare, William, 24–5, 89, 93, 100, 127, 226
Sheridan, Thomas, 134, 135
shifts, communicative, 231–2, 238–9, 244–8: cumulative nature, 235, 244, 246, 247, 255; interrelationships, 232, 241–2, 246, 247, 251, 252; and technology, technique and content, 238–9, 247, 252–5; *see also under* computer technology; printing; speech; writing
Shinto, 195
shorthand, 51, 52, 53, 73
'sic', 104–5, 108
sign language, 12, 46, 232
similes, 20, 26
Sinclair, John, 146–7, 178
Singapore, 111, 127, 129, 207
situationalism, 85
slang usage, 129
Smith, Anthony, 239
snowflake principle, 182
soap operas, 226
social attitudes, *see* bias; class; engineering
socialism, 227
song, 12, 13
sonnet rhyme scheme, 24
sound play, 13, 18, 19
South Africa, 123, 127, 208
Soviet bloc, 230
spaces between words, 44, 45
Spanish speakers, 45, 204
speech: communicative shift to, 231, 239, 244–5, 255; as ELT model, 74, 136–7; physiology of, 11–13, 244–5; spoken prose, 20, 126–7, 128; and words, 42, 44; writing techniques comparable, 253–4; *see also* oral cultures; storage speech
speeches, 20, 126
spelling, *see* orthography
Spenser, Edmund, 93
spoken prose, 20, 126–7, 128
Sprat, Bishop Thomas, 112–13
standard, linguistic, 104–8, 127–9: educated language, 92, 98, 202, 226; establishment, 90–1, 245; five main elements, 127–9; and high varieties/culture, 90, 92, 106–7, 122, 206, 246; history of term, 90, 125

media, 118, 128; printing and, 45, 90, 104–5, 118, 125–6, 127, 202, 225; as teaching model, 85–6
Stanford University, 234–5
stanzas, 24
star maps, 219
Starnes, DeWitt T., 149
statistical words, 47, 51
stenography, 51, 52, 53, 73
Stewart, William A., 145
Stockdale, Dr Frank, 234–5
Stone Age, 233
storage speech, 12–13, 14, 20, 239, 240, 241–2, 252
story-telling, *see* narrative
Straits Times, Singapore, 129
Strang, Barbara, 123
stress, 13, 14–15, 46, 134: stress-timed languages, 14
Strevens, Peter, 103
structuralism, 85
structure–control, 115
structure words, 46
Stuart dynasty, 89
stunt words, 48
Style Council, 126
stylistic words, 59
subwords, Palmer's, 58, 60
Summers, Della, 145, 146, 181, 184, 185
superlative, double, 100
suppletion, 46
Svartvik, Jan, 101, 123–4, 143
Swahili speakers, 45, 204
Sweet, Henry, 137
syllabic consonants, 15
syllables, 4, 12, 35, 45: syllable-timed languages, 14
synonyms, 48, 66, 144–5, 179

tabulations, 219
tally sticks, 233, 239
taste, good, 91, 103
technique in representation of knowledge, 217, 247, 249–50, 253–4
technology: power, and spread of language, 121–3; recording, 252–3, 254; and reference works, 217; in representation of knowledge, 217, 238–9, 247, 249–50, 252; standard English, 118, 128–9

INDEX

telephone, 246, 255: directories, 217, 218, 219
television, 126, 255
text, origin of word, 241
textbooks, 219
thematic order, 149–59, 163–4, 177–90, 198–200, 209–10: and computer technology, 158–9, 164, 167, 182, 199–200, 210–11, 235, 252; cross-referencing, 165, 166, 171, 174, 199, 200 dictionaries, 184, 188, 196, 209–10; and graphic format, 166, 172, 189, 190; historical tradition, 154–8, 179–80, 196–7, 200, 229; hybridization with alphabetic order, 163, 164–7, 219; indexing, 165, 167, 170, 175, 180, 181, 185; range of types, 153–4, 161, 196; and reference rectangle, 151; Roget's, 153, 196, 210; *see also* McArthur, Tom (*Longman Lexicon*; *Oxford Companion to the English Language*): *and under* semantics
thesauruses, 152, 160–1, 196 *see also* Roget, Peter Mark
they, singular, 100
Thompson, Paul, 104, 106
Thorndike, Edward L., 53–7, 60, 65, 67, 68, 72, 140
time-tables, 219
Times-Chambers Essential English Dictionary, 207
timing, syllable- and stress-, 13, 14
Toffler, Alvin, 230, 232, 233, 248
Tok Pisin, 121
tongue, root of, 5, 11–12
tongue-twisters, 20
Tracy, A.-L.-C. Destutt de, 193, 194
trade jargons, 82
trade names, 7
translinguistic words, 48–9
Trappes-Lomax, Hugh: *Oxford Learner's Wordfinder Dictionary*, 185, 190, 210
Traver, A. Aileen, 51, 63, 65, 69–71, 72, 73
Turing, Alan, 238
Tyler, Stephen A., 158, 179

United Nations Organization, 125, 128, 204
United States of America: Dictionary Society of North America, 216; linguistic influence, 203; Native American languages, 18, 19; Plain English campaign, 115, 116; publishing, 127; vocabulary-control movement, 52–3, 53–7; WASP norms in education, 80–1; *see also* American English
universal language, 53, 201–11
universals of knowledge management, 217, 229, 251–2
Urdang, Laurence, 102
usage: books on, 89–97: early, 37, 89, 91–3; Fowler, 93–5; and insecurity, 89, 95, 97; present day, 95–7, 107–8; 'correct', 91, 103; correspondence in *English Today*, 98–108; dynamism, 4–5, 107

varieties of English, 40–1: non–native users and, 124, 205–6; *see also* dialects; standard; *and individual varieties*
Verbatim, 223–7
verbs, 46, 47, 62–3, 70, 142: phrasal, 62–3, 114, 143–4
vernacular languages, 111, 112, 133–4, 197
verse: alliterative, 19; blank, 24–5; *see also* rhyme
Viëtor, Wilhelm, 137
Vincent de Beauvais, 156
visual handicap, 52
visual media, 241
vocabularia, 156, 196
vocabulary control, 50–74: commentators on lists, 69–73; and compounds, 62–3, 66, 71, 74; conflation of lists and words, 51, 54–5; constellations of words, 60, 74; cultural bias, 53–4, 56; and derivatives, 66, 71, 74, 182; and diachronic change, 51, 57; early frequency counts, 50–3; and extensions of meaning, 70, 71, 74, 182; and gender roles, 66–7; and grammatical words, 52, 55, 63–4; and idioms, 63, 66; logical

INDEX

approach, 61–5 *see also* Ogden, C.K.; names, 56–7; objective approach, 53–7, 73, 140; specialized lists, 50–3, 59, 66, 154; and spoken language, 70, 74; and stenography, 51, 52, 53, 73; subjective approach, 57–61, 140; and verbs, 63, 70; West–Ogden feud, 63–5, 115, 140; *see also* Carnegie Report; *General Service List*; Ogden, C.K.; Palmer, Harold E.; West, Michael; *and under* education; ELT; polysemy; writing
vowels, 12, 14–15, 46, 202 *see also* assonance

Wakefield, H., 60–1, 141, 204–5
Walker, John, 92–3, 134–5
Wallace, Michael J., 143
Walter, Elizabeth, 184, 187–8, 210
wasei eigo, 206
waves of humanity, Toffler's, 230–1
Webster, Noah, 37–8, 135, 158, 192, 203
Webster's Third International Dictionary, 37–8, 192
weights and measures, 90, 125, 254
Wells, John C., 139
Welsh language, 202
West, Michael, 56, 60, 61, 65, 142, 204: *New Method* volumes, 60, 140, 141; and Ogden, 63–5, 115, 140; see also *General Service List of English Words*
What's What (Fisher & Bregonier), 154, 164, 196
Whitehall, Harold, 18–19
Whorf, Benjamin Lee, 158
Widdowson, Henry, 54
Wilkins, Bishop John, 157, 158
Wilks, Yorick, 179

Withals, John, 152
wordbooks, 151, 152, 154, 164, 191–200 *see also* dictionaries
words, 42–9: as clusters, 48; definitions, 3, 42–3; division at line-breaks, 108; formation, 3–9; interlinguistic non-equivalence, 44–5; language distinction, 33, 44; literacy and the word, 43–4; as packets of meaning and form, 27–8, 35–8; power of, 27–41: in oral cultures, 36–7, 38; in print cultures, 37–8, 122, 125–6, 137; and rhyme and rhythm, 10–26; in scribal cultures, 37, 38, 253; *see also* bias;
power over, 28, 38–41; as procedural fictions, 27, 33–5; and speech, 42–3, 44; theory of, for vocabulary control, 74; types of, 45–8, 48–9; as visual entities, 44, 45
world English, *see* global English; international standard English
World Englishes, 39
World War, Second, 204
World-Wide Web, 217, 220
writing and written language: and colloquial language, 121; communicative shift to, 12, 92, 231, 239–40, 245, 253–4, 255; and education, 85–6, 121–2, 136; fixity and fluidity, 92, 126, 242, 254; and high culture, 106–7; literacy and the word, 43–4; power of word in, 36–7, 91; and vocabulary control, 53–4, 56, 57, 68, 70, 73; word delimitation, 44, 45
Wyclif, John, 110

zilch, 41